BETWEEN THE LINES
OF THE BIBLE: GENESIS

BETWEEN
the LINES
of the
BIBLE

GENESIS

Recapturing the Full Meaning
of the Biblical Text

Yitzchak Etshalom

OU PRESS

URIM PUBLICATIONS
Jerusalem · New York

Between the Lines of the Bible: Genesis
Recapturing the Full Meaning of the Biblical Text
by Yitzchak Etshalom

Book design by Ariel Walden

Printed in USA

Second Revised and Expanded Edition
First edition originally published by Yashar Books

ISBN 978-965-524-200-3

OU Press – an imprint of the Orthodox Union
11 Broadway, New York, NY 10004
www.oupress.org

Urim Publications
P.O.Box 52287
Jerusalem 91521 Israel

www.UrimPublications.com

Tree oh tree how will I bless you?	אילן אילן
How, in which way, can I bless you?	במה אברכך?
With sweet fruit?	אם אומר לך שיהו פירותיך מתוקין?
Your fruit is sweet...,	הרי פירותיך מתוקין....
With nice shade?	שיהא צילך נאה?
You already have nice shade...	הרי צילך נאה...
With water streaming under you	שתהא אמת המים עוברת תחתיך
You already have it...	הרי אמת המים עוברת תחתיך....
I will bless you	אלא יהי רצון
that all the trees that will come from you	שכל נטיעות שנוטעין ממך
will be like you...	יהיו כמותך...

Dedicated to Joan and Norman Ciment
on your 50th Wedding Anniversary

With love from your children and grandchildren

CONTENTS

PREFACE TO THE REVISED AND
EXPANDED SECOND EDITION

IT HAS BEEN NEARLY A DECADE SINCE THE FIRST EDITION OF this volume was published. In the intervening years, I've published a second volume and have fielded many requests to "update" and add to that first volume. The book you are holding is a modest response to those cherished requests. We have re-sequenced the book so that the essays follow the text of Genesis in its order and have tried to catch all of those small errors that escaped our watchful eyes last time.

More significantly, I've added 7 chapters of all new material to the volume, weaving it into the methodological landscape that was always the vision of this project. One of the chapters was originally conceived as part of another project (Chapter 24) which is why its style is a bit different than the rest of the book.

There are many special people to thank along the way – administrations and faculties of both YULA Boys' and Girls' High Schools, where I am privileged to teach and where my colleagues regularly lend a welcome ear to my questions and musings – some of which became chapters here. I have been fortunate to teach at Young Israel of Century City and the many beautiful friendships I have there have also been vital for spurring me on to write more. My study partner of the past 16 years, Dr. Josh Penn, has been a true friend, a staunch critic and stauncher supporter.

For the past 18+ years, I have been honored to teach a weekly "lunch and learn" shiur at the offices of Mr. Lee Samson and Mr. Larry Feigen, both of whom are good friends and great supporters of the study of Torah. The members of that wonderful shiur have been a marvelous sounding board for most of the material herein and for that I am grateful.

A special thank-you, as well, to the Teichman family who sponsor a weekly lunch class and where I have had the honor of teaching on a monthly basis.

My teachers back home in Israel – Prof. Yoel Elitzur, Zev "Jabo" Erlich, Rav Elhanan Samet, Rav Yoel Bin-Nun and so many others affiliated with the Herzog College have given me, on every visit, much to think about; avenues to follow and find my own insights and positive feedback. I am indebted, especially to the warmth and hospitality of the communities in Ofra and Alon Shvut and the special friends in both places who have opened their homes. A very special thanks to Howard and Sandy, whose Jerusalem home is a special haven. To all of you – your kindnesses will never be forgotten and your love will always be cherished. Thank you.

To those nearest and dearest – my lovely wife, Stefanie and our amazing five children – my deepest gratitude and thanks, for giving me all of those opportunities to sequester myself with a keyboard and to travel to lecture and study. This book is as much yours as it is mine.

During the past year, our Rebbe, Rav Aharon Lichtenstein, *zt"l*, passed away and our world has not been the same. His irreplaceable presence as a voice of Torah, *Yir'at Shamayim* and fundamental *Hessed* was always an anchor for those of us privileged to consider ourselves his *talmidim*. This volume is dedicated to Rav Lichtenstein's memory.

My mother, Miriam Wise, *z"l*, was my first Bible teacher and the biggest reason that I fell in love with the Book of Books; since the publication of volume 2, she joined my father, Rabbi Aaron M. Wise, *z"l*, in eternal rest in the Judean hills. This volume is dedicated, as well, to her memory.

To my teacher, Rav Aharon, *zt"l*, and to my mother, *z"l* – this volume is for you. Thank you for teaching me how to cherish God's words.

Alon Shvut – Los Angeles
Elul, 68th year of Jewish Independence
August 2015

I INTRODUCTION TO THE HISTORY OF BIBLICAL INTERPRETATION

A FULL TREATMENT OF THE HISTORY OF BIBLICAL INTERPRE-
tation would occupy at least one broad shelf and take up many volumes.
That is not my purpose here; however, in order to help define the parameters of how we read the Bible "between the lines," a few background notes
on the history of *Parshanut* (Biblical exegesis) are necessary.

Interpretation of sacred texts is nearly as old as the existence of such
texts—within the Bible itself, clear examples of "inner exegesis" abound.
In this brief introduction, I will introduce the reader to various strains
of interpretation within traditional Jewish circles in order to identify
which of these streams have contributed to the development of the "new
Orthodox School" of *Parshanut*. It is that "school" that informs the methodology that drives this volume.

Parshanut has often been driven by agenda. Many of the exegetical
Midrashim (rabbinic homiletical and exegetical works – see Glossary),
authored during the first eleven centuries of the Common Era, chiefly
in Palestine, were polemical in nature and designed to utilize the ancient
text to address modern circumstances. For instance, the 2nd-century
Palestinian rabbi Shmuel b. Nahman's observation that the phrase "Let
us make man in our image" (Genesis 1:26) is an opening for heretics
to claim support for polytheism apparently was part of a 3rd-century
anti-Christian polemic. (That verse also was used by some of the early
Church Fathers to support Trinitarianism.)

The translation/interpretation of Saadia al-Fayumi Gaon (d. 942,
Baghdad) was both educational and polemical, his chief combatants being
the "literalist" Karaites. Maimonides (d. 1204, Fostat, Egypt) utilized
the text to support his neo-Aristotelian worldview, whereas R. David
Kimhi (d. 1235, Provence) often marshaled his interpretive creativity to
rebut christological claims. The two chief factors motivating exegesis
during the era of the *Rishonim* (early commentators until the middle of

the 15th century — see Appendix A) throughout the Jewish world were explanatory and polemical.

A wide array of new agendas has surfaced in the past few hundred years, and as a result, a much wider range of interpretive literature has been created. The rise of Zionism, secularism, the Emancipation and Reform, the Enlightenment and modernity (not to mention "post-modernity") have each brought in their wake scores of works, authored by traditional Jews, based on the Biblical text. One need look no further than Mecklenberg's *haK'tav vehaKabbalah*, Hoffman's Commentaries on Leviticus and Deuteronomy, Malbim's comprehensive commentary on the entire Hebrew Bible, Rabinowitz's *Tzidkat haTzaddik* and Hirsch's Commentary on the Torah – indigenous residents atop the shelves of every Jewish Bible-phile — to testify to the many challenges that tradition has faced since the late 18th century and the manner in which Biblical interpretation has been used to meet those challenges.

RELIGIOUS ZIONISM AND THE "NEW SCHOOL OF ORTHODOX INTERPRETATION"

The *weltanschauung* of Religious Zionism can be summed up in four words, penned by R. Abraham Isaac Kook (d. 1935, Palestine): *hayashan yit'hadesh vehahadash yitkadesh*—"The old will become renewed and the new will become sanctified."

It should be no surprise that it is within the institutions most closely identified with that approach, that a wedding of the new methodologies of interpretation, including many coming from the world of academia, to the older framework of traditional interpretation has been celebrated. The union is yet young, but the many disciplines that have been tested in the laboratories of secular study, including archaeology, philology, Assyriology, Egyptology, anthropology, and literary theory, have now been marshaled for the cause of Biblical interpretation within the traditional rubric of critical reverence for the text. This is a sanctification of the new as much as a revivification of the old.

The many Orthodox students, scholars, and teachers of this new methodology (which is really a loose confederation of methodologies), who are absolutely committed to the sanctity of the text and to its iron-clad ability to withstand any challenge, see themselves chiefly as *Pashtanim* (see below) who, just as Saadia, Rashbam, and ibn Ezra did in their day, use every available tool to understand the text. The disadvantage from which we suffer – a greater distance from Sinai and from the original *sitz im leben* of the text – is somewhat offset by the more powerful tools at our fingertips. It is with the reverence and the skepticism, the fear and the courage described as the ideal relationship to masters by R. Hayyim of Volozhin, that these exegetes operate. It is that same dialectic that informs the larger works produced by this school (e.g. the *Daat Mikra* series, the Maggid Studies in Tanach and commentary series by R. Elhanan Samet, as well as groundbreaking volumes penned by the likes of R. Yoel Bin-Nun, R. Amnon Bazak and Dr. Yonatan Grossman and the growing archives of articles in *Megadim*).

It is important to note that, surprisingly, there is little that is revolutionary about this method and its various expressions (e.g., works on archaeology, Biblical place names, development of language); it is all well within the spirit of the *Rishonim*, echoing their concerns, furthering their inquiries, and augmenting their solutions. It must be noted that this methodology holds fast to the notion of "accessible data," and will quickly challenge the findings of a highly esteemed commentator if it is clear that his access to the significant information that would ease an understanding of *p'shat* was limited. We are not restrained from challenging the cartography of Rashi, the geography of Ramban, or even the Egyptology of the Midrash when better, more accurate information becomes available. This in no way diminishes the esteem and trust in which we hold these giants of exegesis; but we see ourselves as obligated to allow new information to shed as much light on the sanctified text as possible. Umberto Cassuto and Yehuda Meir Grintz, to name just two academicians of the 20th century, have contributed volumes to a refined understanding of the Biblical text with their input from the many ancient worlds that have unfolded in front of our research-enriched eyes over the past two centuries. R. Mordecai Breuer, whose innovative approach to reconciling redundant or conflicting texts will be adopted in Chapter 7, is commonly considered to be the "grandfather" of the "New School of Orthodox Bible Study."

TARGUMIM

Ever since the Alexandrian community, largely unlettered in Hebrew, commissioned a completion of the translation of the Bible into Greek in the 3rd century BCE (after the Torah was translated by command of Ptolemy II Philadelphus), translations and interpretations have abounded among Jews. The various Targumim (Aramaic translations), the Syriac Peshitta, and Saadia's *Tafsir* were projects that intended to make the text accessible to a non-Hebrew-speaking public. At the same time, the Rabbis of the Talmudic era were developing schools of homiletics that assumed an understanding of the simple meaning of the text and built upon that understanding to extract additional lessons from the text, be they exhortative, illustrative, expressive, or mystical. Yet, there was not a systematic attempt to explain the meaning of the text in a sequential and formalized fashion, undoubtedly due to the widespread assumption that it was well-understood by the reading audience.

PASHTANIM AND DARSHANIM

By the 10th century, the faint challenges to the traditional understanding of the text raised by the various schismatics of the Second Temple became full-blown with the advent of Karaism. R. Saadia Gaon devoted much of his energies and writings to a spirited defense of Rabbinate Judaism, including the first systematic commentary and interpretation of the text. Saadia's contribution opened the door to generations of commentators who took the project, so to speak, in various directions. The medieval period saw the development of Pashtanim ("literalists"; from *p'shat*, which means literal meaning of the text; Pashtanim refers to those scholars concerned with unearthing the original meaning of the word or phrase in question) and Darshanim ("preachers"; the focus is on extracting lessons from the text that may or may not accord with the original frame of reference of the text) who more or less continued the tradition of the Rabbis. Although there is much discussion about his perspective on "*P'shat*,"[1] Rashi (d. 1125, France) is commonly recognized as the most popular of the commentators and as someone closely affiliated with the development of "*p'shat*."[2]

---

1. See *Kamin*: Rashi: P'shuto Shel Mikra uMidrasho Shel Mikra (Heb.), Jerusalem 2000.

2. For an approach to understanding the renewed interest in P'shat among French exegetes in the 12th century and its relation to the a revival of textuality in the church, see *Touito*: Exegesis in Perpetual Motion (Heb) Ramat Gan 2005, chapter 1.

CONTEXTUALISTS AND PHILOSOPHERS

Later centuries saw the rise of two lesser known — but no less significant — schools: The "Contextual" school and the "Contemplative" school. The Contextual school, best represented in the medieval period by Ramban (d. 1270, Aragon, Palestine), Don Isaac Abravanel (d. 1508, Iberia, Italy) and R. Obadia Sforno (d. 1550, Italy) took a "longer" view at the text. Instead of focusing on either the meaning of words and phrases (*"Pashtanim"*) or the lessons to be extracted from them (*"Darshanim"*), the contextualists addressed the larger questions about the text, such as the purpose of Abraham's descent to Egypt, the overall relationship between Joseph and his brothers, and the general scheme of Creation as outlined in Chapter 1 of Genesis. Although these exegetes certainly devoted attention to the meaning of words and, in some cases, the contemporary lessons to be inferred, their overall concern was more with the forest than the trees.

The fourth school of medievalists might best be called "Contemplative." Beginning with Maimonides, including Gersonides (d. 1344, France), R. Nissim of Gerona (d. 1375, Spain), and R. Isaac Arama (d. 1494, Italy), among others, these commentators utilized the text as a means of developing philosophic arguments and axioms. Although Maimonides never completed a commentary on the Bible, much of his *Guide to the Perplexed* functions as a philosophical treatment of the Biblical text. Again, these exegetes (notably Gersonides) also concerned themselves with the meaning of the text as well as the "larger picture," but their unique contribution to interpretation is in the realm of Jewish thought.

The "new school" is partially Contextual — looking at the larger picture of the narrative, the poem, the legal framework, or the prophecy— while being absolutely anchored in a concern for *p'shat*.

It is the aim of this volume to introduce the English-reading public to the various methodologies that the "new school" — which is really a revivified form of the old school — uses in order to bring the text back to life and to deepen our understanding and appreciation of the elegance, the beauty, the vision, and the depth of the Book of Books.

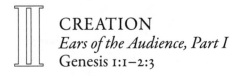

CREATION
Ears of the Audience, Part I
Genesis 1:1–2:3

INTRODUCTION

One of the driving elements behind our methodology is a chief consideration of many of the *pashtanim* (such as Rashbam): Identifying the historic context of a given passage. The significance of this identification is to then "listen" to the passage through the (imagined) ears of the original target audience. As will be developed in Chapter 21, our "omniscience" with regards to the thoughts and intentions of each actor in the story is really a handicap, keeping us from understanding each character's responses. In much the same way – but on the temporal, rather than personal plane – our knowledge of how prophecies will materialize and how plans will reach fruition (or not) impedes our appreciating the impact of the text on its original intended audience.

An important note of caution and clarification: The foregoing in no way delegitimizes or calls into question the significance of every word of the Bible for all people at all times. Just as we transpose laws of damages from oxen and cisterns to automobiles and potholeswe transpose the message from its original context to one that speaks to us.

In order to understand the desired impact of the text — and hence, the implicit lessons, polemics, and allusions — we must adopt the "ears of the audience" and listen through them.

This is, of course, a statement that may be challenged on two points, one doctrinal and the other methodological. The latter is easier to address: The student will eagerly attempt to listen through the "ears of the audience," but they escape him on two grounds. First of all, who is the original audience? When it comes to clear declarations of the text, such as the Revelation at Sinai, Moses's farewell address (the book of Deuteronomy), Joshua's foreswearing of the Israelites in Sh'khem (Joshua 24), and so on, we know who they are. What are we to make of the books of Genesis, Ruth, Judges, Samuel, and Kings, just to name a few of the narrative books of the Bible? Although each of these is placed in a distinct and defined epoch, none of them carries a mention of being recorded and disseminated at a particular time. Who was the first audience to hear the complete version of Ehud's brilliant deflating of Eglon (Judges 3), or of the selection of David as future king (I Samuel 16)? There is no catch-all answer to this question, and each book usually carries some hints that a studied and perceptive eye will pick up, helping to estimate the original audience. In some cases, we have some guidance from tradition that, if bolstered by the text itself, lends great credence to our estimation.

The doctrinal challenge is a bit more complex. Many traditional readers of the Bible have been raised to believe that "the Bible speaks to all people in every generation"; a statement as true as it is misleading. Although there is no doubt that for believers, the messages, values, and mores — as well as the norms of the Book of Books transcend time and place, it is equally certain that some trans-positioning is necessary in order to elicit the proper lesson.

Case in point: The Torah rules that if a master pokes out his slave's eye, that slave immediately earns his freedom. The law seems to be a form of reparation, one that does not necessarily undermine the institution of slavery but merely mitigates its cruelest aspects. However, awareness of the branding practices in the near-east during the Bronze Age, when a slave was permanently marked as such *by having his eye poked out* (see I Samuel 11:2; see also the laws of "ear piercing" for the Hebrew servant who refuses to leave his servitude) brings out a much more powerful statement — the Torah is forcefully opposing the placing of a mark of ownership of one person upon another. This reconfigured attitude towards human bondage is a much more radical statement than a protection against cruelty — but that lesson can only be deduced by listening to the text through the ears of the primary audience to whom the revealed text was first presented.

A clear example of the need for us to reenter the world of the original audience emerges from the opening lines of the Torah and the comment of the most famous of all exegetes, Rabbi Shlomo Yitzhaki. After several other essays relating to the narrative of Creation and its inherent challenges, we will follow this chapter with a related one, assessing the Flood narrative and the story of the Ark from the perspective of the various possible audiences.

RASHI'S OPENING QUESTION

In the first note of his commentary on the Torah, Rashi challenges the very existence of the entire book of Genesis:

> Rabbi Yitzhak said: The Torah should have begun with *This month is unto you the first of the months* (Exodus 12:2) which is the first commandment by which Israel were commanded [this is the commandment of sanctifying the New Moon and of creating a calendar with the month of Aviv (spring) at its head]. What is the reason that it begins with the Creation? On account of "He has declared to His people the power of His works, in order to give them the inheritance of nations" (Psalms 111:6)—that if the nations of the world say to Israel "You are thieves, stealing the lands of the seven [Canaanite] nations", they will respond: "The whole world belongs to the Holy One, Who is Blessed; He gave it to whom He pleased, and according to His will, He took it from them and gave it to us."

Rabbi Yitzhak's question (the source of which is somewhat elusive; it seems to be an alternate version of the homily found in Genesis Rabbah 1:2) seems odd and makes many a student profoundly uncomfortable. How could there be a Torah without the creation narrative, the patriarchal histories, the grandeur of the *Akedah* [binding of Isaac], the shame of Joseph's brothers, and the many other impactful lessons of this first book of books? In order to formalize (and, perhaps, ease) our instinctive discomfort with this comment, we should clarify the assumptions that lie at the heart of Rabbi Yitzhak's question:

1. The Torah is purely a book of commands, proscriptions, and obligations. Besides the many ethical admonitions and exhortations, theological tenets, and principles that suffuse the non-legalistic parts of the Torah, the historic and meta-historic information, glorious poetry, and praise-songs and prophecies are so central to our understanding of God's will and our people's destiny that it is impossible to imagine a Torah bereft of these many texts.

2. The Torah's ultimate message, *weltanschauung*, teleology — as well as its direct series of commands, proscriptions, and obligations — are only addressed to the Israelites. Besides the seven Noahide commands, many of the universalistically-oriented eschatological visions that are found throughout the prophets are founded upon—and are explications of—some of the universalistic elements in the Torah; in addition,

the Torah teaches us that which is "good and right in the eyes of God."
(Deuteronomy 6:18)

As we can see, the premises that drive this opening comment of Rashi
are difficult and somewhat counter-intuitive.

His answer, given in Rabbi Yitzhak's name, is no more satisfying than
the question. First of all, to consider that the first 61 chapters of the Torah
are presented purely to establish our claim to the Land of Israel again
minimizes the impact and import of those weighty chapters.

Rabbi Yitzhak's answer leaves us with a further question: If the sole
purpose of Genesis is to establish God's proprietorship over the earth,
wouldn't the first verse of the Torah have sufficed? His answer does not
account for the patriarchal narratives, the story of slavery, and Exodus — it
doesn't even explain the Eden, flood, or tower narratives.

One further point to ponder in Rabbi Yitzhak's response: If the nations
who will one day challenge our claim to the Land of Israel will be so
easily persuaded by the doctrine of Creation as presented in Genesis, why
wouldn't they also be convinced by verses found throughout Leviticus
(e.g., 18:25–30; 25:38), Numbers (e.g., 13:2, 15:18, 33:50–54), and Deuteronomy (e.g., 11:10–12, 11:31), all of which point to the clear and decisive
divine gift of the Land of Israel to the Children of Israel?

In sum, we have two sets of questions generated by this cryptic comment of Rashi:

1. How could we "do without" Genesis?

2. How does Rabbi Yitzhak's answer solve his quandary?

Before moving on, it is prudent to note that Ramban raised the most
basic of these questions in his first comments on the Torah. His explanation of R. Yitzhak's suggestion is not that we would be left uninformed
about the Creation; rather, that it would be understood from later
references (in the Torah) to Creation, and that the details (including
meta-historic narratives) would be transmitted through oral tradition.

Ramban also explicates Rabbi Yitzhak's answer, such that we understand that much more than the first verse is necessary for the anticipated
polemic against the nations:

> The Torah began with the chapter of "In the beginning God created . . ." and
> recounted the whole subject of creation until the making of man, how He
> granted him dominion over the works of His hands, and that He put all things
> under his feet; and how the Garden of Eden, which is the choicest of places
> created in this world, was made the place of his abode until his sin caused

his expulsion therefrom; and how the people of the generation of the flood were completely expelled from the world on account of their sin, and the only righteous one among them—he [Noah] and his children—were saved; and how the sin of their descendants caused them to be scattered to various places and dispersed to different countries, and how subsequently they seized unto themselves places after their families, in their nations as chance permitted. If so, it is proper that when a people continues to sin it should lose its place and another people should come to inherit its land, for such has been the rule of God in the world from the beginning. This is true all the more regarding that which is related in Scripture, namely that Canaan was cursed and sold as a servant forever. It would therefore not be proper that he inherit the choicest of places of the civilized world. Rather, the servants of God—the seed of His beloved one, Abraham—should inherit it. . . .

In other words, R. Yitzhak anticipates that the international censure of the Children of Israel will be grounded in the claim of the essential injustice of our conquest of the Land—to which we will be able to point to the pattern of Divine justice, involving expulsion, exile, and loss of national sovereignty as a result of sin, and the special relationship enjoyed by the children of Abraham within the matrix of the Divine scheme.

We are still faced with several problems:

1. Many of the Genesis stories — including some of the prominent ones in the first few chapters — seem superfluous within Rabbi Yitzhak's explanation.

2. Again, if the nations are not convinced by our "legal" claims as spelled out in the legalistic portions of the Torah, why would the narratives in Genesis be any more convincing?

RABBI YITZHAK'S ANSWER REVISITED

As noted earlier, the version of the Midrash cited by Rashi is related — with several significant variations — to Genesis Rabbah 1:2. One of the most significant differences is the verb used to describe the response of the Israelites to the nations. Whereas the passage in Genesis Rabbah has "*om'rim . . . m'shivin . . .*" (lit. "say . . . respond . . ."), the version found in Rashi has *om'rim* without the first verb *m'shivin*. In the text of the Midrash, the expectation is that the Israelites will actually respond (verbally) to the nations (i.e., the argument of Divine ownership will be the gist of our defense). It is possible to read Rashi's version differently — that this argument is not a defense, but rather is our claim, presented in a "take it or leave it" manner. In other words, the Israelites will have internalized the truth regarding proper proprietorship of the Land (and the earth) and will make this declaration to the nations.

That being the case, we can re-orient our earlier questions: What information is there in these sections of the Torah that is "more convincing" to us regarding our claim to the Land? And how do we account for the many (seemingly unrelated) stories throughout Genesis?

WHEN WAS GENESIS "GIVEN"?

Before responding to our questions, I'd like to pursue another line of inquiry that will lead us back to Rashi's first comment. The Torah itself tells us that Moses wrote at least one Torah scroll just before his death (Deuteronomy 31:9, 24), and the assumption among the Rabbis is that it was a complete (or nearly complete—note R. Judah's opinion in BT Bava Batra 15a) Torah scroll, including all of Genesis. We may be safe in assuming that this was not the first time that the Israelite nation heard the information contained in Genesis (besides the familiarity that they had with some of the stories in the form of family traditions—see Rashi, Exodus 3:18). When did they first "get to know" the book of Genesis?

Although this may seem an arcane question of dubious worth, this is not necessarily the case. As mentioned in the introduction to this chapter — and as many of the *Rishonim* have stressed — it is crucial to the understanding of the Torah that we read it through the prism of the ears of the original target audience. In other words, the way for us to most effectively and accurately understand the impact of the Torah's message is to try to "hear" it as did the first audience to whom any particular passage was addressed. The many images, word associations, double entendres, and so on that the Torah uses to enrich and deepen the impact of its message are only understood from the perspective of the people to whom these words were originally addressed. Only by "translating" these messages into contemporary terms (one of the most frequent modes of Torah commentary, dating back to the Midrashim) are we fully addressed by the Torah.

Therefore, it makes a big difference when Genesis was first presented to the people. We can understand the importance and implicit messages of the various narratives by placing them against the backdrop of the particular generation that first received them. Once we ascertain the nature and status of the "first audience" of Genesis, we may be able to decipher why these narratives were necessary for them to internalize, as per our understanding of Rabbi Yitzhak.

There are basically three alternatives as to when Genesis was first "presented" to the Children of Israel:

1. *At Mount Sinai.* In Exodus 24:1–7, we are told:

And unto Moses He said: "Come up unto the Lord, you, and Aaron, Nadab, and Abihu, and seventy of the elders of Israel; and worship from afar; and Moses alone will come near to the Lord; but they shall not come near; neither shall the people go up with him." And Moses came and told the people all the words of the Lord, and all the ordinances; and all the people answered with one voice, and said: "All the words which the Lord has spoken will we do." And Moses wrote all the words of the Lord, and rose up early in the morning, and built an altar under the mount, and twelve pillars, according to the twelve tribes of Israel. And he sent the young men of the Children of Israel, who offered burnt-offerings and sacrificed peace-offerings of oxen to the Lord. And Moses took half of the blood, and put it in basins; and half of the blood he dashed against the altar. And he took the Book of the Covenant, and read in the hearing of the people; and they said: "All that the Lord has spoken will we do, and obey."

Regarding the contents of the Book of the Covenant, Rashi avers that it included all of Genesis and all of Exodus until that point (including the Exodus, the Decalogue, and the laws of Chapters 21–23). It seems fairly straightforward that Rashi would maintain that this is the moment of "Genesis revelation." In other words, at this point, the first third (or so) of the Torah was presented to the people, and it was the first time that any of this had been presented (at least in written form) to them (or anyone else).

Rabbi Abraham ibn Ezra (d. 1167, Spain) takes a different approach and maintains that the Book of the Covenant only included those commands given to Moses at Sinai, beginning with the Decalogue. (Ramban concurs.) That being the case, when was Genesis (and the pre-Sinai narrative portions of Exodus) presented to the people?

2. *At the plains of Moab.* As mentioned earlier, Moses finally completed a Torah scroll (the first one presented to anyone else — in this case, the Levites) at the end of his life, in the plains of Moab (on the East Bank opposite Jericho). It is certainly plausible that this was the first time that the specific details of Genesis were revealed to the people, whether they

were given to Moses at that point or he had received them at Sinai and only now revealed them to the people.

3. *In Egypt (pre-Sinai).* The forefathers were prophets — as demonstrated by God's speaking to each of them — and many of their prophecies were intended to be realized in later generations. In addition, many of the symbols and messages given to them were specifically aimed at major historic events. Therefore, it is not implausible to maintain that as the events transpired and the prophecies were given, they were committed to writing. That would place a completed version of Genesis in the hands of the slaves in Egypt. Buttressing this somewhat unconventional perspective is the claim of the Midrash (Exodus Rabbah 5:22), which places a complete book of Genesis in Moses's hands at the beginning of his mission, well before the arrival at Sinai.

In sum, we have three viable alternatives as to when and to whom the book of Genesis was first revealed. It thus seems reasonable that the major impact of the narratives of Genesis must be viewed against these three "target audiences." And, since it is unclear which one was the true "original recipient," we would do well to suggest implications for each. In other words, by discerning the implications and import of any particular narrative in Genesis for the particular target group, we can respond confidently to Rabbi Yitzhak's question: "This is why Genesis had to be written — to get this particular message across to these particular people."

This is not to suggest that any of the narratives in Genesis are less than 100 percent accurate, but the fact of their inclusion (as opposed to others that are excluded, such as the early parts of Abraham's life) and how they are described (the particular uses of God's Names, word associations, etc.) carry implications that are, again, best understood by taking the original target audience into account.

SURVEYING PARASHAT B'RESHEET

In order to home in on the issue here, we will confine the rest of the analysis to the central themes of the opening weekly reading in Genesis, commonly called *Parashat B'resheet* (1:1–6:8). The interested reader can then apply these principles to the remainder of the pre-Sinaitic narrative.

There are 10 themes in *Parashat B'resheet*:

1. First Creation Story (1:1–2:3)
2. Second Creation Story (2:4–8)

3. Description of Garden (2:9–25)
4. Sin, Curse, and Exile #1 (3:1–24)
5. Fratricide (4:1–8)
6. Sin, Curse, and Exile #2 (4:9–16)
7. Generations ("Begats") (4:17–5:32)
8. Divine Disappointment (6:1–4)
9. Divine Consideration to Reverse Creation (6:5–7)
10. "Saving" Presence of the Righteous Man (Noah 6:8)

THE IMPACT OF PARASHAT B'RESHEET
ON THE EARLIEST TARGET AUDIENCE

I would like to analyze these major themes against the background of the Midrashic claim that Genesis was in the possession of the Israelites during their slavery. By taking their situation into account, we can revisit Rabbi Yitzhak's question and note how the messages of Genesis, implicitly or explicitly presented through these narratives, would have fortified their resolve and helped shape their understanding of their own future and destiny. By doing so, we can more fully understand Rashi's comment, as explicated by Ramban, that these lessons would serve the people well in readying them for their return to the Land and for a proper interaction with the neighboring nations.

The Israelites in Egypt, before and during the period of their slavery, had a proud past but (without the information in Genesis) an uncertain future and an oppressive present. Although some Hebrews evidently assimilated into Egyptian culture, others maintained fidelity to national faith, customs and, most significantly, aspirations. As such, the impact of these messages would have reasonably resonated with some of the most cherished and necessary beliefs and values that helped them survive and ensured the return of their children and grandchildren to the Land.

Here is a review of the 10 major themes in *Parashat B'resheet* and suggestions as to how the slave nation would have reasonably responded to these narrative passages:

1. First Creation Story (1:1–2:3)

The order that is the "signature" of this presentation of Creation (note how each day has its own orderly schema, each species reproducing according to its kind, etc.) is a powerful antidote to the harshness of exile and slavery. If God's universe is orderly and just, then the basic injustice of slavery will ultimately be rectified, especially following the implications of the end of *Parashat B'resheet* (#10 below).

2. Second Creation Story (2:4–8)

In the second story, the entire universe revolves around Man and, as we see further, it is Man's happiness that drives the Divine plan. As such, the essential unhappiness of slavery — as well as the "unnatural" subjugation of one man under another — is contrary to the Divine will and plan of creation.

3. Description of the Garden (2:9–25)

As beautiful as Egypt may be (see Genesis 13:10), it cannot compare with the "choicest of all places" (to use Ramban's phrase). The Land that our ancestors knew, were given, and had to leave is the closest thing on earth to this beautiful garden, thus giving hope for the future. In addition, the knowledge that both the Trees of Life and of Knowledge reside there create a longing for return to this paradise on earth, further inspiring these slaves to accept the burden of liberation and return home.

4. Sin, Curse, and Exile #1 (3:1–24)

Note that this first sin, curse, and exile sequence begins in the "choicest of places." The message is quite clear: As paradisiacal as this garden may be, that is the level of scrupulousness and piety that must be maintained there. Our "present" behavior in Egypt will not be acceptable there. (See the beginning of Leviticus 18 — the parallels are self-evident. See an alternative treatment of the sin-curse-exile sequence in Chapter V)

5. Fratricide (4:1–8)

The threat of dissension is great, especially for a people trying to regenerate their own national existence (cf. Exodus 2:11–15 and Rashi ad loc. v. 14). Even (perhaps especially) in the realms of piety and Divine worship, the dangers of "one-upsmanship" are prevalent.

6. Sin, Curse, and Exile #2 (4:9–16)

Unlike the earlier sequence, this one takes place outside of the Garden. There are some crimes that are so heinous, no land can bear the felon— and murder (especially fratricide) is at the top of that list. Note that here, unlike the earlier exile from the Garden to the East, Cain the murderer finds no place to rest. The Land to which the slave nation is coming will not bear its iniquities; even here they are not exempt from the onus of moral waywardness.

7. Generations ("Begats") (4:17–5:32)

Although this is often seen as "filler" text, which bridges the ten generations from Adam to Noah, there is a profound and sociologically impactful message here. Over the course of ten generations and hundreds of years, humanity sunk from the man who carried the breath of God to a generation so vile that they deserved destruction. Note that these changes do not occur overnight; they are the product of many years of down-spiraling immorality, idolatry, and wanton behavior. Perhaps the clue to the shift is given when we are told that "during the days of Enos, people began to call out the name of God" (see Rashi at 4:26; Mishne Torah *Avodah Zarah* 1:1).

8. Divine Disappointment (6:1–4)

Man is engaged in a contract with God and God is profoundly invested in man's behavior. Although this may be comforting regarding the Egyptian taskmasters, it is also the source of a great sense of responsibility towards our own present and future behavior, as well as our job to help perfect all of humanity (a job that cannot even be started as slaves in a foreign land).

9. Divine Consideration to Reverse Creation (6:5–7)

This brief passage, the theology of which seems so obvious to us, is highly significant. If God can "reconsider" creation, then He is not merely the "Prime Mover," but also the "Constant Mover," Whose will maintains creation at all times. In other words, this is a fundamental rejection of deism; God not only created, He continues as master of the universe who can, at any point, revert His creation to the primordial chaos.

10. "Saving" Presence of the Righteous Man (Noah 6:8)

The role of the individual person/nation who is righteous must have been very impactful to our ancestors in Egypt. If one person's righteousness can spare the world, that puts immense power and responsibility on the individual — all the more so on a nation whose credo is doing righteousness and justice (18:19). This nation which was temporarily exiled and enslaved but knew that a brighter future was their destiny must have been stirred and inspired by the opportunity to continue the role of Noah (and, later,

Abraham, Isaac, and Jacob) as "the righteous one [who] is an everlasting foundation." (Proverbs 10:25)

CODA

Rabbi Yitzhak's question is now clear: Since the Torah is fundamentally a book of instruction for the nation of Israel, why do we need to be taught all of the lessons of Genesis?

His answer is equally clear: In order for the Israelites, who were exiled and enslaved, to be able to maintain an understanding of Divine justice, national self-identity, and the special nature of the Land where they were destined to return, along with profound sociological and anthropological lessons necessary for the success of their national enterprise, they had to be given the full book of Genesis.

AFTERWORD

By utilizing the first component of our methodology — reading the text through the eyes of the original target audience(s) — we were able to discern the great significance of the (putatively) "extra" narratives that comprise the first 61 chapters of the Torah. Although we confined ourselves to the first 6 chapters, the principle holds true and can be applied throughout the pre-Sinaitic narrative.

TWO CREATION STORIES
Biblical Criticism – Countering the Critics (I)

OVER THE PAST 300 YEARS, NEARLY ALL ACADEMIC WORK IN
Biblical study and related fields has been undertaken within the accepted
axioms of the various schools of "Biblical Criticism." A full history of
these schools is beyond the scope of this work; that which is relevant to
the burgeoning world of "neo-Orthodox" *Parshanut* will be sketched
out here.

The first "red flag" for adherents of the school of Biblical Criticism
(specifically Higher Criticism – see below) is the various versions of similar stories in the Torah, each seeming to have its own lexicon, emphasis,
and worldview.

The first texts to which these critics point are the first two stories of
Creation (1:1–2:3 and 2:4 ff). Each story, when read as is, presents an
internally consistent and comprehensive story of creation, but the stories
differ in style, substance, and focus. The length of the creation process,
the order of creation, the Name of God used in the text, the "orderliness"
of the world and so on – each of these is presented in nearly antithetical
fashion in the two stories.

These differences are among the stronger "arguments" marshaled by
the school of Higher Criticism, which has set the tone for all academic research and scholarly discourse regarding the Bible. This school of thought
(which is really many different schools, each with its own variation) sees
the Torah as a patchwork of narratives, legal texts, and prophecy/poetry,
each produced by a different community of priests and scholars during the
10th–6th centuries BCE, which were woven into the Torah as we know
it sometime around the era of Ezra's leadership (5th century BCE, with
more modern minimalists dating parts into the Hellenistic period of the
4th and 3rd centuries BCE). The Bible critics maintain that each of these
communities had a different "version" of Creation, a different Name for
God etc. – thus explaining the many apparent discrepancies and stylistic
variations within the text.

For a myriad of reasons, both in the areas of creed and scholarship, we reject this "Documentary Hypothesis." Our belief is that the Torah was given by God and that the authorship is not only singular, it is exclusively Divine. These two statements of belief—whether or not they can be reasonably demonstrated (and there is much literature, medieval and contemporary, coming down on both sides of this question)— are part of the bedrock of traditional Jewish *"Hashkafah"* (worldview).

It has become a staple of neo-Orthodox *Parshanut*, beginning with the groundbreaking work of Rabbi D. Z. Hoffman (see Appendix), to address the issues raised by the critics. Serious commentators and scholars, familiar with the literature and approaches developed by the "Documentary Hypothesis," recognize the challenges raised by the text, but also recognize the essential vacuousness of the approach taken by the critics and, thus, respond to the same questions independent of the "doctrines" of the critical schools.

This chapter introduces a new approach to the old problem: reconciling the two stories of Creation, with all of their differences, into one document and one Author.

In Chapter 7, we will present a similarly styled development of the two "versions" of the Flood narrative; although we have maintained fidelity to the sequence of the text, for methodological purposes it is recommended that the two be read as one continuum. Chapter 10 will complete this series with an essay on a "lightning rod" for the critical schools found later in Genesis.

B'RESHEET: THE "GENESIS" OF A PROBLEM

Following the Torah's recounting, how long did Creation take? When (in that sequence) was Man created? When were the animals created? Where does the creation of Woman fit within this matrix?

Although most people would give singular answers to each of these questions (Creation took six or seven days, depending on whether you reckon the Sabbath; Man was created on the sixth day; the animals were created just before that; Woman was created from Man's rib), the reality of the Torah's narrative is far more complex.

Not only are there two different stories of Creation (the first story continues from 1:1 until the middle of 2:4; the second continues from there), but, from a purely text-driven read of the information, the accounts are contradictory! In the first story, Creation takes six or seven days, Man is created as a complete (single male-female) being at the apex of Creation. In the second story, Creation takes one day, Man is created as a lonely being at the beginning of the process. Woman is formed from Man — and is his "completion" — at the end of this creation process. Among the most pronounced differences between the two stories is the name for God; in the first story, God is exclusively referred to as the generic "Elohim," whereas in the second story, He is consistently called "Hashem[3] Elohim."

Because both intellectual honesty and religious tenet prevent us from positing that the Divine Author presents inconsistent information, how can we explain the "multiple versions" and apparent contradictions within the text?

TWO BASIC APPROACHES

From the perspective of tradition there are several ways to resolve these apparent contradictions. Most of them can be categorized into one of two basic approaches.

APPROACH #1: EACH VERSION COMPLETES THE OTHER

Fundamentally (no pun intended), we could try to "meld" the stories together. Rashi adopts this approach; for instance, in his commentary on the first verse in the Torah, Rashi notes that the first version of Creation uses the name "Elohim" for God, denoting strict justice (a court of law is also called *Elohim*—see Exodus 21:6), whereas the second version includes both the "Hashem" and "Elohim," indicating that although God's original intention was to create a world that would operate according to strict justice, He saw that that world could not last, so He integrated compassion (indicated by the Tetragrammaton—see Exodus 34:6) into the process.

The Talmud (BT Ketubot 8a) takes a similar approach to the two versions of the creation of Woman: "originally God intended to create them as one being, but in the end He created them as separate individuals."

There are many examples of this approach, which is a distinct thread of exegesis in Rabbinic and medieval commentary. The upshot of this approach is that each version tells part of the story, and the "alternate version" completes the picture.

This approach has been adopted by some contemporary authors who

---

3. References the Tetragrammaton – Y-H-V-H.

attempt to "reconcile" science and Torah (why this attempt may not be necessary and may, indeed, be misleading and harmful, is taken up in Chapter 7). The thinking goes as follows: Because each version provides only "part" of the information, it stands to reason that we may "synthesize" the versions together in various ways, including those that appear compatible with modern scientific theories about the origin of the universe, age of the earth, and origin of the species. In any case, this approach is both well-known and ubiquitously applied throughout Rabbinic exegesis regarding the Creation story (stories).

For purposes of our discussion, we will introduce another approach, which has its roots in Rabbinic literature and which was adopted by several of the *Rishonim* and more recent commentators.

APPROACH #2: CHANGING THE FRAME OF REFERENCE

Both the problem and the various solutions proposed by the proponents of the first approach are predicated on an understanding of the role of the Torah that is not the only valid one.

TWO TYPES OF TRUTH

A brief segue on the nature of "Truth" is in order here: There are statements that fall under the category of "Mathematical Truth"; for instance, that 7 times 9 equals 63 is not only an uncontested statement, but also the only acceptable one. In other words, 7 times 9 MUST equal 63; if it equals anything else, something is wrong with the computation. Mathematical Truth is not only consistent, but also exclusive.

If we maintain that the Torah is speaking the language of "Mathematical Truth," we have no recourse but to satisfy the two sides of the contradiction and either demonstrate that there is no contradiction at all or "weave" the information together (as demonstrated above).

There is, however, another type of statement that does not admit to "Mathematical Truth"; we will refer to it as "Ontological Truth" (the reality about living, growing, and dynamic beings). For instance, whereas it would be accurate to say that a certain boy loves to play baseball, that does not tell the full story of the boy. He is also afraid of spiders, excited about his upcoming trip to Washington, and has great aptitude in science. Whereas 7 times 9 cannot equal anything but 63, the boy can simultaneously be a baseball fan, a science whiz, and an arachnophobe.

As many commentators have pointed out (e.g., see Sforno's introduction to Genesis and S.D. Luzzato's introduction to his commentary on the Torah; note also Rashi's second comment on Genesis), the goal of the Torah is not to present "Mathematical Truths" in the realms of biology, mathematics, or "the origin of Man"; rather, the Torah is geared to teaching us basic principles of faith, shaping proper attitudes towards the world around us, towards God, and towards fellow humans. In addition — and most critically — the Torah's aim is to build a holy nation that will ultimately teach the basic truths and ethics of the Torah (note Deuteronomy 4:6) to the entire world.

That being the case, we may certainly understand the various versions of Creation as relating to different aspects of the world and of Man—and, notably, of Man's relationship with both the world around him and with the Creator.[4]

We can then look at each story not as a mathematical statement that is either true or false and that is vulnerable to contradiction from another, equally valid source (such as the next chapter!); rather, we look at each version as a series of ontological statements, geared toward teaching us significant and focal perspectives about who we are and how we should act.

TWO STORIES: HEAVEN AND EARTH; EARTH AND HEAVEN

We may find a clue about the "dual" nature of the Creation narrative via a careful look at the point where the two stories "meet," immediately after the Sabbath narrative: "These are the generations of the heaven and of the earth when they were created, On the day that *Hashem Elohim* made earth and heaven." (2:4)

Note that the first half of this verse is a perfect conclusion to the "first version"; it utilizes the common "*Eleh*" (these . . .) concluding formula. Note also that just as the first story began with the creation of "*Shamayim va'Aretz*" (heaven and earth), this half-verse seems to conclude that creation.

The second half begins a new "story," or another perspective of the same story: "On the day that *Hashem Elohim* made **earth** and **heaven**."

---

4. As far back as pre-millenial Alexandria, Jews were resolving the two stories of creation in a similar manner. See Philo's *On The Creation of the Cosmos According to Moses*, par. 134

Note that the order is reversed — this is a deliberate move on the part of the text to shift the emphasis and the perspective of the story.

Now let's see what the two stories are — which two perspectives of Creation are being presented here.

VERSION #1: THE STORY OF THE WORLD

The first version is, indeed, the story of the creation of the heaven and the earth; in other words, it is the story of the creation of the world from a Divine perspective. It begins with the Heaven, presenting an orderly world structured in a hierarchical manner in which every manner of life has its place (note the refrain of "according to its species" in the third, fifth, and sixth days). Man is created as the final, crowning touch of this glorious labor, and is formed "in God's image" in order to be His "agent," as it were, on earth: ". . . replenish the earth, and subdue it; and have dominion over the fish of the sea . . ." (1:28) Man is complete, Man is a master over his world, and Man needs nothing. Man here is also not commanded — God blesses him with fertility, but there is no direct relationship between Man and God in this version.

This is truly the story of the world; an orderly world created by God in which Man can be His partner, His agent—but not His "servant." The Name for God that denotes compassion—*Hashem*—is totally missing from this account, because there is no need for Divine compassion where there is no Divine command and no Divine worship.

VERSION #2: THE STORY OF MAN

There is another side to the story — the story of "*the* EARTH *and the* HEAVENS" — the story from the perspective of Man. (God is still "telling" the story, but from Man's point of view.)

From the human perspective, everything created serves a human purpose; even the animals can serve as Man's companions (and thus are "created" after him), but Man is not nearly as complete as the "detached" view would have it. Man is lonely; Man seeks out God as he seeks out meaning in this world of alienation and discord. This is a world where nothing grows because ". . . there was not a man to till the ground." (2:5) God forms Man and then, around him and for his sake, creates a beautiful world of orchards and rivers. Immediately, the most crucial point in their relationship is realized: God commands Man! Man is no longer lonely, on one level, because he is in relationship with God. From a different perspective, however, he is lonely because there is no one with whom to share this new life. Unlike the first "detached" story, in which everything is assessed as "good" (and, ultimately, "very good"), the first "non-good" thing is introduced — loneliness (2:18). As we follow Man through his bouts with temptation, guilt, cowardice, and the like, we learn more about who he is — and who we are.

The Torah is not telling us two conflicting versions about Creation; rather, we are seeing two sides of the same coin. The world is, indeed, an orderly place of hierarchical systems, where Man is the ultimate creature; yet, the world is also a place where Man feels alien and distant, seeking out companionship and meaning in his relationships with fellow humans, with a mate, and with God.

TWO CREATION STORIES
Structure and Meaning: Chiasmus

INTRODUCTION

Literary Structure: The Chiasmus

Throughout this volume, we will investigate modern methods of *Parshanut* that involve contextual reading, utilization of historic background, and numerous other hermeneutic tools, some of which were used, albeit without much fanfare, by the classical commentators and even by the Rabbis of the Talmudic/Midrashic era. One feature with which all of our traditional predecessors were familiar is literary structure. Literary structure refers to the strategic and deliberate placement of common, parallel, or antonymic words or phrases at key junctures within a pericope that help to establish a sense of setting or a mood, or perhaps telegraph a subtextual message to the sensitive reader. Because the Torah expects us all to be thoughtful and sensitive readers, we have a responsibility to analyze the potential structural nuances within a given literary unit in order to dig underneath the words of the text and identify an underlying theme, if possible, that serves to inform the entire unit.

One common literary structure that is liberally used within the canon is the chiasmus. The letter "chi" in Greek is shaped like an "X" (χ); a chiasmus is a unit that is structured in an ABBA or ABCBA fashion. The subunits may be phrases, groups of verses, paragraphs (*Parashot*), or even larger units. Scholars have even proposed seeing the entire hexateuch (Torah and Joshua) as a chiasmus.[5] We will not venture that far, but it is easy to demonstrate both the existence and significance of both types of chiasmus within each of these units.

---

5. See *Between the Lines of the Bible*, volume 2, chapter 10

Here are examples of both ABBA and ABCBA (they are by no means limited to four or five stages) in phrases within one verse.

- ABBA: (1 Samuel 1:2): And he had two wives:
  - the name of the one was Hannah,
    - and the name of the other Peninnah;
    - and Peninnah had children,
  - but Hannah had no children.

The order here is Hannah, Peninnah, Peninnah, Hannah. Peninnah is highlighted — by virtue of her having borne children — and Hannah is "marginalized." This accurately reflects Hannah's status, in spite of El-kanah's love for her, within the family. It serves to inform the rest of the narrative, which is focused on Hannah's prayer for a son.

- ABCBA: (Judges 5:24): Blessed above women shall Jael be, the wife of Heber the Kenite, above women in the tent shall she be blessed.
  —Hebrew:

> *T'vorakh*
>   *miNashim*
>   *Ya'el Eshet Hever haKeini*
>   *miNashim ba'Ohel*
> *T'vorakh*

This verse, towards the end of Deborah and Barak's song of victory, praises Jael for her liquidation of Sisera. By using the paired *T'vorakh* (blessed is) as the framework of the verse, and then introducing the group over which Jael is to be praised (more than women in the tent), her name and family connection are highlighted. Reading through the associated narrative (Judges 4) gives the necessary background: Jael was able to finish off Sisera because he made the fatal mistake of relying on the alliance between the Canaanites and the Kenites.

The chiastic structure—a sort of inverted parallelism—may be a "pure" chiasmus, as in the two examples given above, where A and A' match each other. Alternatively, they may be a "progressive" chiasmus, where the actors, in their parallel spot within the structure, have developed (for better or for worse) and, as such, the chiasmus is not made up of parallel descriptive statements, but rather of progressive statements that allude to a dynamic.

THE GENESIS PROBLEM REVISITED

In the previous chapter, in addressing the challenges presented by the schools of Biblical Criticism, we analyzed the "two creation stories" found at the beginning of Genesis. As mentioned there, and as was quite clear to the Rabbis of the Talmudic/Midrashic era, as well as the classical medieval commentators, there are two distinct and radically different presentations of the Creation within the first three chapters of Genesis. In that chapter, I suggested that we look at the two stories as complementary, each presenting a different perspective on this world.

We will now revisit the problem, adding a literary component to that analysis, and thereby bringing to light a significant "message" that is being communicated in these opening chapters.

As mentioned earlier, the Midrashic authors were aware of these discrepancies. In some approaches, the second story was understood to be a detailed clarification of the first; in others, the first represented "idealized Creation," whereas the second was the "actual Creation" of the world and of mankind. Still others saw the first story as representing the goal of each component of Creation, and the second story describing the way in which it served man and, thus, served God's purpose. Each of these approaches, among others, was adopted by one or more of the medieval commentators in their assessment of the text.

I would like to suggest that although a superficial perusal of the text leaves the impression that we are dealing with two distinct — and diametrically opposite — stories that demand reconciliation, this is not necessarily the case. If we take a closer look at the literary structure of these two descriptions, we will note an interesting pattern that suggests one integrated presentation.

DEFINING THE METHOD

As presented at the beginning of this chapter, the Biblical text is often presented in chiastic form. A chiasmus (as with any parallelism) can be identified in one of two manners:

1. common words or phrases are used, or
2. similar ideas are presented.

I would like to suggest that if we look at both Creation stories, we will find some interesting parallels between them that suggest a chiastic structure. For our purposes, the second Creation story ends at the conclusion of Chapter3 (v. 24), with the exile of Man from the Garden.

Within the analysis presented below, we will use the letters followed by number 1 or 2 (e.g., A1 and A2) to represent the parallel statements. What may be confusing is that all of *x2* (A2, B2, etc.) will be reckoned in reverse order, because the chiasmus builds from the outside in. The parallel to the first passage is the final one, the parallel to the second is the penultimate, and so on.

As we have done before, we will use "Hashem" to indicate the appearance of the Tetragrammaton and "God" to represent "Elohim."

THE STRUCTURE

A. Ultimate separation

A1: "In the beginning God created the *Shamayim* (heavens?) and the *Aretz* (earth?)."

Although some have interpreted the entire first story as one of repeated and intensified separation, where each species is assigned a role, the text itself suggests a different approach. As *Netziv*[6] points out, *Shamayim* (which cannot mean the same as the "Heaven" of v. 8, as pointed out by Ramban ad loc. — it hadn't yet been created) refers to all sources of giving, impacting, and influencing. *Aretz* refers, in kind, to all spheres of receptivity. In other words, the first thing that God created was the possibility of giving and receiving, of impacting and of being impacted. Everything that unfolds is the development of the interaction between those two poles.

That being the case, the Torah begins with a description of total separation between the spheres. There was *Shamayim* and there was *Aretz* — as yet, there was no interaction between the two.

A2: "And Hashem God sent him out from the Garden of Eden, to till the ground from where he was taken. So He drove out the man; and He placed Cherubim at the east of the garden of Eden, and a flaming sword which turned every way, to guard the way of the tree of life." (3:23–24)

Man is permanently and forcefully barred from his abode — the model for exile. Not only is this a parallel model of separation, it also parallels

---

6. R. Naftali Tzvi Yehuda Berlin, commonly known by his acronym "Netziv" – d. 1893, Poland. See Appendix A.

the disengagement of impact described in the first verse. Man, whose job (as we will see further on) is to work the Garden and protect it, has been removed from his sphere of influence.

B. Anticipation of interaction

B1: "Now the earth was *Tohu* and *Bohu*, and darkness was upon the face of the deep. And the spirit of God hovered over the face of the waters" (1:2). (*Tohu* and *Bohu* have been interpreted in several ways; hence, they have been left without translation. Ramban understands *Tohu* as matter and *Bohu* as form.)

We are riveted by anticipation that God's spirit, hovering over the water, is going to act in such a way as to cause dynamic interaction, thus enabling the process of Creation. That is, of course, what happens in the very next verse.

B2: "And Hashem God said: 'Behold, the Man is become as one of us, to know good and evil; and now, lest he put forth his hand, and take also of the tree of life, and eat, and live forever.'" (3:22)

Note that the concern—that Man might "live forever"—neatly parallels the "spirit of God" in B1. The spirit that animates Man, as described in 2:7, is the spirit of God. More significantly, this verse, the motivation for Man's exile, anticipates Man's inappropriate interaction in the Garden, which necessitates his removal.

C. Vehicle for interaction: The creation of light

C1: "And God said: 'Let there be light' And there was light. . . . And there was evening and there was morning, one day." (1:3,5)

As is clear, both from the textual evidence and from a plethora of statements in Midrashic literature (followed by all of the classical commentators), the "light" created on the first day was not the sunlight with which we are accustomed. The implication of the creation of light here is best put by the comment in Genesis Rabbah:

> R. Isaac says, the light was created first [before the world]; this is similar to a king who set out to build a castle in a dark place. What did he do? He lit candles and torches in order to ascertain how to establish the foundation. (Genesis Rabbah 3:1)

The light is presented here as the vehicle for creating interaction between the *Shamayim* and the *Aretz*.

C2: "And Hashem God fashioned for Adam and for his wife *Kot'not 'Or* (garments of skins), and clothed them." (3:21)

In response to the punishments meted out to the first couple and the serpent (see below), God fashioned clothes for Adam and his wife. This should not be seen only as a preparation for their ouster from the garden; even while there, they fell out of harmony with their surroundings to the point where they were in need of protection from their own environment.

Whereas the light created on the first day was a vehicle for more intense interaction, the clothes fashioned by God were a vehicle for a more disjointed and isolated existence.

Curiously, we find a textual "emendation" in the Midrash attributed to R. Meir (who had a reputation as a reliable scribe — see BT Megillah 18b). In R. Meir's Torah it says "*Kot'not Or*" (*Or* with an *Alef*, meaning "light," as opposed to the conventional *Or with an Ayin*,, meaning "skin" — see Mirkin's illuminating comments at Genesis Rabbah 20:12[7]). R. Meir understood that their garments were fashioned from the light of the first day's creation.

D. Establishing boundaries

D1: "And God said: 'Let there be a firmament in the midst of the waters, and let it divide the waters from the waters.' . . . And there was evening and there was morning, a second day." (1:6, 8)

Before enabling any interaction, clear boundaries between the actor and recipient must be drawn, as well as defining the various recipients. For example, any successful classroom experience will only take place once the difference in the roles of the teacher and students is established and clarified to all, as well as identifying the range of needs of the various students. This is the sense of the "accomplishment" of the second day of Creation.

D2: "And Hashem God said to the serpent, 'Because you have done this, you are cursed . . . And I will put enmity between you and the Woman' . . . To the Woman he said 'I will greatly multiply the pain of your child bearing; in sorrow you shall bring forth children; and your desire shall be to your husband, and he shall rule over you.' And to Adam he said '. . . cursed is the ground for your sake; in sorrow shall you eat of it all the days of your life; Thorns also and thistles shall it bring forth to you; and you shall eat the herb of the field; In the sweat of your face shall you eat

---

7. *Mirkin*, Midrash Rabbah, Tel-Aviv 1957 (Heb.) vol. 1 pp. 156–157.

bread, till you return to the ground; for out of it you were taken; for dust you are, and to dust shall you return.' And Adam called his wife's name Eve; because she was the mother of all living." (3:14–20)

Subsequent to the sin, and the consequential finger-pointing (man to his wife, she to the serpent), all three actors are punished. The one thread that holds these punishments together is the absolute disharmony from environment. The serpent, previously able to converse with Man (see R. Obadia Sforno's approach to this and, more radically, Gersonides's take on the entire story), is now a mortal enemy to Man. The Woman, created as a helper to Man, becomes his subject (politically incorrect though this may be, that is exactly what the text says), and Man, given the job of tilling the garden, is now at odds with the earth.

The profundity of this separation can be discerned in the verse that follows Adam's punishment: Adam gave his wife a name. Why wasn't this name mentioned earlier?

Before the creation of Woman (in Chapter 2), Man was given the opportunity to find a companion among the animals. What indicated that none of these matches was appropriate? Man gave names to all of the animals (2:19–20), the result of which was "but for Adam there was not found a helpmeet for him." From Woman's entry onto the stage of creation, Adam does not name her, except to call her "Mrs." (*Ishah* — female *Ish*[8]). It is only when they have been turned against each other, as their environment has been turned against them, that Adam has the dispassion of separation that allows him to name her.

Just as we found on the second day, we see a description of clear boundaries established, not only limiting the range of operation (the serpent), but also creating a permanent divide between the species.

E. Fidelity of the species

E1: "And God said: 'Let the earth put forth grass, herb yielding seed, and fruit-tree bearing fruit after its kind, whose seed is in itself, upon the earth' And it was so. And the earth brought forth grass, herb yielding seed after its kind, and tree bearing fruit, whose seed was in itself, after its kind; and God saw that it was good. And there was evening and there was morning, a third day." (1:11–13)

The *leitwort* (see Chapter 12) in this section is *l'Mineihu* — "according

---

8. This is an example of textual homiletics, as the two words are based on nearly antonymic roots!

to its kind." In one form or another, it shows up three times in the two central verses here. The creation of regenerative vegetation is built on fidelity to the species — each seed brings forth its own kind. In Chapter 6, we will use this model to explain the "reversal of creation," which was the underlying theme of the flood narrative.

Although the creation story has now moved towards active integration, allowing the forces of heaven and earth to combine to create the environment that man will enjoy, the integration is still bound by *l'Mineihu*.

E2: "And they heard the voice of Hashem God walking in the Garden in the cool of the day . . . And Hashem God called to Adam, and said to him, 'Where are you?' . . . And He said, 'Who told you that you were naked? Have you eaten of the tree, which I commanded you that you should not eat?' And the Man said, 'The Woman whom you gave to be with me, she gave me of the tree, and I ate.' And Hashem God said to the Woman, 'What is this that you have done?' And the Woman said, 'The serpent beguiled me, and I ate.'" (3:8–12)

Until this point, as indicated by the first verse quoted here, there is a sense not only of harmony, but of boundlessness in the Garden. Not only are Man and Woman "of one flesh" (2:24), but God Himself "walks in the Garden." (For a beautiful example of this imagery in Midrashic literature, see Ecclesiastes Rabbah 7:19.)

At this point, God and Man are (for the first time) turned against each other. God seeks Man, who hides from him, denying any wrongdoing. When faced with the reality of his sin, Man points to an "other," the Woman. She, in turn, points to an "other," the serpent. Each species (and gender) is drawing the lines for themselves. As opposed to R. Aryeh Levin's legendary statement to the doctor "my wife's foot hurts us," every actor here is isolating him- or herself from the others. Just as the third day of Creation focused on "each after its own kind," that's exactly how this scene was played out. (On a related note, the Midrash explains that the "task" of the second day was not completed until the third day, which is why there is no assessment of "it is good" on the second day. Similarly, the separation between the species and the genders outlined in this segment of the Garden narrative becomes complete when God announces the punishment, presented in section D above.)

F. Illumination and power

F1: "And God said: 'Let there be lights in the firmament of the heaven to divide the day from the night; and let them be for signs, and for seasons, and for days and years; and let them be for lights in the firmament of the heaven to give light upon the earth' And it was so. And God made the two great lights: the greater light to rule the day, and the lesser light to rule the night . . . and there was evening and there was morning, a fourth day." (1:14–19)

This description, in the first Creation story, of the establishment of the "heavenly lights" highlights their purpose: to rule over the day and night, as well as to divide those two realms. (The Midrash developed this theme of "rulership" in a beautiful legend—BT Hullin 60b.) The link between the power to illumine and the ability to rule and control is firmly established here, as is the interrelationship between visual acuity and discernment (the ability to distinguish one day from another).

F2: "'. . . For God knows that in the day you eat of it, then your eyes shall be opened, and you shall be as gods, knowing good and evil.' And when the Woman saw that the tree was good for food, and that it was pleasant to the eyes, and a tree to be desired to make one wise, she took of its fruit, and ate; and gave also to her husband with her; and he ate. And the eyes of them both were opened . . ." (3:5–7)

The essential seduction of the serpent is power, to wit, "by eating of this fruit, you will gain a vision heretofore reserved for God, and, as a result, you will have a godly power"; indeed, that is not far from what actually transpired. Just as the purpose of the lights of the fourth day of Creation was their dominion, similarly, the vision acquired through eating of the fruit was designed to empower Man.

G. Reptiles

G1: "And God said: 'Let the waters swarm with swarms of living creatures, and let fowl fly above the earth in the open firmament of heaven.' And God created the great sea-monsters, and every living creature that creepeth, wherewith the waters swarmed, after its kind, and every winged fowl after its kind; and God saw that it was good. And God blessed them, saying: 'Be fruitful, and multiply, and fill the waters in the seas, and let fowl multiply in the earth.'" (1:20–22)

Among all of the birds and fish (and beasts, created on the sixth day), the only one that is deemed to be "created" (*Bara*) is the *Tanin* (crocodile/sea monster?). The verb *Bara* appears in only three contexts in this chapter: the general introduction (1:1, 2:3), the creation of Man (v. 27), and the creation of these sea-beasts. The first two are easy to explain — the overall act being described here is creation, even if the individual components were, as Ramban describes it, the evolution and unfolding of all of the potential in that original Creation. The second one, referring to Man, is eminently reasonable as it highlights the unique nature of Mankind, being formed singularly in God's image. The mention of creation in reference to the *Taninim* is a bit odd; commentators have raised several suggestions to solve this riddle. I'd like to suggest that this sea monster, something of an amphibious reptile, is portrayed as the marine parallel of the primordial serpent. The serpent is presented as the cleverest of all beasts, able not only to communicate with, but even to seduce Man. Yet, by the time the story is over, his station is severely reduced to that of the snakes we all know. In the same manner, the early sea monsters were clearly the most powerful and/or significant of the non-human beasts, thus explaining their being described as "created" (and singled out for a detailed listing of their creation), even though, from our perspective, they are a thing of the very distant past and occupy no place in our world. See the parallel quote from the second story:

G2: 1. "Now the serpent was more subtle than any beast of the field which Hashem God had made. And he said to the Woman, 'Has God said, you shall not eat of every tree of the garden?'" . . . and the serpent said to the Woman, 'surely die.'" (3:1–4)

H. Creation of beasts

H1: "And God said: 'Let the earth bring forth the living creature after its kind, cattle, and creeping thing, and beast of the earth after its kind' And it was so. And God made the beast of the earth after its kind, and the cattle after their kind, and every thing that creeps upon the earth after its kind; and God saw that it was good." (1:24–25)

The animals, unlike Man, are "formed" from the ground. In addition, they have no specific purpose, except, as we will soon see, to serve Man (1:28).

H2: "And Hashem God said, 'It is not good that the Man should be alone; I will make him a help to match him.' And out of the ground Hashem God formed every beast of the field, and every bird of the air; and brought them to Adam to see what he would call them; and whatsoever Adam called every living creature, that was its name. And Adam gave names to all cattle, and to the bird of the air, and to every beast of the field; but for Adam there was not found a help to match him. And Hashem God made Adam fall into a deep sleep . . . And they were both naked, the man and his wife, and were not ashamed." (2:18–25)

The entire purpose of the creation of animals is to alleviate Man's loneliness. When that doesn't work, Woman is fashioned from his rib (or "side") — but, even after her creation, the two of them are described in animal-like terms. Note especially, the description of their lack of shame at their nakedness. Although we may wish to see this as child-like innocence, the lack of shame explicitly mentioned seems to point more to the "animal" side of Mankind.

I. Uniqueness of man

I₁: "And God said: 'Let us make Man in Our image, after Our likeness; and let them have dominion over the fish of the sea, and over the birds of the air, and over the cattle, and over all the earth, and over every creeping thing that creeps upon the earth.' So God created Man in His own image ... And God blessed them; and God said unto them: 'Be fruitful, and multiply, and replenish the earth, and subdue it; and have dominion over the fish of the sea, and over the birds of the air, and over every living thing that moves upon the earth.'" (1:26–28)

Man is the crown of Creation, formed in God's Image. In addition, Man is presented as the caretaker of the earth, who will rule (as proxy for the Creator?) over all of the other creatures.

I₂: "And Hashem God formed Man of the dust of the ground, and breathed into his nostrils the breath of life; and Man became a living soul. And Hashem God planted a garden eastward in Eden; and there He put the Man whom he had formed. and out of the ground made Hashem God every tree to grow that is pleasant ... And a river went out from Eden to water the garden ... And Hashem God took the Man, and put him into the garden of Eden to cultivate it and to keep it. And Hashem God commanded the man, saying..." (2:7–16)

The description of God lovingly forming (as it were, with His own hands) Man from the dust and breathing the spirit of life into his nostrils highlights, again, Man's esteemed station in God's universe. Man is the only creature capable of being commanded, as he is the only one endowed with the ability to err — and the conscience to keep from erring.

J. Man's responsibility

J₁: "And God said: 'Behold, I have given you every herb yielding seed, which is upon the face of all the earth, and every tree, in which is the fruit of a tree yielding seed — to you it shall be for food; and to every beast of the earth, and to every bird of the air, and to every thing that creeps

upon the earth, where there is life, I have given every green herb for food'
And it was so." (1:29–30)

Man is given charge of the earth, even to make sure that the other
creatures stand in proper relation to each other.

J2: ". . . in the day that Hashem God made the earth and the heavens,
and every plant of the field before it was in the earth, and every herb of
the field before it grew; for Hashem God had not caused it to rain upon
the earth, and there was not a man to till the ground. And a mist went
up from the earth, and watered the whole face of the ground." (2:4–6)

The whole world is waiting for the arrival of Man, who will take charge
– "and there was not a man to till the ground." Man's unique character,
exalted among all creatures, obligates him to act responsibly towards all
lesser creatures.

K: Shabbat

This section, which has been marked off in two opposing manners, sits at
the convergence of our inverted parallelism. Whereas our traditional divisions (*s'darim*) have placed this paragraph at the end of the first creation
story, the "chapter" divisions (of Christian origin) reckon this section as
part of the second story (or an independent unit). Within the scheme we
are suggesting here, it is both the end of the first story and the beginning
(or introduction) to the second:

> And God saw every thing that He had made, and behold, it was very good,
> And there was evening and there was morning, the sixth day. And the heaven
> and the earth were finished, and all the host of them. And on the seventh day
> God finished His work which He had made; and He rested on the seventh
> day from all His work which He had made. And God blessed the seventh
> day, and sanctified it; because in it He rested from all His work which God in
> creating had made. These are the generations of the heaven and of the earth
> when they were created . . . (1:31–2:4)

The pinnacle of Creation, where every creature stands in perfect and
ideal relation to every other component of creation, is realized with the
Sabbath. Ultimately, all things return to God, as do all of His creatures.
The focus on Man, so prevalent in the previous (and coming) section, is
absent here, as the world of the Sabbath, a world filled with the sanctity
and blessing of God's "rest," overwhelms Creation itself.

ANALYZING THE STRUCTURE

As in any inverted parallel, the focus point is at the fulcrum, or nexus, of the parallel. The extreme points of each story describe a total and ultimate separation. With each step, interaction and integration are enabled, enhanced, and realized. At the final step, not only are all creatures in place, but they all stand in proper relation to each other. Man, the crown of Creation, is charged with implementing God's plan of dynamic growth and synthesis on earth, all within the Divine mandate.

In these two, chiastically related stories, we have seen:

A. Total separation
B. Anticipation of interaction
C. Vehicle for interaction
D. Firming of boundaries
E. "Species fidelity"
F. The power associated with illumination
G. The formerly unique station of some unique beasts
H. The creation of animals
I. The unique creation of Man
J. Man's role on earth
K. The Sabbath

ASSESSMENT: WHAT HAVE WE LEARNED?

The "neat symmetry" presented here not only renders the challenges raised by the conflicting reports of Creation moot, but also serves to reorient our appreciation of the entire presentation of Creation in the first three chapters and to see it as one integrated story. This is all fine and good, but what's the lesson here?

The pointing of each story as beginning with a total separation of God from His world, as it were, and culminating in unity, places *Teshuvah* as the glorious background on the tapestry of the world. All things stem from God's will and all things are profoundly connected to God. All of Creation points towards God and yearns to return to its source. However we understand *Teshuvah* (repentance/return to God) in its pure legal sense (as an independent *Mitzvah* or one that attaches to all others as a contingency), we see a powerful thread of *Teshuvah* woven throughout these two stories of creation.

Teshuvah, in its fullest sense (most beautifully defined and illuminated by Rabbi A. I. Kook in his *Orot haTeshuva*), does not attach itself only (or chiefly) to specific acts and omissions. *Teshuvah* is, rather, the very life-spirit of all of Creation. As we have seen in this analysis, the separation and isolation, be it heavens from earth or Man from the Garden, stand at the polar extremes from the holiness of the Sabbath. The Sabbath is that singular experience, which we are blessed with each week, where all of Creation stands at its perfect place in relation to the Creator — and to itself. Is it any wonder that the Rabbis attributed the "Song of the Sabbath" (Psalm 92) to Adam, after he learned of the power of *Teshuvah* (Genesis Rabbah 22:13)?

"Great is *Teshuvah*, that it preceded the creation of the world." (Midrash T'hillim 90:12)

"*Teshuvah* preceded the world, therefore it is the foundation of the world. The fulfillment of life occurs specifically through the unfolding revelation of its essential nature."[9]

AFTERWORD

The tools of literary analysis, only a few of which are presented in this volume, can be used with great efficiency to uncover layers of meaning in the text and help us read between the lines. By looking at the "greater picture," we were able to discern an inversion pattern that placed the Sabbath at the nexus of Creation.

---

9. R. Abraham Kook, *Orot haTeshuvah* 5:6.

SETTING THE STAGE
Primordial Sins

INTRODUCTION

The book of Genesis, unlike the other four books, is nearly all narrative; even the one legalistic text (the presentation of *B'rit Milah* at 17:10 – see Chapter XI *q.v.*) and the various prophecies and poetics (e.g., the various blessings given by fathers to their sons) are couched in a narrative context. We are accustomed – and quite comfortable – reading Genesis from "the beginning" as a narrative flow, each story pushing towards the next, seeing (or sensing – and sometimes seeking) the causal relationship between them. Yet, even a cursory read of the book leaves us with a strong sense that the first eleven chapters stand out as distinct from the rest of the book; the first real character that we get to know and see in protagonist terms is Abraham, who is introduced at the end of chapter 11. The stories, the characters, their actions – even their life-spans – have a mythic aura to them; indeed, we read those first sequence of stories as "universal history" whereas, beginning in chapter 12, "Israelite history" begins. However we choose to interpret Creation, the garden, the flood and the tower – and our tradition has a wide range of approaches to each of these – we intuit that these narratives are foundational and speak to Man's nature and de-scribe the course of humankind, serving as a backdrop against which to view the history of the Abrahamic nation and ultimately the covenant forged between God and Jacob's descendants at Sinai.

Following this perspective, I'd like to suggest that we ought to view the "pre-history" of the first two Parashot ("Beresheet" and "Noach") as serving a particular goal which necessitates reading the text in a non-linear fashion.

Subsequent to the Creation of the world, which was deemed to be "very good" (1:31), Man descended from the august position he held at the moment of his own birth to a point of perdition so severe that the

Creator "regretted" creating Man and decided to destroy all, turning the creation sequence backward by flooding the earth. There was but one family that was relatively innocent and served as the nucleus of a new creation – note the similarity in language between the first Creation at the end of Chapter 1 and the new – postdiluvian "creation" covenant of Chapter 8.

The new creation, however, does not fare well and mankind again sinks into an abyss of sinfulness, such that God again intervenes – far more mildly – by actively disrupting the construction of the Tower in Shin'ar (11:1–9). However, as God has bound Himself by an oath to never again destroy the earth, a different model of starting over is introduced. In lieu of destruction, the new model is instruction – and Abraham is chosen to carry that message to a globally central location, from where "all families of the earth will be blessed through him" (12:3). In other words, Abraham's task is to heal a world gone awry and to restore the Divine to the mundane and to sanctify the profane. Our rabbis hinted to this notion by observing the parallel between the span from Creation to the flood (10 generations) and the span from the flood to Abraham (again, 10 generations). The rest of the narrative, the covenant, the singular mission of Abraham and his seed, is a response to the patterns of behavior since Creation – in other words, it is Abraham's job to fix a broken world. It is to that end that we are privy to the stories which are, prima facie, foreign to our nationhood – the foundational stories of the pre-Abrahamic world; we read these in order to see the stage which Abraham ascended, to understand what was broken about the world and to understand what it was that he and his progeny were to repair. In that light, we ought to read the first eleven chapters with Abraham – and his descendants – in mind, as describing the challenges that we are all called to overcome and the rupture we are summoned to mend. Much as we read the foundational history to get a sense of a potential beautiful and just world, we also read it to understand the covenant and mission given to us at Sinai.

Note: it is advisable to read this chapter with Bible in hand; read the indicated passages before each section.

THE FIRST VIOLATION – SIN OF APPETITE   Genesis 3

The first transgression in human history, the earliest recorded time of Man's disobedience to God's command is the trespass against the "Tree of

Knowledge of Good and Evil" in Eden. There are nearly as many ways to understand this story as there are commentators, ranging from the literal to the symbolic, metaphoric and metaphysical; yet we must always begin our investigation with *P'shuto Shel Mikra* – the simple, straightforward meaning of the text. That is to say – regardless of our understanding of *what happened*, we must first ascertain what the text is teaching us – in other words, to understand what the text wants to communicate about what happened.

The environment of the garden is replete with sexuality; indeed, the terms used in this narrative speak to desire and lust – ... ותרא האשה כי תאוה הוא לעיניים – *"and the Woman saw that the tree was ... lustful to the eyes"*; many post-Biblical traditions exposit some form of sexual desire, awakening, or pollution in this story, including ascribing sexual jealousy to the snake as his motivation for seducing the Woman to eat from the tree. Indeed, our Rabbis suggest that the "tree" in question may have been a grapevine, as the association between wine and promiscuity is well-attested in the Biblical canon.

The driving force behind promiscuity and other sexual violations is one of appetite – the eyes see, the heart desires, and the body follows in tow. This is the beginning of Mankind's "road to perdition." For the first time, God seeks out Man – "where are you?" – and metes out the consequences for this desire gone awry. Mankind is banished from the elite location and is e'er mired in a battle against his environment, pitting Man against the soil, Woman against her own body, and both of them against the animal kingdom.

Important to note: the text does not, here or elsewhere, criminalize desire itself, except insofar as it leads to an outright violation of the law. But a desire that impels Man past his responsibilities is an appetite which, once sated, only becomes more ravenous.

THE SECOND VIOLATION(S) – SIN OF VIOLENCE   Genesis 4

The first murder recorded in the Bible is the slaying of Abel by his elder brother Cain. The story is well-known and, as the Rabbis suggest, it is indeed possible that Cain did not intend to snuff out his brother's life – but nonetheless reacted violently and with (apparent) intent to inflict bodily harm on his brother – as a result of his jealousy over the Divine favor which Abel's offering had garnered over his. Again, God confronts the criminal, leaving him an opening to confess by asking an "innocent" question and, when the violator does not confess, hands down the decree and the sentence is executed.

Within a few generations, what began as an unintended tragic consequence of anger unbridled (the death of Abel) has become a strategy and a known part of the human landscape. Five generations later, Cain's descendant Lemekh, the first documented polygamist, threatens his wives with violence if they do not accede to his sexual demands. Murder has become a threat, a tool to be used for the powerful man to get his way.

THE FINAL VIOLATION – SIN OF IDEOLOGY   Chapter 4, verse 26

The concluding verse of Chapter 4 is – like so many in these chapters – opaque and enigmatic. Whereas the first stich is easy to understand – Seth (Adam's third son) gave birth to a son and named him "Enosh" (literally "mortal"), the final phrase אז הוחל לקרוא בשם ה' has all of the classical commentators taking variant and, in some cases, diametrically polar positions. While some read the phrase to mean "then people started to publicize God's Name" (akin to Abraham's mission), others understand it to mean that people began to call *other things* "God" – or that people *ceased* (הוחל – stopped) to call out to God. Oddly enough, the overwhelming majority of commentators see the passage as ominous – even Seforno understands that "calling out God's Name" (which we would typically read as an upbeat verse) was due to the many sins of the generation – and those "calling out" were the righteous few, trying to correct society's ills.

Idolatry is unlike violations driven by appetite/desire or anger/jealousy. When embracing an idolatrous creed, the opportunities for correcting wrongful behavior and attitudes is severely diminished as those perspectives and actions are now justified. Further on, we will explore the relationship between these three stages of wrongdoing; suffice it for now to point out that this is the last "crime" identified in the text until just before the Flood narrative.

It is interesting to note that an even more enigmatic passage which presages the Flood and seems to be the proximate cause of that utter destruction – the "*B'nei ha'Elohim*" and their taking of human women by force (6:2) – incorporates all three of our motifs: taking women (sexual desire); "that they chose" (implication of force, the motif of violence); and calling them "*B'nei ha'Elohim*" (implying some sort of divinity).

INTERLUDE: DESTRUCTION AND A NEW WORLD   Chapters 7–8

The direct result of Man's fall is the Flood – and, as mentioned above (and is more fully explored in Chapter 6), the aftermath of the Flood is a new start, a new humanity. *B'nei Adam* – children of Adam, are now *B'nei Noach* – children of Noach, the "new" father of humanity. We expect, we hope, we pray that this time Mankind will "get it right"; and avoid the patterns of behavior which led to the near-total destruction of the world.

THE FIRST VIOLATION – SIN OF APPETITE (REDUX)
Genesis 9:20–29

Subsequent to the various covenanting and blessing scenes which follow Noah's exit from the ark, the first story to which we are privy takes place in a tent – ostensibly Noah's (but note the Midrash's read of the written form אהלה – "her tent") where Noah lies, drunk and asleep, as his son Ham engages in some nefarious sexual activity. Although a literal read of the text has Ham merely looking at his father's nakedness, the rest of the narrative cannot support this understanding, on two counts:

First of all, uncomfortable as we might be with the image of a son staring at his father's nakedness and even relating this to his brothers outside the tent, this hardly warrants the curse heaped upon Ham and his progeny by his father. More to the point, Noah wakes from his drunken slumber and "knows what his younger son had done to him" – but if all the son did was stare, what was there for Noah to know? This may be the motivation behind the Rabbinic interpretation that Ham either sodomized or castrated his father, thus doing something to Noah that he would certainly realize upon awakening. Some have suggested that Ham had relations with his own mother, reading the Leviticus-trope of וירא חם את ערות אביו אבי כנען as meaning that Ham had sexual congress with Noah's wife and that Canaan was the illegitimate progeny of that incestuous and adulterous union. All variations aside, there is no escaping the sexually tinged context of this scene. Unlike the first "go-around," however, this narrative speaks to issues of violence and power as well as sexuality. The Midrashic approach that Ham castrated his father is explained as his move to prevent further co-heirs from being born; the approach that he sodomized his father seems to represent a power-play for control over the family, which the more recent take – that Ham had relations with Noah's wife[10] – certainly supports.

THE SECOND VIOLATION– SIN OF VIOLENCE (REDUX)

Genesis 10:8–11

While Chapter 10 seems innocuous enough – a list of "begats" and the basic framework for the Biblical "seventy nations" and apparently a bridge between the sin in Noah's tent and the Tower – a more careful read brings an insidious development to light.

We are introduced to one Nimrod, a grandson of Ham, who is presented as one who was the first to be a גבור בארץ – a powerful man in the land. Nimrod is not only the first one to be called גבור – such that any powerful hunter was referenced by Nimrod – he is also the first one to be called מלך. Verse 10 relates that the beginning of his monarchy was Babylonia, throughout the land of Shinar – and that land eventually gave birth to the Assyrian Empire and its capital Nineveh (a city with frightening associations for the Jewish people during the First Commonwealth). Monarchy is not necessarily a bad thing – but there are kings who *lead* their people, as idealized in 1 Samuel 12 and those that *rule over* their people by force and threats – the leadership of Samaria rebuked by Amos (see Amos 4:1) and described in 1 Kings 21. Ecclesiastes – himself a king (Ecc. 1:1) observes the evil done when "a man rules over another to do him evil" (Ecc. 8:9). If we ponder, for just a moment, how one man could have, for the first time in history, taken control over others (outside of his family) – we need look no further than the description of Nimrod – "a valiant archer." Evidently, Nimrod utilized his prowess as a predator to control others – again, violence and the threat of death as a strategy. Unlike the violence we encountered in the first series, however, this is not limited to internal family power struggles – rather to regional and "national" politics as one man crowns himself over others and rules them by dint of his power and the threat of violence. The many Midrashim which interpret Nimrod's name as associated with מרד – rebellion – testify to his rebellion against God. Perhaps the intent of those Midrashim is that any flesh-and-blood who usurps God's position as "King of the Universe" is, *ipso facto*, a rebel.

---

10. *Torat ha-Elokim*, (Heb.) Heydenheim, 1797, pp. 108–109; see, more recently, *Bergsma and Hahn*: Noah's Nakedness and the Curse on Canaan, *JBL* 124/1, pp. 25–40.

THE FINAL VIOLATION – SIN OF IDEOLOGY (REDUX)

Genesis 11:1–9

The final blow to the postdiluvian world was the construction of the Tower at Shinar. Commentators have puzzled over this "sin," trying to identify what it was that the builders did that merited God's intervention to stop their project, the bold move of upsetting their communication and their rather immediate dispersion throughout the world. Among the *Pashtanim*, various approaches linked to the move to one city may be found. Rashbam sees the sin as transgressing (or, "deliberately ignoring") the Divine command to spread out and populate the earth (9:7); ibn Ezra interprets the violation as one of civic aggrandizement – "let us make for ourselves a name"; Abravanel (after summarizing many of the other approaches, each of which he rejects) suggests that their sin was the urbanization of society itself, which taxed their energies and time and took them away from the essential purpose of Man – to develop himself intellectually and spiritually.

The Rabbis have a different understanding of the sin of the community at Shinar. They see the Tower as a nefarious attempt to build a structure that will rival God (or, alternatively, go to battle against God) and will have an idol at the top of the structure. They even describe this structure – which was in the "backyard" of the Babylonian sages – as a building so tall that even with one third burned and one third sunk, a person could go to the (remaining) top and see Jericho.

The last two hundred years of Biblical Archaeology, beginning with the Babylonian Exploration Fund, have unearthed dozens of structures in the Mesopotamian valley. These structures, pyramid-like with stairs reaching to the top, all had cultic uses and are known as "ziggurats." The purpose of these structures (dubbed by their builders/devotees with names like "Pillar of the Earth" etc.) was for the priests to ascend and worship atop the structure. The tower described in our chapter fits this model perfectly and supports the Midrashic contention as to the nature of the sin – thus explaining the invasive Divine reaction and the pillorying of *"Anshei Dor haPalagah"* (the people of the generation of the separation) in one breath with *"Anshei Dor haMabul"* (the people of the generation of the Flood).

So, we've come full circle. The final nail in the coffin of the generations following the Flood, which sets the stage for Abraham's entry onto the stage of world history, is one of ideology and idolatry.

The pattern of sin we have uncovered within the foundational period of Mankind is clear and repeated in sequence:

- sexual appetite unbound, *followed by*
- violence as a response and then as a strategy, *followed by*
- ideological perversion to idolatry, *followed by*
  - God's intervention (destruction or instruction)

AND BEFORE ABRAHAM . . .
ASSESSING THE SEQUENCE

As proposed earlier, the first eleven chapters of Genesis are foundational and reflect the Torah's perspective on the "nature of things" – how the world works and, far more to the point – how people work. This cycle of sin which was repeated after the Flood – with an increase in impact and reach (from families to societies) is one which speaks of the human experience and, to which, the Torah addresses its societal norms and values.

The sequence is one which is readily understandable in human terms, both psychological as well as social. Man is born with desires and is taught, in most social settings, that he must delay or, in some cases, utterly curb his desires if the object of that desire is forbidden now – or forever. When appetite overcomes inhibition, the bounds of personal responsibility – and social propriety – are shattered. As noted above, appetite breeds appetite – the notion of satiation is illusory, as each rung for which lustful man reaches soon becomes the floor for his next reach.

Sooner or later, man will find someone standing in his way – a protective father, a courageous home-owner, a heretofore unwilling subject. To that end, appetite drives power – if accessible, the lustful man will utilize whatever subjugating means at hand to get what he wants. Note that the sequence is always appetite, *followed* by power.

Ah, that brings us to the ideology. Here is where we must be honest about one of Mankind's lesser known foibles. Man abhors internal conflict – which is why, for instance, so many ridicule those who work hard; if we do not deride them, we experience internal conflict about our own sloth and the lesser achievements we can boast. By reducing their accomplishments, we can feel less conflict about our own shortcomings.

One of the historically consistent methods used by individuals and groups who wish to deviate from acceptable norms is to devise an ideology which not only allows, but encourages such behavior. In other words, man wants and so he takes (appetite unbound); when someone gets in the way of what he wants, he will use his power to erase the obstacle (power unbound). Feeling remorse and conflict over his childish, self-centered behavior, he has the choice to own up to his own inadequacies which is too much for most. Alternatively, he can devise a religion, a dogma, or political schematic that justifies and encourages his behavior. From scourge, he can become a hero – all without having to overcome his appetites.

It is all too easy for a generation raised in the shadow of Auschwitz to appreciate this point. The butchers who ruthlessly killed so many millions of innocents had somehow convinced themselves that their victims were less than human; that it was an act of ideological fidelity to kill babies, pregnant women and elderly scholars – and everyone in between.

This last point is likely the intent of the Talmud's observation that the Jewish people only worshipped idols (which they knew to be vain) in order to permit them otherwise forbidden sexual liaisons.[11]

This is the world that Abraham inherited; the society which his message was intended to address and repair.

ENTER ABRAHAM

Perhaps the most telling feature of our first father is his isolation. "The Lonely Man of Faith" is Abraham – as the Rabbis put it, he is called "עברי" because the whole world is one side and he is (alone) on the other. During the course of his journeys, besides the many followers and (at least) one wife, Abraham has to separate from his nephew Lot and from his son Ishmael. Isaac later follows suit and only Jacob remains in the Land (see Genesis Chapter 36). Each of these families – the families of Lot (Ammon and Moav), the Ishmaelites and Esau's descendants (Edom) are, to some extent, included in the Covenant. When the Israelites are circling back to Canaan after their years of wandering in the desert, they are warned by God not to violate the territory of Lot's children as well as that of Edom.

The Rabbis have an interesting observation about these three "cast-off" tribe-nations of Abraham's seed; although included in a broader covenant, they do not gain the inner-circle of the Sinai covenant. The Midrash Halakhah[12] relates that before God gave the Torah to His people, he offered it to the children of Lot, the children of Ishmael and the children

---

11. BT Sanhedrin 63b, citing Rav (3rd century, Babylonia).
12. cf. Sifrei Devarim, par. 343

of Esau. Later Midrashim subsequently extend this to "all the nations of the world," but at first it only allows for the possibility that Abraham's kin would enter into the covenant with God.

Each nation first asks which rules are included in the covenant – they won't sign on to the Divine covenant "sight-unseen." Esau learns that there is a ban on murder – to which they respond that their entire life is "lived by the sword"; the children of Lot learn that adultery is forbidden, which they cannot abide, since both of their eponymous ancestors were born of incest (Genesis 19). Subsequently, the Ishmaelites find out that stealing is forbidden by this law – and they flinch as well. Note that both sins of appetite (stealing, adultery) as well as violence ("by the sword") are included in the life-styles of Abraham's *rejected* seed. Indeed, Abraham himself contended with challenges to sexual propriety (with Sarah in Egypt and in Gerar) and ultimately taught lessons to neighboring kings about fidelity. He also went to war, combatting the evil done against the people of Sodom and rescuing his king – contending against the approach of "might makes right." And, of course, Abraham was the great teacher of monotheism, taking his message of one God of justice and human moral accountability everywhere he traveled.

Note that Abraham set out to repair this rift in the human condition in reverse order – first "calling out in God's Name," then leading a war of rescue and, finally, purifying the human appetite through the command of circumcision. At this point, he is finally ready to be called "father of many nations" and to realize the great blessing that "all the families of the earth will be blessed through you."

The societies that Abraham taught were driven by ideologies created to justify the use of power in pursuit of sating an abyss of an appetite.

In the aftermath of the Bar-Kokhba rebellion, at one of the lowest points in post-millenial Jewish history, the Romans frequently threatened Jews with death if they publicly practiced any number of Mitzvot. Many Jews were martyring themselves for any number of commands, until the collegium met in the attic of Beit Nith'za and ruled that "if a person is told that he should violate the law or die, he *must* violate the law and not die – except for three laws for which he must martyr himself. He must martyr himself rather than worshipping other gods; rather than engaging in forbidden sexual liaisons; and he must prefer his own death to murder."[13] These three "cardinal sins," the only ones for which, under any

13. BT Sanhedrin 74a

circumstance, a Jew is obligated to give his life, are the "foundational sins" of humanity, the trespasses which Abraham had the task of combatting.

AFTERWORD

In studying the Bible, we often look (or should be looking) for patterns – not only textual patterns (much of which have been discussed in both this volume as well as Volume 2) but also patterns of behavior and attitude. When we discern a sequence or pattern of behavior or expression, it may – and usually will – help us gain a more panoramic view of the text and give us fresh insight into the specific nuances of the Torah's narrative.

VI TWO FLOOD STORIES
Ears of the Audience, Part II

INTRODUCTION

"For as the new heavens and the new earth, which I will make, shall remain before Me, says the Lord, so shall your seed and your name remain." (Isaiah 66:22)

In the same spirit as we've already done in Chapter II, we will analyze some significant features in the description of the Flood and its eventual subsiding, then take note of how these features would have impacted each of the three possible original target audiences of the book of Genesis.

THE FLOOD—A SECOND CREATION

The world that God created, as presented in Genesis 1:1–2:3, is markedly similar to the world that was redeemed after the Flood. Even a cursory look at the description of the "new (postdiluvian) world" reveals numerous literary associations with the Creation. (This comparison itself does not represent an innovative approach — see Rashi's comments at 7:11.)

Here is a comparison of the major stages of Creation, as presented in the first chapter of Genesis, and the significant stages of "re-creation" (or "restoration") of the postdiluvian world as outlined in Chapter 8 of Genesis:

Day 1: ". . . and the spirit of God hovered over the face of the waters." (1:2)
After the Flood: "God made a wind to pass over the earth." (8:1)

Day 2: "Let there be a firmament in the midst of the waters, and let it divide the waters from the waters." (1:6)

After the Flood: "...the fountains also of the deep and the windows of heaven were stopped, and the rain from heaven was restrained" (8:2)

Day 3: "Let the waters under the heaven be gathered together unto one place, and let the dry land appear." (1:9)
After the Flood: "...in the tenth month, on the first day of the month, were the tops of the mountains seen." (8:5)

Day 3: "Let the earth put forth grass, herb yielding seed, and fruit-tree bearing fruit after its kind, wherein is the seed thereof, upon the earth." (1:11)
After the Flood: "And the dove came in to him at evening; and in her mouth there was a freshly plucked olive leaf; so Noah knew that the waters were abated from off the earth." (8:11)

Day 4: "Let there be lights in the firmament of the heaven to divide the day from the night; and let them be for signs, and for seasons, and for days and years." (1:14)
After the Flood: "While the earth remains, seedtime and harvest, and cold and heat, and summer and winter, and day and night shall not cease." (8:22) (Note also that in 8:11, the dove comes to Noah "at evening," the first mention of any distinct time of day after the Flood; evidently, night and day were blurred during the entire cataclysm.)

Day 5: "Let the waters swarm with swarms of living creatures, and let fowl fly above the earth in the open firmament of heaven." (1:20)
After the Flood: "And he stayed yet another seven days; and sent forth the dove; and she returned not again unto him any more" (8:12) (i.e., the dove returned to its earlier station as a "bird that flies above the earth").

Day 6: " 'Let the earth bring forth the living creature after its kind, cattle, and creeping thing, and beast of the earth after its kind,' and it was so ... 'Let us make Man in our image, after our likeness ....' And God blessed them; and God said unto them: 'Be fruitful, and multiply, and replenish the earth, and subdue it; and have dominion over the fish of the sea, and over the fowl of the air, and over every living thing that creeps upon the earth.'" (1:24, 26, 28)
After the Flood: "Go out from the ark, you, and your wife, and your sons, and your sons' wives with you. Bring out with you every living thing

that is with you, of all flesh, both fowl and of cattle, and every creeping thing that creeps upon the earth; that they may swarm in the earth, and be fruitful, and multiply upon the earth." (8:16–17)

(Note that here, unlike the "first" Creation, mankind comes before the animals; we will address this below.)

Besides these fairly clear parallels, the denouement of the first Creation is, of course, the institution of the Sabbath. Even though there is no explicit parallel in the Noah narrative, the final phrase of Chapter 8, "While the earth remains, seedtime and harvest, and cold and heat, and summer and winter, and day and night shall not cease," uses the same root (שבת), as does the word used twice in the Sabbath narrative (2:1–3) to describe God's ceasing creative activity.

All in all, the Torah does seem to be telling us that the world that Noah re-entered was a re-creation of the first world, a world that became so polluted and corrupt that it was sentenced to "non-worldhood."

Here we pose two questions:

1. How was this world different from the first — what would guarantee its survival?

2. What possible import could this message contain for each — or any — of the three generations who first read the book of Genesis?

VIOLATIONS AND LIBATIONS

Before addressing these two questions, I'd like to raise a tangential question in reference to two comments of R. Obadia Sforno.

The Torah refers to the daily offering brought in the Tabernacle as "a continual burnt-offering, which was offered at Mount Sinai, for a sweet savor, a sacrifice made by fire unto the Lord" (Numbers 28:6). In other words, the daily offering is a reminder/re-experience of the offerings brought at the foot of Sinai in the wake of the Revelation. Sforno notes that although there were no libations or meal offerings brought with the original offerings at the foot of Sinai, they were commanded as part of the daily regular offering from that point on:

> "and the tenth part of an *ephah* of fine flour for a meal-offering, mixed with the fourth part of a *hin* of beaten oil. . . . and the drink-offering of it shall be the fourth part of a *hin* for one lamb . . . ." (Numbers 28:5, 7)

Sforno is also sensitive to the fact that the command regarding bringing libations and grain offerings to accompany personal offerings is presented in the Torah directly in the aftermath of the sin of the scouts. (Numbers 15:1–16)

He sees these two introductions of the obligation of libations and grain offerings as more than coincidental: Until the sin of the golden calf (Exodus 32), there was no Divine intent to have libations (nor grain offerings) brought with any animal offering; subsequent to that grievous transgression, we were commanded to bring libations and grain offerings to accompany communal offerings (such as the daily offering).

As a consequence of the sin of the scouts (and the people's rejection of the Land; see Numbers 14:1), God commanded us to bring libations and grain offerings with personal offerings as well.

Our third question is one of cause and effect:

Why does Sforno align these particular sins with the increased obligations regarding wine and meal offerings? In other words, what is the relationship between the sin of the golden calf and the obligation to bring libations and grain offerings with communal offerings? And what is the relationship between the sin of the scouts and the obligation to bring libations and grain offerings with personal offerings?

We will return to this question after addressing our first question: How was this world different from the recently destroyed "first" world?

THE ARK EFFECT

As several commentators have pointed out, the timing scheme in the Flood narrative is arranged in a chiasmus, as follows:

A (7 days): "Come you and all your house into the ark; for you have I seen righteous before me in this generation. Of every clean beast you shall take to you seven pairs, the male and his female; and of beasts that are not clean one pair, the male and his female. Of birds also of the air by seven pairs, the male and the female; to keep seed alive upon the face of all the earth. For in another seven days I will cause it to rain upon the earth . . . ." (Genesis 7:1–4)

B (40 days): "And the rain was upon the earth forty days and forty nights." (7:12)

C (150 days): "And the waters prevailed upon the earth a hundred and fifty days." (7:24)

C' (150 days): "And the waters returned from off the earth continually; and after the end of the hundred and fifty days the waters were abated." (8:3)

B' (40 days): "And it came to pass at the end of forty days, that Noah opened the window of the ark which he had made." (8:6)

A' (7 days): "And he stayed yet another seven days; and sent forth the dove; and she returned not again to him any more. And it came to pass in the six hundred and first year, in the first month, the first day of the month, the waters were dried up from off the earth; and Noah removed the covering of the ark, and looked, and behold, the face of the ground was dry. And in the second month, on the twenty-seventh day of the month, was the earth dried. And God spoke to Noah, saying: 'Go out from the ark, you, and your wife, and your sons, and your sons' wives with you.'" (8:12–16)

When the Torah presents a chiastic structure, whether in narrative or legalistic text, it does so in order to highlight the "center." What sits at the center of this "reversed chiasmus?" ("Reversed" because the movements described in the first set of verses — entrance into the ark and the onset of the Flood — are reversed in the second.) In other words, what changed to allow Noah to come out and to allow the world to be restored?

One of the significant differences between the "old world" and the postdiluvian world is the introduction of a covenant. Adam had no covenantal relationship with his Creator. God blessed Man, provided him with all of his needs, commanded, chastised, punished, and exiled him — but at no point was Adam a "covenantal partner" with God. Indeed, there is very little (aside from naming animals and siring the next generation) that Adam "does" that is productive. Adam is presented in the Torah chiefly as the passive recipient of Divine favor.

No member of humanity is any different, including Noah. (The one exception may be the offerings brought by Cain and Abel.) This is true only up until the time of the Flood (I am following Sforno's interpretation at 6:18). Note what has changed between the first set of verses, where Noah enters the Ark, and the second set, announcing his impending exit:

Whereas, in the first set, we are told that ". . . the Lord shut him in" (7:16), in the aftermath of the Flood we read: ". . . and Noah removed the covering of the ark . . ." (8:13). Noah, who had entered the ark not of his own volition (see Rashi at 7:8) and who was sealed in by God, suddenly becomes an active participant in his own rescue, opening the cover of the ark. Note that the Hebrew word used to describe God's sealing him in

(סגר) is a direct antonym of the word used for Noah's opening of the cover (פתח). The center of this entire narrative, the highlight of the Flood, is Noah's active involvement in the affairs of the world.

"AND IT WAS VERY GOOD . . ."

At this point, it is prudent to note one more similarity between Creation (Chapter 1) and re-Creation (Chapter 8). Both narratives end with a description of God's pleasure:

Day 6: "And God saw every thing that he had made, and, behold, it was very good; and there was evening and there was morning, the sixth day." (1:31)

After the Flood: "And the Lord smelled the sweet savour; and the Lord said in His heart: 'I will not again curse the ground any more for man's sake; for the imagination of man's heart is evil from his youth; nor neither will I again destroy every living thing, as I have done." (8:21)

Note, however, a significant difference between these two: In the first narrative, the Divine affirmation of Creation comes after His blessing to mankind (1:28); after the Flood, God takes pleasure and "removes the curse" from the earth — and only after that blesses mankind: "And God blessed Noah and his sons, and said to them: 'Be fruitful and multiply, and replenish the earth.'" (9:1) (Note the strong similarity between this blessing and that given to Adam in 1:28.)

Again, we see that it is man's role in the cCreation, which comes along with the first covenant (9:9–17), that is cause for his blessing. Unlike the first Creation, where blessings were part and parcel of the Divine mandate and were, perforce, unearned by the recipient of that blessing, the antediluvian world is built on a covenanted relationship where man "earns" God's favor and blessing.

How was that accomplished? What did Noah do—besides taking his own steps to leave the ark — to gain Divine favor?

THE OFFERING: THE SYMBOL OF MAN'S ROLE IN THE COVENANT

"And Noah built an altar to the Lord; and took of every clean beast, and of every clean bird, and offered burnt-offerings on the altar." (Genesis 8:20)

Noah's response to salvation was bringing offerings to God. Although Cain and Abel already offered up sacrifices, this is the first instance where an offering is presented as emblematic of a relationship that the one bringing the offering has with God. Noah's reaction to being saved, to weathering the ordeal of the Flood, and to being given a second chance, was to offer up some of his bounty to God.

This offering motivated God's blessing for Noah, his descendants, and his new world: "And the Lord smelled the sweet savour; and the Lord said in His heart: 'I will not again curse the ground any more for man's sake; for the imagination of man's heart is evil from his youth; nor will I again destroy every living thing, as I have done.'" (8:21)

Noah has assumed a measure of responsibility for his relationship with God by taking an active role, so there is now room for a covenant — which "obligates" God to maintain the world, its seasons, and its inhabitants.

BACK TO SFORNO

We can now understand Sforno's cryptic comments regarding the introduction of libations and meal offerings as accompanying offerings. When the people sinned by constructing and worshipping the golden calf, they were blemished as a nation and sentenced to die (see Exodus 32:10). After Moses begged, negotiated, and demanded God's forgiveness, it was necessary for the people to demonstrate a greater level of involvement in their own side of the covenant. A symptom of that greater involvement was the innovation of the "Second Tablets." Unlike the "First Tablets," given at the end of the first set of forty days at Sinai, this set was carved by Moses. The human engraving of these second tablets, so much inferior to the Divine inscription on the first set, has its own glory. Man's greater role in maintaining his own "side" of the covenant ensures an adherence to that covenant commensurate to the greater investment on the part of the people.

The added offerings of libations and grain, just like Noah's offering at the genesis of the new world, are a reflection of a greater level of commitment and investment in the covenant on the part of the Israelites.

However we understand the sin of the golden calf, it is abundantly clear that the sin of the scouts is deliberately portrayed as a "sister sin" to it. Note, for example, how Moses utilizes the Divine attributes of compassion — first revealed in the aftermath of the calf episode — in his plea for Divine forgiveness of the sin of the scouts (compare Exodus 34:6–7 with Numbers 14:17–18).

If the nation sinned as a whole at Sinai, worshipping the golden calf, their crime was much more personal and private when they wept "on that night" after hearing the report of the scouts. Although the nation congregated, the Torah portrays their fears and weeping as private and individualistic, in contradistinction to the communal "celebration" around the newly constructed calf.

It stands to reason that if the Torah's antidote to the communal sin of the golden calf was the addition of the libations and grain offerings to accompany communal offerings, that the appropriate response to the (mass) private sin of the scouts was to add the obligation of libations and grain offerings to private offerings.

Now that we understand Sforno's explanation of the relationship between offerings and increased responsibility on the part of the worshipper, we can explain the difference between the world that Noah left when he entered the ark and the one he rebuilt when he exited.

In the antediluvian world, man was the passive beneficiary of God's bounty and blessing (which is why mankind is introduced after the animals — man is the ultimate creature, but no more than a creature).

On the other hand, the postdiluvian world presents mankind as actively invested in the survival and success of this venture. This is the essential difference, first alluded to in Noah's behavior inside the ark. Note that when Noah opened the cover, the Torah tells us that he "looked" (Hebrew וירא) — the exact word used to describe God's observations of the antediluvian world. (Compare this with 1:4, 12, 18, 21, 31, and, most significantly, 6:5 and 6:12.) Noah is now taking on a greater "partnership" with God in his responsibility for the welfare of the world.

THE "MESSAGE"

We are now in position to properly address the second question above: What possible import could this message contain for each — or any — of the three generations who first read the book of Genesis?

For the generation of slaves in Egypt: Their oppressed existence and suffering under the heel of a foreign power will ultimately end, as did the unjust world before the Flood. They must understand, however, that the "new world" awaiting them beyond the Red Sea will be one that obligates them to play a more active role in their covenantal relationship.

For the generation at Sinai: The "fall" in the shadow of Sinai, that terrible crime of the golden calf that sullied the pristine purity generated by the Revelation (see BT Shabbat 146a), impacted on their entire lives, as well as the rest of Jewish history (see Exodus 32:34). For this generation, the message of the Flood and the "new world" is that they would have another chance, but that they would have to bear an increased share of the responsibility for the covenant with God. (Note how closely the "post-calf" covenant is linked to scrupulous observance of God's commands — cf. Exodus 34:10–11.)

For the generation at the plains of Moab: The message of the Flood and its aftermath would have the most significant impact. Subsequent to the many failures during their sojourn in the desert, the story promises the possibility of building a new world once they enter the Land — but concomitantly commits them to assuming a greater sense of responsibility for the success of their national endeavor, to build a "kingdom of priests and a holy nation."

AFTERWORD

In much the same fashion as we did in Chapter II, we reexamined the import of the text in question from the perspective of the possible original audiences. By carefully employing other structural tools of analysis — which were more fully explicated in Chapter IV we were able to understand the intended impact of the narrative on the "first readership," and thus have a greater grasp of the message for us, the generations that follow.

VII TWO FLOOD STORIES (II)
Biblical Criticism – Countering the Critics (II)

INTRODUCTION

Just as we encountered in dealing with Creation, the Flood and its after-math seems to be told twice, in conflicting versions. The existence of these "rival versions" can best be demonstrated by using each to answer basic questions about the Flood and its aftermath. (We will refer to "V1" and "V2" here; the thread that binds them will be suggested later on. As we have done throughout the volume, we will also use "Hashem" to denote the Tetragrammaton, and "God" to represent the name "Elohim." In some cases, the verses of "V1" will follow those of "V2".)

A. *The nature of evil*

V1: "The earth became corrupt before God, and the earth was filled with violence . . . for all flesh had corrupted their way upon the earth." (6:11–12)

V2: "Hashem saw that the wickedness of man was great in the earth, and that every imagination of the thoughts of his heart was only evil continually." (6:5)

In the first version, we are told about specific actions and behaviors that warranted destruction. Our Rabbis explain that the "corrupted way" mentioned here was sexual impropriety of the most egregious sort; the "violence" refers to thievery, for which the Heavenly decree was finally sealed.

In the alternate version, we are not given information about specific behaviors, just general *evil*. In addition, a factor not mentioned in the first version is presented — man's thoughts.

B. The merit of Noah

V1: "Noah was in his generations a man innocent[14] and wholehearted; Noah walked with God." (6:9)

V2: "Noah found favor with Hashem . . . 'for you alone have I found innocent before Me in this generation.'" (6:8, 7:1)

In v. 9, Noah is described as "innocent" (*tzaddik*) and "wholehearted" (*tamim*), walking "with God." This description speaks of someone who is innocent of the corruption of the generation and who walks in God's path (see Genesis 18:19).

The verse immediately preceding it addresses a different aspect of Noah — not his "objective" merit, but rather how God "sees" him. Noah found favor in God's eyes — is a much more sympathetic and subjective statement. Even the later statement (7:1), when God addresses Noah, speaks more about their relationship – *innocent **before me**—*than does the earlier one.

C. How many animals?

V1: "And of every living thing of all flesh, you shall take two of each into the ark, to keep them alive with you; they shall be male and female. Of the fowl after their kind, cattle of every kind, every kind of creeping thing on earth, two of each shall come to you to stay alive." (6:19–20)

V2: "Of every clean (*tahor*) animal you shall take seven pairs, males and their mates, and of every animal that is not clean (*asher lo tehorah*) two, a male and its mate." (7:2)

The differences here are clear — not only numerically, but also teleologically. What is the purpose of "collecting" the animals? In the first version, two animals of each kind are gathered in order to maintain the species (hence, one male and one female). In the second version, the purpose of gathering these animals becomes clear only after the Flood — to bring a thanksgiving offering with the pure animals.

Note that in the first version, the terms used for male and female are the "clinical" *zakhar* and *neqevah*, terms which say nothing about the relationship between them. On the other hand, the second story, where animals are classified by ritual definitions and seven pairs of the "pure" animals are taken, also refers to the "couples" as *ish v'ishto* — a "man and his mate."

---

14. see below at Chapter XII for an explanation of this translation

D. *Covenant or commitment?*

V1: "... I establish My covenant with you, and with your seed after you; and with every living creature that is with you, the fowl, the cattle, and every beast of the earth with you; of all that go out of the ark, even every beast of the earth. And I will establish My covenant with you; neither shall all flesh be cut off any more by the waters of the flood; neither shall there any more be a flood to destroy the earth. ... This is the token of the covenant which I make between Me and you and every living creature that is with you, for perpetual generations: I have set My bow in the cloud, and it shall be for a token of a covenant between Me and the earth. And it shall come to pass, when I bring clouds over the earth, and the bow is seen in the cloud, that I will remember My covenant, which is between Me and you and every living creature of all flesh; and the waters shall no more become a flood to destroy all flesh. And the bow shall be in the cloud; and I will look upon it, that I may remember the everlasting covenant between God and every living creature of all flesh that is upon the earth." And God said unto Noah: "This is the token of the covenant which I have established between Me and all flesh that is upon the earth." (9:9–17)

V2: Then Noah built an altar to Hashem, and, taking of every clean animal and of every clean bird, he offered burnt offerings on the altar. Hashem smelled the pleasing odor, and Hashem said to Himself: "Never again will I doom the earth because of Man, since the devisings of Man's mind are evil from his youth; nor will I ever again destroy every living being, as I have done. So long as the earth endures, seedtime and harvest, cold and heat, summer and winter, day and night shall not cease." (8:20–22)

Here we have a clear and obvious difference between the "versions." In the first version, God enters into a covenant with Noah, who is presented as a representative of all living beings and of the earth itself. God makes a covenant, complete with a visible sign (the rainbow), wherein He agrees to never again destroy the earth (at least, not with a Flood). The motivation for this covenant isn't readily obvious, unless we include the commands that immediately precede this section. These commands, which serve as a flashback to the creation of Man, include the prohibition of murder and the responsibility to judge such behavior (8:4–6).

In the second version, on the other hand, there is a clear catalyst for God's commitment: the pleasing odor of the offerings brought by Noah. In addition, the commitment that God makes is not stated to anyone, nor is there any "covenant" form to it. Man is not asked to do anything in response, nor is there any sign of the covenant. God makes this commitment "to Himself," as it were; the commitment is grounded in the tragic reality of man's imperfection," . . . for the imagination of man's heart is evil from his youth. . . ."

SUMMARY

A cursory reading of Chapters 6 through 8 of Genesis presents two different pictures of the Flood: Why it happened (violence or "evil intentions"); the merit of Noah (walking *with* God or innocent *before* God); the number and purpose of the animals (two pairs to save the species or seven pairs for offerings); and the Divine promise to never repeat the Flood (covenant or commitment).

The careful reader will note — at least if he or she follows in the original — that the name for God used throughout "version 1" is "Elohim," the generic name for God. The name used throughout "version 2" is "Hashem."

How many stories are there here? Are there two different narratives, or one multifaceted one? Bottom line: How many animals were there? What was Noah's merit? Which "version" is "accurate"?

(It is both prudent and imperative to note that most of the *Rishonim* who addressed this issue used the same approach here to the "two stories" of Creation. They combined the two versions, seeing each as completing what is "missing" from the other. We will try to present another viable option here.)

SCIENCE VS. TORAH: CONFLICT OR ILLUSION?

Before addressing the specific question of the "two stories" of the Flood, a larger question should be addressed. Much has been made of the apparent conflict between science and the Bible. Because the world has embraced the methods of scientific reasoning and has been willing to challenge a fundamentalist reading of the Bible, these two versions of reality have been regularly thrown against each other. Is the world 6,000 years old — or several billion? Were there six days of creation — or innumerably more? Did Man evolve from "lower species" — or was he formed *ex nihilo* as the crown of creation?

Responses to this apparent problem have fallen into three groups, discussed in the following sections.

GROUP A: THE REJECTIONISTS

There are those who maintain that the Bible must be understood as being a literal account of Creation, the Flood, and so on. Besides the internal contradictions, this clearly pits the Biblical account against science. This leaves adherents to this perspective with two options: either accept the Biblical account *in toto*, and reject the findings of the scientific world, or reject the Biblical account *in toto*. Each of these "rejectionist" approaches is rarely confined to the issues in question. Someone who believes that the Bible is trying to promote a specific version of Creation — one that he rejects on account of science—will not be likely to accept the Biblical mandate in other areas of wisdom, ethics, or personal obligations. Similarly, someone who rejects the scientific approach to Creation, evolution and the like, out of hand is not likely to "buy into" the scientific method in other areas.

The result of this first approach is the rejection of one or another of the disciplines as the bearer of truth. Although some of our fellow traditionalists have opted for such an approach (to the extreme of maintaining that God placed fossils on the earth in order to test our belief in the age of the world), most contemporary Orthodox thinkers are too committed to the scientific method as a valuable expression of "Creative Man" to reject it so totally.

GROUP B: THE INTEGRATIONISTS

Of late, there has been a good deal of study and literature devoted to an attempted harmonization between the disciplines of Torah and science. Some modern "integrationists" try to demonstrate that the latest findings of the scientific world are, not only corroborated, but also anticipated by the Torah. A marvelous example of this is Ramban's comment on the phrase "Let us make man in our image"— troubling enough on theological grounds. Ramban explains that God is talking to the earth, creating a partnership whereby the earth would develop the body of Man and God would, upon completion of that process, fill that body with a Divine spirit. The notion of the earth "developing" the body is curiously close to the process outlined by Darwin—in the widest of strokes.

The advantages of this approach over the first one are obvious — there is no need to reject either area of study and a person can live an intellectually honest life as a member of modern society without sacrificing religious creed.

The downside is not so clear. Besides some forced readings (in both disciplines—bending science to work with Torah is sometimes as tricky as bending Torah to achieve compatibility with science), this method canonizes the products of the scientific method; because the claim is that these theories are already found in the Torah, that makes them somewhat immutable. What happens when (not *if*, but *when*) a particular theory that we have heretofore identified in the Torah becomes outdated in the world of science? Will we still hold onto it, claiming religious allegiance?

Although the integrationist school has won many adherents in recent decades, I believe that the danger outlined above — along with resting on a very questionable foundation — makes this approach a shaky one at best.

GROUP C: THE TELEOLOGISTS

Before asking any of these questions about contradictions within the text or conflicts between our text and the world of scientific hypotheses, we have to begin with a most basic question: What is the purpose of the Torah? Why did God give us "His golden treasure, which existed for 974 generations before the creation of the world" (BT Shabbat 88b)?

This question is not mine — it is the focus of the first comments of both Rashi and Ramban on the Torah. The assumption that drives each of their comments is that God's purpose in giving us His Torah is to teach us how to live (note especially Ramban's critique on Rashi's first question). Besides specific actions to perform or avoid, this includes proper ethics, attitudes, and perspectives — towards each other, our nation, the earth and, of course, the Almighty.

R. Shmuel David Luzzatto put it as follows in the introduction to his commentary on the Torah:

> Intelligent people understand that the goal of the Torah is not to inform us about natural sciences; rather it was given in order to create a straight path for people in the way of righteousness and law, to sustain in their minds the belief in the Unity of God and His Providence. . . .

Therefore, our approach to issues of "science vs. Torah" is that it is basically a non-issue. Science is concerned with discovering the "how" of the world; Torah is concerned with teaching us the "why" of God's world. In clearer terms, whereas the world of science is a discipline of discovery, answering the question "how did this come to be?", the world of Torah is concerned with answering a different question: "granted that this exists, how should I interact with it?" (whether the "it" in question is another person, the world at large, my nation, etc.).

Based on this principle, not only do we not regard the concerns of science as similar to that of the Torah, but also we can approach apparent contradictions in the Torah with renewed vigor and from a fresh perspective.

Since the goal of the Torah is to teach us how we should live and proper beliefs about God and His relationship with the world (and the relationship we should endeavor to have with Him), it stands to reason that "multiple versions" of narratives are not conflicting products of different schools (as the Bible critics maintain); rather, they are multi-faceted lessons about how we should live — different perspectives of (and different lessons about) one event.

THE "TWO ADAMS"

We will need one more brief interlude before responding to our question about the Flood narrative. We will adapt the dual description of Man as adumbrated by R. Joseph Soloveitchik in his *magum opus* "The Lonely Man of Faith"[15]. He coined the terms "Adam I" and "Adam II", which we will reference below.

The goal in creating Man (Adam) was twofold. As we read in the conflation of Creation narrative(s), Man was to be a commanded being — facing God, having a relationship with Him, a relationship that includes commandedness and guilt, loneliness and reunification (Adam II). At the same time, he was to be a majestic being, bearing the Image of God and acting as His agent in the world (Adam I).

Neither of these goals was met. Not only did Adam fail to observe the one command he was given — and failed to own up to his responsibility in that regard — but his progeny violated the most basic principle of God's agency, the maintenance and furthering of the natural and social order, when Cain murdered his own brother.

These double failings continued for generations until God decided to "wipe man from the earth"— but not before identifying the seeds of a new hope. Noah was to be the next Adam, with the potential for both types of human ideal (majesty and humility) in him.

We can now return to our questions.

---

15. First published in *Tradition*, vol. 7, no. 2 (1965).

BACK TO NOAH

Why did God decide to destroy the earth? From the perspective of man's duty to maintain and promote the order-out-of-chaos of Creation: "The earth became corrupt before God; the earth was filled with violence.... for all flesh had corrupted its ways on earth." (6:11–12) Man had failed to promote order, violating both sexual and social (financial) boundaries. However, "And the Lord saw that the wickedness of man was great in the earth, and that every imagination of the thoughts of his heart was only evil continually." (6:5) Man had also failed to develop spiritually, to grow in his relationship with the Almighty.

This easily explains why Noah was chosen: On the one hand, he was the one person in that generation who "walked *with* God," promoting the perfection of Creation. On the other hand, he "found favor in God's eyes" and was "innocent before Me"— he was able to stand in front of God as a servant. We now understand the dual purpose of taking the animals onto the ark. As "majestic Man," God's agent in the world, Noah took two of each kind — one male and one female — in order to ensure continuation of each species. As "worshipping Man," standing before God and focused on a dialogic relationship with Him, he took "clean animals" for purposes of worship.

We also understand the covenant and commitment presented in the aftermath of the Flood. Noah, who stands before God in worship, is pleasing to God and God responds by committing to never again disrupt the seasons. God "realizes" that Man is incapable of the sort of perfection previously expected, and He fine-tunes the rules by which the world is governed.

But Noah is also the (potential) embodiment of "majestic Man," who acts not only on his own behalf as a worshipper, but also on behalf of all existence as their king. With this king, God enters into an explicit agreement (King to king, as it were), complete with a publicly displayed sign of that covenant. That covenant, however, comes with a codicil: Man must live by the basic rules of God's order, filling and dominating the land but taking care never to shed the blood of a fellow. Ultimately, God says, I will act to correct the order if you do not. The world is Man's to perfect, but God will intervene if Man fails in this task.

The Torah tells us two stories because there are two different relationships and duties being re-evaluated here. In Man's role as God's agent, where God presents himself as "Elohim," the God of all Creation, it is his lawlessness and reckless abandon towards the order of creation that must be corrected. In order to do so, Creation is reversed (the "upper waters" and "lower waters" are no longer divided) and must be reestablished, by taking the one man who promoted that order, having him take enough of each species to repopulate the earth, and forging an agreement with him by which such destruction would never again take place. Man, for his part, is responsible for the promotion of God's order on earth.

In Man's role as God's servant, where God presents himself as "Hashem," highlighting Divine compassion, it is his failure to develop himself spiritually that must be corrected. To that end, the one man who is *"before Me"* is saved, along with enough animals to afford him the opportunity to re-forge the relationship of worship.

The Divine hope that Noah would prove to be a successful "second Adam," embodying both roles, was only realized ten generations later, with the entrance of Abraham onto the scene.

AFTERWORD

R. Mordecai Breuer, commonly considered to be the intellectual "grandfather" of the modern school of Orthodox Bible Interpretation (most of the prominent teachers and scholars of this school are his students) developed and systematized the approach which sees redundant, alternate, or conflicting passages in the Torah as representing different perspectives of the law, story, or message. He referred to this approach as *Shitat haBehinot* ("The Perspective System").[16] Taking a page from Breuer's system, we were able to discern two different perspectives on the causes of, plot, and aftermath of the Flood story, taking much of the wind out of the sails of the "Higher Critics."

---

16. See, *inter alia*, his Pirkei Mo'adot (Jerusalem, 1986), Pirkei Beresheet (Alon Shevut 1999) and Pirkei Mikraot (Alon Shvut 2009), as well as a collection of articles reflecting on his trail-blazing approach, in *Yosef Ofer (ed.) Shitat haBehinot shel haRav Breuer* Alon Shvut 2005. All of these titles are in Hebrew.

NOAH'S BIRDS
The Raven and the Dove

In the aftermath of the Flood, as the waters receded, Noah lifted off the cover of the ark and sent out a raven, which flew in circles (or to and from the ark) until the earth was dry. He subsequently sent a dove to see if the waters had receded – which is odd, since the raven had already stayed that long . . . or had it? The dove, oddly, could not find a resting place and returned; seven days later he sent the dove out and she came back at the end of the day with an olive branch in her mouth; seven days later, he sent the dove out and it never returned.

THE TEXT   Genesis 8:6–14

And it came to pass at the end of forty days, that Noah opened the window of the ark which he had made. **7** and he sent forth a raven, and it went forth to and fro, until the waters were dried up from off the earth. **8** and he sent forth a dove from him, to see if the waters were abated from off the face of the ground. **9** But the dove found no rest for the sole of her foot, and she returned unto him to the ark, for the waters were on the face of the whole earth; and he put forth his hand, and took her, and brought her in unto him into the ark. **10** And he stayed yet other seven days; and again he sent forth the dove out of the ark. **11** And the dove came in to him at eventide; and lo in her mouth an olive-leaf freshly plucked; so Noah knew that the waters were abated from off the earth. **12** And he stayed yet other seven days; and sent forth the dove; and she returned not again unto him anymore. **13** And it came to pass in the six hundred and first year, in the first month, the first day of the month, the waters were dried up from off the earth; and Noah removed the covering of the ark, and looked, and behold, the face of the ground was dried. **14** And in the second month, on the seven and twentieth day of the month, was the earth dry.

THE MISSIONS: SEQUENCE AND PURPOSE

Scholars, medieval and modern, traditional and "otherwise," have puzzled over this sequence for centuries. The three "missions" of the dove seem to be unusual – after all, if the land was already visible well before Noah sent out the dove the first time, why did it not find any rest? And why did it return after its second voyage – but with an olive branch – and why specifically a branch of an olive tree? And if it was able to gain access to such trees, why did it come back at all – after all, when it was sent the third time and evidently found the water yet lower, it didn't return.

One parenthetic note about the sequencing problem as it relates to v. 7; it is possible that Noah sent out the raven and he kept circling; while the raven was circling, he began the dove-dispatches, such that the phrase *'ad y'voshet hamayim me'al ha'aretz* (until the waters dried up from the land) may not have happened before the dove was sent. Thus the seeming contradiction between v. 7 and v. 11 is reconciled.

I'd like to put these questions aside for the meanwhile and look at the un-feted bird of Noah's ark – the raven. What was the purpose of Noah's sending it out and what could it accomplish that the dove couldn't do – and vice-versa? What did Noah learn from the raven's return and why did that cause him to send out the meeker dove?

The history of interpretation of this conundrum is not overly rich; there has always been such a focus on so many other "major" components of the immediate postdiluvian world (the offering, the covenant of the rainbow, the renewed moral code, etc.) that the birds in general – and the raven in particular – have been generally overlooked.

Among the moderns, there are some who, predictably, argue for two traditions and see the two birds as two versions of the same; others, going as far back as Philo of Alexandria, have argued that the birds are purely symbolic; the raven representing vice (and, in his version, never returning as it is comfortable in the destroyed world) while the dove represents virtue (hence must return as it cannot bear to live among the remnants of such havoc). A suggestion was recently made that Noah, by sending out the raven, hovering "to and fro" over the water, was reenacting God's "spirit hovering over the waters" in Genesis 1:2.

REEXAMINING THE EVIDENCE –
AND ASKING THE "RIGHT" QUESTION

The key to understanding this narrative twist lies in assessing, as best as we can, Noah's considerations and intentions at this point in the voyage.

First of all, the rain had stopped, which meant that, sooner or later, the earth would be able to begin absorbing the waters, thereby allowing the water level to recede. The ark came to rest when the water receded to the level of the high mountains, thus giving some ground (perhaps still underwater) for the ark to rest. This is detailed in Chapter 8:1–4; in v. 5, approximately seventy days pass and the mountain tops are now visible as the waters continue to recede. It is only at that point or sometime later (the reference point of "forty days" in v. 6 is unclear – is it forty days after the rains ended? forty days after the mountain tops were visible? forty days after the ark came to rest?) that Noah opens the window/cover of the ark and sends out the raven, followed by the dove.

What was Noah trying to ascertain by sending out the raven? Noah had to wonder what life remained – if any – underneath all of that water; on a more immediate level, he wanted to find out how low the water level was at this point.

Noah remembered the beginning of the Flood – it wasn't that long ago. When the torrential rains came and springs opened up, people's natural instinct would have been to try to survive. Where do people go when there is a flood – regardless if the flood is the result of an over-swelled river or a torrential downpour? They seek higher ground. The upper ground, as high an area as could sustain animal and/or human life, would have been filled with all sorts of mammals for the raven to feast on. Noah was trying to find out if the water level had gone so low as to allow for a habitable place, at which point he could (at least) let the predatory mammals out of the ark, knowing that they would have access to plenty of sustenance. Keep in mind that Noah could not see how far the water had receded from his vantage point – all he saw was the very mountain tops as his ark was grounded at Ararat – so the raven's behavior would serve him well as an indicator of how low the water had gone down.

The raven continued to circle until "the waters were dried from the land" – meaning, the land that he was sent to explore. When the raven stopped circling and, presumably, disappeared from view, Noah could safely assume that habitable areas were now exposed and not water-logged. However, that would not help the great herbivore population on the ark – nor would it help the humans who were only permitted meat after leaving the ark.

His next step was to send out a dove, who would not be able to rest until it found a tree with branches appropriate for resting – in other words, the tree-line for nesting trees (which are typically low) would be visible. Since the dove could not find any rest, Noah understood that the broad world of vegetation, needed by so much of his mammalian cargo, was not yet accessible.

He then sent the dove a second time, and it returned that same day (at evening) with an olive branch in its mouth. This was quite informative, as Noah now knew several critical things that would help him in assessing how to restart life on earth. He knew that low trees (an olive tree, while it can grow in mountainous areas, is a typically short tree) were now visible and that they hadn't been destroyed by the flood – a most vital piece of data. Secondly, he now knew that that level was visible – but he also understood something else. If the dove returned to him so quickly – or at all – it meant that the dove could not find a proper place to nest. Why couldn't the dove nest on that olive tree? Simply put – birds build nests from twigs on the ground. The final test of human and herbivorous mammal viability would be to see if the ground was exposed and dry – dry enough that twigs could be used to make a nest.

One week later, Noah got his answer. The dove went out for a third time and evidently was able to build a nest, as she never returned. At that point, Noah was ready to open up the ark, as all of the cargo – human and "animal" – now had access to habitable areas and vegetation.

AFTERWORD

It is vital to view the narrative from a "real-world" perspective, remembering that the characters only know what they know and that the various questions posed, observations made, and tests passed (or not) may be designed to further the actor's grasp of the situation. We find ourselves at the disadvantage of having read the story so many times that, in this instance (for example) we already know that the earth is completely dry (well, at least by the end of the narrative). We have to sensitize ourselves to the reality that Noah doesn't know that – to anticipate the questions in his mind and view his actions in that light – as intelligent and thoughtful attempts to give him the information necessary to move forward.

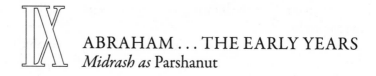

IX ABRAHAM ... THE EARLY YEARS
Midrash as Parshanut

INTRODUCTION: Midrashic Literature

This chapter presents a vital key to understanding the methodology of *Parshanut*. Instead of introducing "new tools of interpretation," we will now discover that the Rabbis of the Midrash used them as well.

That genre of Rabbinic literature commonly known as "Midrash" has been widely misunderstood — and has taken a proverbial "beating" in more than one circle of late. In order to properly assay the issue and begin our inquiry, we must first clarify and distinguish between two terms that are often confused in discussions of Rabbinic homiletics.

The term "Midrash," which means exegesis, a particular type of textual expansion and application, is properly used to describe any of a number of exegetical methods. Generally speaking, there are two types of Midrash: Midrash Halakhah and Midrash Aggadah.

Midrash Halakhah is an exegetical analysis of a legal text with a normative result. For instance, when the Torah defines fit animals as being *min haB'hemah* ("of the animals" – Leviticus 1:2), the Midrash Halakhah infers from that particular phrase that not all animals are fit to be brought to the altar (and then goes on to list which are excluded). Because the results of a legal discussion are practical, the exegetical method is (relatively) tightly defined and is subject to challenge and dispute.

Midrash Aggadah can be loosely defined as any other sort of exegesis on Biblical text. This includes exhortative, poetic, prophetic, narrative, epic, and any non-normative text in the Bible. As expected, the range of texts available for Midrash Aggadah is much broader and the methodology is less strictly defined than for Midrash Halakhah. In addition, multiple approaches can be tolerated and even welcomed because there is generally no legal implication to the inference. Even in those cases where such an inference may be claimed, the general methodology of the study of Midrash Aggadah allows (indeed, encourages) a wider range of approaches and perspectives. As such, we may find a series of alternate *Midr'shei Aggadah* on a given passage (e.g., the "test" of Abraham in Genesis 22:1) that, although representing different perspectives, do not necessarily preclude one another.

Hence, the term "Halakhah" when standing alone (and describing a type of Rabbinic statement) would most properly be associated with a normative statement independent of the text. The word "Aggadah" refers to a statement that is non-normative and, again, is not derived from or associated with a given text.

The study of Midrash Aggadah has always been challenging: to identify which interpretations are exegetical as an attempt to discern the straightforward meaning of the text; which are polemic (often against the early Christians); which are veiled attacks (e.g., on the Roman Empire); which are traditional lore that the author of the homily is "hanging" on a particular text, and so on. Much of the derision shown by many towards statements in the Midrash Aggadah (indicated by phrases such as "it's *only* a Midrash") is rooted in an inability (or unwillingness) to rigorously address the text and analyze its various components, understanding that some are intended as literal interpretations and an actual retelling of history, whereas others are poetic and artistic devices intended to drive home a critical point. Maimonides neatly divided the students of Aggadah into three groups — those who take everything literally, who are fools; those who take nothing literally, who are heretics; and those who wisely analyze each passage and discern how each passage ought to be studied. A proper and incisive approach to the study of Midrash Aggadah, knowing which passage to approach with which perspective, consistently rewards the student with a discovery of depths of wisdom and profound sensitivity.

There has been a considerable renewal of interest in Midrashic literature of late. In traditional circles this was spurred on by Maharal[17] and his systematic approach to Aggadah which suffused his many compilations. Nineteenth and twentieth century rabbinic figures such as R. Hayyim of Volozhin,[18] the "Netziv," and R. Abraham Isaac Kook,[19] among many, developed a repertoire of Aggadic tools which they wove into their worldviews. In the academic world, Joseph Heinemann, Jonah Fraenkel, and

---

17. R. Judah Loew of Prague, d. 1609
18. d. 1821, Russia
19. d. 1935, Jerusalem

Avigdor Shinan, all of Hebrew University, have done much to promote the analytic study of Midrash.

A proper presentation of the various facets of Midrash Aggadah is well beyond the scope of this forum; however, that does not exempt us from, at the very least, reexamining our attitude towards this central branch of Rabbinic literature and strengthening our awareness of the sagacity and trust of the Rabbis that is, after all, one of the forty-eight methods through which Torah is acquired (Avot 6:6).

To that end, we will assay a famous Midrash Aggadah (which is, *prima facie*, nearly bereft of Midrashic method) whose point of origin is an oblique reference at the end of Genesis 11. The central thesis here is that there is, of course, much more to the Midrash Aggadah than meets the eye. The fuller thesis will be presented after the following text.

THE MIDRASH

A. Preface

As developed above in Chapter 5, one of the central figures — if not the pivotal one — in Genesis is Abraham. We are given rich descriptions of his interactions with kings, family members, angels, and God Himself, several of which will occupy our attention in the next few chapters of this book — but all of that begins with his selection at age 75. We are told nothing in the text about his early life. The few vague verses at the end of Chapter 11 help little (if at all) in explaining why this son of Terah, scion of Shem, was selected as the progenitor of God's people.

There are several well-known Aggadot that partially fill in the "missing years" of Abraham's youth. Perhaps the most well-known Aggadah appears in several versions and has, as its point of departure, a minor difficulty in the Torah's retelling of Abraham's family life:

> And Terah lived seventy years, and fathered Abram, Nahor, and Haran. Now these are the generations of Terah; Terah fathered Abram, Nahor, and Haran; and Haran fathered Lot. And Haran died before his father Terah in the land of his birth, in Ur of the Chaldeans. And Abram and Nahor took wives; the name of Abram's wife was Sarai; and the name of Nahor's wife, Milkah, the daughter of Haran, the father of Milkah, and the father of Yiskah. But Sarai was barren; she had no child. And Terah took Abram his son, and Lot the son of Haran his grandson, and Sarai his daughter-in-law, his son Abram's

wife; and they went forth with them from Ur of the Chaldeans, to go to the land of Canaan; and they came to Charan, and lived there. And the days of Terah were two hundred and five years; and Terah died in Charan. (11:26–32)

The death of הרן (not to be confused with the place חרן, located in northern Syria or southern Turkey) during the life (literally "in the presence of") his father was a first. Although Abel died before Adam, we're not given any information about the relationship between the bereaved father and his murdered child. Here, the text clearly marks the death of Haran as happening before the death of Terah — the first recorded case of a child predeceasing his father where we can actually place the two of them in any sort of relationship.

The Midrash addresses this problem of the premature death of Haran and, along the way, does much to inform us of Abraham's life before the command of *Lekh Lekha* (12:1).

B. *The text of the Midrash:* Genesis Rabbah 38:16

"And Haran died in the presence of his father Terah."
R. Hiyya the grandson of R. Ada of Jaffa [said]:
Terah was an idolater.
One day he went out somewhere,
and put Abraham in charge of selling [the idols].
When a man would come who wanted to purchase, he would say to him:
"How old are you?"
[The customer] would answer: "Fifty or sixty years old."
[Abraham] would say: "Woe to the man who is sixty years old
And desires to worship something one day old."
[The customer] would be ashamed and leave.
One day a woman came, carrying in her hand a basket of fine flour.
She said: "Here, offer it before them."
Abraham seized a stick,
And smashed all the idols,
And placed the stick in the hand of the biggest of them.
When his father came, he said to him:
"Who did this to them?"
[Abraham] said:, "Would I hide anything from my father? a woman came, carrying in her hand a basket of fine flour.
She said: "Here, offer it before them."
When I offered it, one god said: "I will eat first,"

And another said, "No, I will eat first."

Then the biggest of them rose up and smashed all the others.

[His father] said:, "Are you making fun of me? Do they know anything?"

[Abraham] answered: "Shall your ears not hear what your mouth is saying?"

He took [Abraham] and handed him over to Nimrod.

[Nimrod] said to him: "Let us worship the fire."

[Abraham] said to him: "If so, let us worship the water which extinguishes the fire."

[Nimrod] said to him: "Let us worship the water."

[Abraham] said to him: "If so, let us worship the clouds which bear the water."

[Nimrod] said to him: "Let us worship the clouds."

[Abraham] said to him: "If so, let us worship the wind which scatters the clouds."

[Nimrod] said to him: "Let us worship the wind."

[Abraham] said to him: "If so, let us worship man who withstands the wind."

[Nimrod] said to him: "You are speaking nonsense; I only bow to the fire."

"I will throw you into it.

Let the God to Whom you bow come and save you from it."

Haran was there.

He said [to himself] Either way;

If Abraham is successful, I will say that I am with Abraham;

If Nimrod is successful, I will say that I am with Nimrod.

Once Abraham went into the furnace and was saved,

They asked [Haran]: "With which one are you [allied]?"

He said to them: "I am with Abraham."

They took him and threw him into the fire and his bowels were burned out.

He came out and died in front of Terah his father.

This is the meaning of the verse: "And Haran died in the presence of his father Terah."

C. *The overall question*

Reading this Aggadah, one is immediately struck by the non-Midrashic style. There is absolutely no association with text here. Instead, there is a detailed story, down to the specifics of the debate between Abraham and Nimrod, the manner in which Abraham would shame his customers, and the story he concocted to explain the decimation of the "inventory" to his father. The question one must pose here is one of source: from where did the Rabbis derive this information? How do they know that Terah was an idol salesman; that Abraham spoke this way to his customers, the other way to his father, and in such a manner to Nimrod; and why would we even think that Abraham and Nimrod ever met?

The one answer that is always available is *Mesorah* (tradition). To wit, the Rabbis had a reliable tradition going back to Abraham himself that this is how this particular series of events played out. That is appealing, although anyone embracing this approach would have to contend with variations in alternate versions. Yet there are two serious problems with this response. First of all, if this was a reliable tradition dating back to Abraham, why isn't it mentioned in the text of the Aggadah? After all, when the Rabbis have reliable traditions dating back to a much more recent time, they indicate this (see, inter alia, M. Peah 2:6) or, at the very least, refer to the statement as *Gemara* or *Halakhah l'Moshe miSinai* or, in Aggadic contexts, "This matter is a tradition in our hands" (BT Yoma 21a). Second of all, why is the entire Aggadah credited to one authority (R. Hiyya the grandson of R. Ada of Yafo)? Shouldn't it be presented as an anonymous text?

There is another direction — perhaps as much to the "skeptical" side as the first answer was to the "believer" side —that has its roots in some Rabbinic scholarship, although certainly not the mainstream. Some will suggest that this Aggadah reflects a polemic against idolatry; it is a product of its time in the sense that it stakes no claim to knowing anything about Abraham's actual activities, but uses Abraham as a convenient foil for "making a point" about principles, idols, loyalty, and so on. As stated, this is not as foreign an idea as one might think, and is sometimes the most appropriate way to view an Aggadah. Unfortunately, this is often an "easy way out" of contending with the difficult question of, "How did they know this?"

I would like to suggest an alternative approach to understanding this Midrash, one that maintains the integrity of the report and its association to the historic character of Abraham, while defending against the two challenges raised to the *Mesorah* argument noted above.

D. The thesis

Although direct derivations are not found in this Aggadah (albeit the opening and closing lines anchor the Aggadah in a Midrashic attempt to identify the reason for Haran's early demise), I'd like to suggest that the entire reconstruction of Abraham's life here is the result of *Parshanut* — textual interpretation. In other words, every one of the major components of this selection is the result of a reasonable read of the Bible. This is not to argue that every detail of the Aggadah is exegetically derived from the text, especially given the variations of those details as found in the versions of the passage. It is the suggested thesis here, however, that each general component of the Aggadah is directly derived from a careful reading of the Biblical text.

In order to accomplish this, each text in the Abraham narrative (and other selections that shed light on this period) must be read carefully, keeping an eye out for parallel texts and allusions to related passages. Indeed, the same "reading between the lines" that is the *raison d'etre* of this book was practiced by the Rabbis of the Midrashic era.

RECONSTRUCTING THE MIDRASH

There are six principle components to the Aggadah; we will demonstrate that each of them can be supported by a sensitive and careful read of the Abrahamic narrative and related texts:

A. Terah the idolater
B. Terah the salesman
C. Abraham's style of argumentation
D. Abraham's meeting with Nimrod
E. Abraham in the fire
F. Haran and "Pascal's Wager"

A. Terah the Idolater

The source for this component is an explicit text (Joshua 24:2). At the end of his life, Joshua related a historiosophy to the people, which begins with this line:

> And Joshua said to all the people, Thus said The Lord, God of Israel, 'Your fathers lived on the other side of the river in old time, Terah, the father of Abraham, and the father of Nahor; and they served other gods.'

Even though this translation renders the last pronoun unclear, such that we do not know who worshipped foreign gods (it may have been Nahor and Abraham, which would give us a whole different history), the cantillation marks (*Ta'amei haMikra*) make it clear that those who worshipped foreign gods are "your fathers"; Terah is the representative of that group mentioned by name.

When the Aggadah begins by stating "Terah was an idolater," it isn't innovating a new idea or revising history—this is the information found in Joshua's farewell address.

B. Terah the Salesman

This one is not as straightforward and accessible as Terah's idolatrous affiliation. A few pieces of information about the ancient world that can be inferred from the text will help us.

First, society in the ancient world was not transient. People stayed in one area for generations except for cases of war or famine (which is why the call to Abraham of *Lekh Lekha* is so extravagant and reckoned by rabbinic tradition as the first of his tests). Only people whose livelihood allowed them to move easily did so — and, as the text tells us, Terah took his family from Ur towards Canaan, getting only as far as Haran. Terah was the first person who we are told uprooted from one location to another without direct Divine intervention (such as Adam, Cain, and the people in Shinar who were exiled). Hence, he must have had a profession that allowed him to easily move, which leaves him either as a shepherd, an artisan, or a salesman. A careful look at the Genesis narratives will show that Abraham and Jacob were traders whose chief livelihoods and fortunes were made in that fashion. The use of camels, owned by both, and their possession and use of precious metals (gold and silver) are clear indications of mercantile behavior.[20]

In addition, we have other records of idolaters who were, in addition to devotees of the pagan religion, men who engaged in the sale of ritual objects. In Judges 17–18, we are told the story of Micah who lived on Mount Ephraim. He took money given to him by his mother and had an idol fashioned, which he then set up in a temple. When his idol, its appurtenances, and his priest were seized (by members of Dan), the townspeople chased after the thieves to try to restore their goods. Although not stated explicitly, it seems that the reason for their distress at the loss of the idol and its "support system" was an issue of livelihood. Evidently, the temple was a source of revenue for the town, whether as a result of travelers staying

---

20. See *inter alia*, Bin-Nun *Parashiot Yitzhak* (Heb.) Megadim 25, Alon Shvut 1996, pp. 35–77 and the extensive footnotes there.

there or because they sold *Teraphim* (household gods); in any case, the association between idolatry and trade seems clear.

C. Abraham's Style of Argumentation

At three points in the Aggadah, Abraham engages in some form of theological debate (or rebuke): with the usual customer, with his father, and with Nimrod. His style of arguing is consistent—at no point does he come out and state his beliefs, strong though they may be. Instead, he elicits information from his disputant, and then, in classical Socratic fashion, turns that person's own words against him, using the disputant's premise to bolster his own argument.

For instance, he doesn't ridicule or rebuke the customer for purchasing a "god fresh from the kiln"; rather, he asks him (seemingly off-handedly) as to his age. One almost gets the sense that Abraham's response is muttered under his breath: "How ridiculous, a man of fifty worshipping a day-old idol." In shame, the customer slinks out of the shop.

That we have every reason to believe that Abraham would have worked to promote the belief in one God is evident from the verses that highlight his selection (12:1–3) and his activities in Canaan (calling out in the name of God). We don't need to look far to find sources that support the content of his interactions, but how do the authors of this Midrash Aggadah know his somewhat unconventional form of argumentation?

The answer can be found, I believe, in the interaction between Abraham and Abimelech (Chapter 20). Unlike the first "wife-sister" episode (in Egypt), which was necessitated by the famine, there is no reason given for Abraham's descent to Gerar (20:1). Abraham knew, in advance, that he would have to utilize the "wife/sister" ruse in order to spare his life (v. 11)—but why go there at all?

Note that in that interaction, Abraham does not rebuke the king (and, indirectly, his constituents) for their moral turpitude until they come to him, ready to hear an explanation for his curious behavior. If he went to Gerar in order to spread the word and attract more adherents (see Rashi at 12:5 and Sforno at 12:9), why didn't he immediately come in and decry their low standards? Alternatively, if he knew that Sarah would be endangered as a result, why go there at all?

It seems that Abraham went there in order to engage in debate, a debate that could only begin once the people challenged him and were receptive (as a result of their great fear) to what he had to say. It seems to have succeeded, at least partially, because Abimelech (or his son) recognized God's support for Isaac (26:28), implying that they had some understanding of—and respect for—the God of Abraham.

Utilizing the one instance we have of argumentation and chastisement in which Abraham participated that is explicit in the text, the authors of the Midrash are able to apply that style to earlier interactions in Abraham's life.

(The claim here is not that each of the specific events—or the details, such as the age of the customers—can be inferred from the text, nor that we need to accept each of them as an exact historic record; the thesis is merely that the general information and messages of the Aggadah are the result of a careful reading of the text.)

D. Abraham's Meeting with Nimrod

The Torah is not only silent about any meeting between these two, the entire Nimrod biography (10:8–12) is completed well before Abraham is even introduced in the text. From where did the Midrashic authors get the notion that Nimrod and Abraham had any direct interaction?

One feature shared by these two men is power — both were recognized as kings. Indeed, Nimrod was the first person to be considered a king:

> And Cush fathered Nimrod; he was the first on earth to be a mighty one. He was a mighty hunter before The Lord; therefore it is said, 'As Nimrod the mighty hunter before The Lord.' And the beginning of his kingdom was Babel, and Erech, and Accad, and Calneh, in the land of Shinar. (Genesis 10:8–10)

Abraham is also considered royalty:

> And the Hittites answered Abraham, saying to him, Hear us, my lord; you are a mighty prince among us . . .' (Genesis 23:5–6)

There is one more component to the Nimrod story that is vital for understanding the Aggadah. The attitude of the Bible is generally negative towards human rulers — note Gideon's response to the people of Manasseh in Judges 8 and Samuel's diatribe against the people's demand for a king in 1 Samuel 8. Nimrod being the first self-declared king, he was also the first to form a direct challenge to the Rule of the one true King. Abraham's entire life was dedicated to teaching the world about the one true God and to encouraging everyone to accept His rule. As such, Abraham and Nimrod are natural combatants and antagonists. Since Nimrod's life overlapped that of Abraham, and he ruled in the district where Abraham operated (at least during part of his younger years), the land of the Chaldeans, it is most reasonable that the two of them would have interacted. Once we add in the salvation from fire (see next section), following the model of the latter-day king of the same area (Nebuchadnezzar) throwing loyal monotheists into the fire, their meeting is almost a foregone conclusion.

E. Abraham in the Fire

When God addresses Abraham in anticipation of the first covenant (Chapter 15), He states: "I am the Lord that brought thee out of Ur of the Chaldees." (15:7) Before assessing the allusion to a later verse, we need to clarify the meaning of *Ur Kasdim*. The word "*Ur*" may be a place name (hence "Ur of the Chaldees" in most translations); alternatively, it may mean "the *Ur* that is in the Chaldean land," the word "*Ur*" meaning furnace (cf. Isaiah 31:9, 50:11). Even if it is a place name, it may have been named after a great furnace found there.

In any case, God took Abraham out of this place — how do we understand the verb *Hotzeitikha* (I took you out)? Does it refer to the command to "Get thee from thy land . . ." ? Does it allude, perhaps, to a more direct and interventionist evacuation?

The only other place in the Torah where the phrase *Asher Hotzeiti* appears is in the first statement of the Decalogue: "I am The Lord your God who took you out of the Land of Egypt . . ." (Exodus 20:2, Deuteronomy 5:6) In that case, the "taking out" was accomplished through miraculous, interventionist means.

If we accept the theory (which we have explained and utilized in this volume) that unspecified terms in the canon are best clarified through parallel passages in the Bible where those same terms are used, then we have a clearer picture of the "exodus" of Abraham from Mesopotamia. God intervened, miraculously, to save him, in some manner that would later be approximated in Egypt.

Although we have a great deal of information about the miracles leading up to the Exodus, there is little in the Bible to describe the servitude from which we were redeemed. There is, however, one description of the Egyptian sojourn that appears in three passages. In Deuteronomy 4:20, 1 Kings 8:51, and Jeremiah 11:4, the Egypt from which we were redeemed is called *an iron furnace*. So, if God presents Himself, as it were, to Abraham, with the words "that took you out," and we have no information as to what it was from which Abraham was saved, we can look at the parallel passage and, using the description of Egypt found throughout the canon, conclude that Abraham was saved from — a furnace!

F. Haran and "Pascal's Wager"

The final point in the Midrash that we will address is the role of Haran here. He engages in what is commonly referred to as Pascal's Wager. Blaise Pascal (1623–1662), a French mathematician and logician, suggested that it is a good idea to believe in God, based on "the odds." If one doesn't believe in God and turns out to have erred, he will be eternally damned. If he is right, he will achieve salvation. If, on the other hand, he believes in God and turns out to have erred, he will have lost nothing.

Haran's faith, unlike that of Abraham, is depicted as opportunistic. The point of this segment of the Aggadah is quite clear: Declarations of faith are not cut from one cloth, and the faith that can withstand the furnace is one that has already been forged by the crucible, not one of momentary convenience.

How do the authors of the Midrash know that this was Haran's failing? Why couldn't he have predeceased his father for some other sin?

Again, we are not looking for a clue to help determine the exact wording used by Haran in his response to Nimrod, nor even to substantiate the manner of his death; we are, however, searching for some revelation of the text regarding the general temperament of Abraham's brother that would inform the Rabbinic reconstruction of this event.

Because we have no other information about Haran in the text, we have to go to the next best source: his son, Lot.

As we find throughout the Abrahamic narratives, Lot is someone who always took the easy path and the most convenient road, even if it deleteriously affected his family.

When Abraham and Lot needed to separate, Abraham offered Lot his choice: "If you go to the left, I will go to the right; if you go to the right, I will take the left," meaning that they will divide up the mountain range between north (left) and south (right). Abraham abjured Lot to remain in the mountains, a place of greater faith and solitude (see, inter alia, Deuteronomy 11:10–12). Instead, Lot chose the "easy life" of Sodom, which, at the time, appeared as "the garden of The Lord, the land of Egypt"—lush and fertile.

When fleeing from that selfsame city, he begs the angels to allow him to stay nearby, as he cannot go further; this leads to the shameful scene in which his daughters get him drunk and become pregnant. We don't know a lot about Haran, but his son bears the shameful badge of an opportunist; hence, the first child to predecease his father (aside from murder) dies as a result of that opportunistic attitude when applied to the great faith of Abraham.

AFTERWORD

Instead of viewing Midrashic literature as separate from the canonized text, by seeing it as a type of *Parshanut* (exegesis), we can see the great sensitivity with which the giants on whose shoulders we stand looked between the lines of the sanctified text.

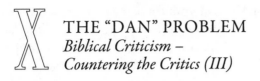

THE "DAN" PROBLEM
Biblical Criticism –
Countering the Critics (III)

INTRODUCTION: THE PROBLEM

The Abrahamic narrative, which begins at the end of Chapter 11 and follows Abraham to Canaan, on to Egypt, and back to Canaan, is interrupted by a story in which the central actors are other than Abraham and his family. Chapter 14 details an alliance of four Mesopotamian kings who subdue and enslave five Canaanite city-states (the "five cities of Sodom") for twelve years. The city-states finally rebel and the overlords come to crush them — and succeed. Among those taken captive are Lot and his household; at this point, we'll let the text take over:

> And there came one that had escaped, and told Abram the Hebrew — now he
> dwelt by the terebinths of Mamre the Amorite, brother of Eshcol, and brother
> of Aner; and these were confederate with Abram. And when Abram heard
> that his brother was taken captive, he led forth his trained men, born in his
> house, three hundred and eighteen, and pursued as far as Dan. And he divided
> himself against them by night, he and his servants, and smote them, and
> pursued them unto Hobah, which is on the left hand of Damascus. (vv. 13–15)

Subsequently, Abraham is involved in a powerful entente involving the king of Sodom and the mysterious Melchizedek. We now turn our attention to a small geographic note in the narrative of the war. This phrase is the cause of much consternation for those of us who maintain our belief in the unity and divinity of the text of the Torah — and is the source of much "banner waving" among those who would challenge our tradition.

According to the report, which, according to our tradition, was given to Moses at Mount Sinai a full forty-seven years before the conquest of the Land of Israel — or, at the very latest, in the plains of Moab just before entering the Land — the northern town near Damascus that marked the end of the first leg of Abraham's pursuit of the four kings was named Dan. We, the modern readers, find no difficulty with the use of this landmark. We know all about the northern town of Dan, which, during the early years of the first Commonwealth, was considered our northern border (see I Kings 5:5). We also hear about its being designated as the northern worship site by Jeroboam ben Nebat (ibid. 12:29). It should not be surprising, then, that the Torah uses Dan as a marker to identify a point along Abraham's path.

Alas, the issue is not so simple. The Land of Israel was divided, subsequent to the Joshuan wars, by Joshua and Eleazar the Priest. The details of each tribe's borders and the major towns that fell to each tribe are detailed in Chapters 15–19 of the book of Joshua. (Chapter 15 details the holding of Judah; 16–17 are the land of the House of Joseph, including Menasseh and Ephraim; 18 presents the boundaries and towns of Benjamin; and Chapter 19 completes the list for Simeon, Zebulun, Issachar, Asher, Naphtali, and Dan. We will eventually attend to the "2.5 tribes" of the East Bank of the Jordan.)

The territory apportioned to Dan was nowhere near Damascus:

> The seventh lot came out for the tribe of the children of Dan according to their families. And the border of their inheritance was Zorah, and Eshtaol, and Ir-shemesh; and Shaalabbin, and Aijalon, and Ithlah; and Elon, and Timnah, and Ekron; and Eltekeh, and Gibbethon, and Baalath; and Jehud, and Bene-berak, and Gath-rimmon; and Me-jarkon, and Rakkon, with the border before Jaffa. This is the inheritance of the tribe of the children of Dan according to their families, these cities with their villages. (19:40–48)

In other words, the area allotted to Dan was in and around the hub of modern Israel—Tel Aviv. (Indeed, all Israelis are familiar with the designation of Greater Tel-Aviv as "Gush Dan"—the local bus company is even named "Dan.") How did a northern town get associated with Dan?

The complete story is found in Judges 18, but begins at the end of the first chapter of Judges. The first chapter details each tribe's success — or lack thereof — in conquering the land allotted them. The sequence of the chapter is quite clear; it begins with the perfectly successful Judah and spirals down to the utter failure of Dan:

> And the Amorites forced the children of Dan into the hill-country; for they would not suffer them to come down to the valley. But the Amorites were

resolved to dwell in Harheres, in Aijalon, and in Shaalbim; yet the hand of the house of Joseph prevailed, so that they became tributary. (1:34–35)

All other tribes conquered all or most of their designated territory; Dan was unsuccessful in conquering any of their allotment.

In Chapter 18 (which happened towards the beginning of the period of the Judges—see v. 30), we are told that the Danites were encamped in Judah's territory, such that their settlement was a Danite camp within Judah. Several representatives went out to scout land for conquest and, eventually, found the town of Layish in a northern valley. The text describes what the scouts found:

> . . . [They] saw the people that were therein, how they dwelt in security, after the manner of the Zidonians, quiet and secure; for there was none in the land, possessing authority, that might put them to shame in any thing, and they were far from the Zidonians, and had no dealings with any man. (v. 7)

They subsequently returned to the Danite camp, reported what they found, and returned with an army of 600 men, who massacred the town and renamed it as Dan, in honor of their eponymous father.

This story is summed up in the book of Joshua in one sentence (note that "Layish" here is called "Leshem"):

> And the border of the children of Dan was too strait for them; so the children of Dan went up and fought against Leshem, and took it, and smote it with the edge of the sword, and possessed it, and dwelt therein, and called Leshem, Dan, after the name of Dan their father. (19:47)

Our question on Genesis 14 is clear: How can the Torah refer to Abraham's pursuit to "Dan" when, at the time of the giving and completion of the Torah (even according to the latest approach within traditional attitudes), Dan's territory was to be on the south-central coast of Israel? The immediate response that springs to mind is "prophecy"—doesn't God know where Dan is going to end up? Why can't the identification of the locus be a prophetic statement? (See, e.g., Rashi ad loc.)

This answer is easily dismissed without encroaching on our well-held belief in prophecy. Whereas prophecies, such as the poetry of Balaam (Numbers 23–24) and Moses (Deuteronomy 32), certainly are presented in oblique fashion, such that a proper understanding of the words and ideas may only happen—if at all—over time. This must be said for all "distant" prophecies, such as any apocalyptic or eschatological visions.

Keep in mind, however, that Genesis 14 is a narrative; the narrative only has meaning if its primary audience can understand it. What would be the point of presenting a detail in this narrative that makes no sense to the readership?

It is easy to see how the "Bible critics" (see the beginning of this section) take this phrase as proof positive that the Torah could not have been given at Sinai or any earlier than the Danite conquest of the north. Truth to tell, by the middle of the 19th century the axioms of the critics had been so widely accepted that this became a mere footnote. (John Skinner noted in 1910,[21] in reference to our passage: "It is singular that such a prolepsis should occur in a document elsewhere so careful of the appearance of antiquity.")

Nonetheless, it is challenges such as the one posed by the "Dan problem" that form part of the theories that are the foundations of the "School of Higher Biblical Criticism."

Professor Yehuda Kil argues[22] that the referent "Dan" in our verse cannot mean the same town captured and renamed by the Danites in the period of the Judges. He suggests that the Bible refers to changed place names by their older name, along with the new one. For instance, "And he [Jacob] called the name of that place Beth-el, but the name of the city was Luz at the first." (Genesis 28:19)

Therefore, concludes Kil, our text should have said "and he chased them until Dan, which is Layish" or something of that sort (see Genesis 14:17 for an example of this formula).

Kil suggests that the "Dan" referred to here is not the (yet-to-be-named) town, but rather the whole area, named Dan on account of the Jordan, which flows through there. Alternatively, he takes a cue from R. Baruch Epstein in his Torah Temimah (followed by Y. M. Grintz in his significant work *Yihudo veQadmuto Shel Sefer B'resheet*) and suggests that "Dan" here may be "*D'dan*", one of the children of Keturah whom Abraham sent east (Genesis 25:6). In defense of this somewhat extravagant suggestion, he notes that there are places where doubled letters are dropped when preceded by another instance of the letter, such as *Ad D'dan*. His proof,

---

21. *Skinner, John*: Genesis – International Critical Commentary, New York 1910, p. 267.

22. *Kil, Yehudah*, Genesis – Da'at Mikra vol. 1 (Heb.), Jerusalem 1997, p. 382 f.n 55.

however, involves an elided "*heh*" (בלילה ההוא) which is much more easily overlooked than a consanantal "*daled*".

Kil's observations are interesting but not compelling. He has no textual support for the area to be referred to as Dan —certainly not before the Danite conquest — and the Jordan connection is weak. As to the *D'dan* suggestion, it suffers on two counts: The example he brings loses much less by eliding the middle "*heh*"; here, it leads to a misidentification of the location. In addition, Abraham sent them "eastward, unto the east country," which is never assumed to be in or near the Golan. It is usually understood as Mesopotamia or beyond.

Professor Yehuda Elitzur presented an approach to the problem within the context of a larger issue. His oral presentation was published post-humously in the prestigious journal of biblical studies *Al Atar* in 1999 (vol. 4–5, pp. 243–249). We will utilize his approach to solve the "Dan problem," along with several other enigmas in the Bible—but, first a few more questions.

A FEW MORE QUESTIONS

The final scene in the Torah posits Moses atop Mount Nebo as God shows him the entire land:

> And Moses went up from the plains of Moab unto Mount Nebo, to the top of Pisgah, that is over against Jericho. And the Lord showed him all the land, even Gilead as far as Dan; and all Naphtali, and the land of Ephraim and Manasseh, and all the land of Judah, as far as the hinder sea.
>
> (Deuteronomy 34:1–2)

Following the sweep of vision described, Moses's eyes follow from north (Gilead) around the northeast (Naphtali), moving south and west until reaching the sea. If Dan's land is supposed to be on the south-central coast, the panoramic view of Moses is anything but smooth — why describe it in such a herky-jerky fashion?

Just before that farewell scene, Moses blesses nearly all of the tribes. His blessing to Dan reads, "And of Dan he said: Dan is a lion's whelp, that leapeth forth from Bashan." (33:22)

The land of Bashan is in the Golan (see, inter alia, Deuteronomy 4:43). Why is Moses blessing Dan in association with this place, so far from their intended territory?

Besides these two questions about Dan, there are several passages in the Torah where we are given names of the third and fourth generations from Jacob. Some of these names are curious, as they are the names of places in Canaan:

1. Machir, Manasseh's eldest, names his first son "Gilead." Gilead is the name of the mountain range on the East Bank of the Jordan and, generically, *Eretz haGil'ad* refers to the land north of the Jabbok river. The name Gilead is well known from Genesis, as that is the place where Jacob and Laban have their fateful meeting and covenant ceremony (31:21, 23, 47–53—note Jacob's clever pun in v. 47).

2. Another of Manasseh's sons is named Sh'khem (Joshua 17:2).

3. Yet another of Manasseh's sons is named Hepher (ibid.). Hepher is the name of one of the 31 city-states conquered by Joshua (Joshua 12:17).

4. This same Hepher has a granddaughter named Tirzah (Numbers 26:33)—yet another of the city-states conquered in the Joshuan wars (Joshua 12:24).

5. Issachar names one of his sons Shimron (46:13). Shimron is one more city-state (Joshua 11:1).

6. One of Kohath's sons (grandson of Levi) is Hebron (Exodus 6:18), a city that later becomes a Levitical city, given to the priestly children of Kohath (Joshua 21:11)!

The mystery deepens once we realize that these children —all born on Egyptian soil — carry names of locations that ended up in the territory conquered by their tribe (or, in the case of Hebron, granted to their family). The "eastern half" of Manasseh basically settled the land of Gilead. The city of Sh'khem falls in Ephraim's territory, very close to the border with Manasseh. Hepher and Tirzah are both city-states that fall within Manasseh's land. Shimron ends up in Zebulun's territory, just inside the border with Issachar.

How are we to understand these odd phenomena? We cannot posit that the towns were named after the people, since both textual evidence and, in some cases, extra-textual evidence indicate that the names used predated the conquest, and most likely the birth of these children.

Why did Manasseh's family members give these names to their descendants? Why did Issachar name his son — born in Canaan before the famine — Shimron, a city that would fall a few kilometers outside of his boundaries?

TWO TRIBES—OR TWO AND A HALF?

We have one more narrative to peruse; our analysis takes us next to Numbers 32. That Chapter records the events that took place after the Israelite army soundly defeated Sichon and Og, the two Emorite chieftains on the East Bank. Subsequent to that victory, there is an intense and detailed negotiation between Moses and the two and a half tribes that wished to remain in Gilead. Except that that is not exactly the case — only Reuben and Gad approach Moses, although half of Manasseh is included, later on, in the story. Note these selections, all from Numbers 32:

> Now the children of Reuben and the children of Gad had a very great multitude of cattle; and . . . the children of Gad and the children of Reuben came and spoke to Moses, and to Eleazar the priest, and to the princes of the congregation, saying . . . "If we have found favor in your sight, let this land be given to your servants for a possession; bring us not over the Jordan." And Moses said to the children of Gad and to the children of Reuben: "Shall your brothers go to war, and shall you sit here?" (vv. 1–6)
>
> And Moses said to them: "If the children of Gad and the children of Reuben will pass with you over the Jordan, every man that is armed to battle . . . then you shall give them the land of Gilead for a possession; but if they will not pass over with you armed, they shall have possessions among you in the land of Canaan." And the children of Gad and the children of Reuben answered, saying . . . "we will pass over armed before the Lord into the land of Canaan, and the possession of our inheritance will remain with us beyond the Jordan." And Moses gave to them, even to the children of Gad, and to the children of Reuben, and to the half-tribe of Manasseh the son of Joseph, the kingdom of Sichon king of the Amorites, and the kingdom of Og king of Bashan, the land, with its cities in the borders, even the cities of the country around. (vv. 29–33)

How did the tribe of Manasseh get involved here? They made no request of Moses or the elders. They were not accused by Moses nor did they negotiate with him regarding their status as vanguards.

THE EARLY DIVISION

In order to get a handle on this, we need to go back to the earliest Divine Promise of the Land and its contingent Covenant. The first Covenant that God made with Abraham condemns Abraham's descendants to servitude as strangers in a foreign land. Although we retro-fit this prophecy to the great events in Egypt culminating with the Exodus, the text is ambiguous on several fronts, including the timing of its fulfillment.

Note that Abraham was promised

> ... that your seed will be a stranger in a land that is not theirs, and shall serve them; and they shall afflict them four hundred years; and also that nation, whom they serve, will I judge; and afterward will they come out with great substance. ... And in the fourth generation will return here ... (Genesis 15:13–16)

Upon examination of the terms of this promise, we find that they all fit with Jacob's exile in Aram (Chapters 28–31):

1. He was stranger in a foreign land (Aram).
2. He was worked and oppressed for a long time (31:6–8, 38–41), which is Biblically expressed as 400 years .
3. Jacob returned with great wealth, as can be seen from the gifts he sent to Esau (32:14–15).
4. The return of the fourth generation is eerily mirrored by Jacob's response to the birth of Joseph: "And when Rachel gave birth to Joseph, Jacob said to Laban: 'Send me, that I may go to my place, and to my country.'" (30:25)

Jacob's reaction indicates that he thought that his mission in Aram was achieved with the birth of a son to Rachel, his beloved, and that son was the fourth generation to Abraham. Following this explanation, Jacob would have thought that the exile/return condition of the covenant had been fulfilled; no further exile need occur.

That being the case, it stands to reason that the children of Jacob, once they had returned to the Land, began dividing it up (once they reached maturity). In Chapter XXII, I support this thesis by pointing to the brothers' shepherding of father Jacob's flock about sixty miles away from his home in Hebron, Reuben's disappearance from the brothers during the discussions about Joseph, and Judah's development of business relations in Timnah (all of this is found in Genesis 37–38).

The brothers began dividing up the land and, at least in the case of Judah, were settling into their future territory (Timnah, the location of Judah's interaction, is included among the cities of Judah [Joshua 15:57]). It stands to reason, then, that the brothers, knowing full well that God would eventually grant them (or their children) the land, divided it up along general lines.

THE IDEAL APPORTIONMENT

Before putting all of this information together, a quick look at Jacob's death-bed scenes (including the blessing to Joseph in the presence of Menasseh and Ephraim) will give us an additional perspective on the argument.

In blessing Joseph, Jacob concludes with an odd phrase: "And I have given to you one *Sh'khem* above your brothers, which I took from the hand of the Amorite with my sword and with my bow." (48:22) However we may translate *Sh'khem* (the conventional understanding is "portion," referring to the extra portion given to Joseph as the firstborn), the use of this word is a clear allusion to the city of Sh'khem, which is not only to be Joseph's burial site, but also sits right at the border of the territories of his two sons.

In his blessing to Judah, Jacob states: ". . . Binding his foal to the vine, and his ass's colt to the choice vine; he washed his garments in wine, and his clothes in the blood of grapes; his eyes shall be red with wine, and his teeth white with milk." (49:11–12)

In his blessing to Zebulun, Jacob says: "Zebulun shall dwell at the shore of the sea, and he shall be a shore for ships, and his flank shall be upon Zidon." (v. 13)

Regarding Asher, the blessing is: "As for Asher, his bread shall be fat, and he shall yield royal dainties." (v. 20)

These blessings refer to (at least by allusion) geographic areas. The finest area for vineyards in the Land is in the mountains of Hebron, in the middle of Judah's territory. Zebulun is given land by the sea, and Asher is blessed with rich and royal produce, belonging to the northern coast.

In sum, not only did the sons divide up the land, but their father also affirmed their division in his final words.

(Regarding the "lottery" via which the land was divided, it is quite clear both from the relevant passages in Joshua and from Rabbinic tradition that the purpose of the lottery was not to determine the location of each tribe's territory, but to provide Divine affirmation for that apportionment. Cf. BT Bava Batra 122a.)

NAMES AND PLACES

We now understand why Manasseh's son, born (second generation) in Egypt, named his first-born Gilead. Those beautiful mountains were always intended to be given to Joseph's two sons; evidently they divided his broad territory while in Egypt and Manasseh received Gilead. This explains why names such as Tirzah, Hepher, and Sh'khem are given in the Manasseh family, and why Issachar names a son Shimron. These were all ancient city-states that existed at the time of Jacob's years of fatherhood in the land — places that were destined to belong to the respective tribe.

We also understand the anomaly in Numbers 32, in which Reuben and Gad approach and negotiate with Moses, who then gives them land, along with half of Manasseh. That half of Manasseh was always destined to inherit that part of the land, which extends deep into the Golan (see Numbers 34:11). They were given the land along with Reuben and Gad because it was as a result of the wars with Sichon and Og that any of the East Bank became available for apportioning. However, unlike the request of the two tribes, that half of Manasseh did not desire anything outside of the territory always intended for them.

RETURN TO DAN

We have solved some of our ancillary problems; however, from the theory presented so far, we haven't yet explained the Dan phenomenon. According to what we've presented so far, we would expect there to be Danites with names like Jehud and Jafo (which we don't find).

Professor Elitzur suggests that at this point we have to rethink the implications of Numbers 32. Since Reuben and Gad requested land on the East Bank—land to which they were not rightfully entitled—that means they had some land waiting for them on the West Bank. Once they completed their settlement with Moses, that land had to be redivided. We have no idea where they were meant to settle, but it is reasonable to posit that as a result of their new territory, Dan was moved to the south-central coast. (Dan is one of the few tribes about whom we have no geographical hints in Jacob's blessing.)

When Dan was unsuccessful in conquering their "new" territory, their next move was to scout out their old home, up in the north. When they found that Naphtali had not conquered this town, they took it themselves and (re)named it Dan. In other words, the city had always been known as Dan within the family, but now that they conquered it, they gave it the formal name in honor of their eponymous father. This is alluded to in Moses's blessing: "And of Dan he said: Dan is a lion's whelp, that leapeth forth from Bashan." (Deuteronomy 33:22) Dan is compared to a lion, and Layish, the (temporary) name of that town, is another word for lion. Moses is blessing Dan that they should somehow return to their ancestral home.

Once we understand that the northern town had always been known as Dan within the nation — even if it didn't have that formal name (much as we always referred to Palestine as *Eretz Yisrael* even when that wasn't the internationally recognized name for our Land) — the reference to Dan as a landmark in Abraham's pursuit is most reasonable and to be expected. Standing at the Plains of Moab, or even at Sinai, we all knew what the town "Dan" meant and where it was.

AFTERWORD

Instead of shying away from the challenges raised by the adherents of the school of Higher Biblical Criticism, we courageously address them head-on. The questions they ask are questions; the inconsistencies indeed exist. That does not mean that the conclusions that they offer are foregone or even necessary. To acknowledge a challenge does not mean to embrace the answer of the challenger.

By changing our frame of reference and bringing it into line with the overall oeuvre of the Torah, we were able to assign each story of Creation to a different perspective of the truth about this world and our relationship with its Creator. By accepting and confronting the doubled story of the Flood, we came to a deeper understanding of the great failure of mankind that precipitated that great precipitation. By employing an older tool—reading the text through the eyes of the earlier generations—we understood that the assignment of Dan was an early one that would be a proper landmark to a generation standing at the foot of Sinai.

TWO BRITOT
Doublets and Doubts

In Chapter III we addressed one of the common "points of interest" of the school of Higher Criticism – apparently contradictory narratives. In this chapter, we will turn our attention to another, related "target" – the apparent redundancy of narrative or law. The three wife/sister encounters (Chapters 12, 20, and 26) involving Abraham/Sarah and Isaac/Rebekah; the several Divine promises to Abraham regarding his future ownership of the Land; the two distinct times when Jacob's name is changed — all these and more are fodder for the skeptical eyes of these critics.

As is usually the case — and as we discovered in our assessment of the Creation "doublet" and the Flood narratives — by assigning each "version" to a unique perspective, we are able to not only respond to the challenges of the critics, but also gain a deeper and more engaging understanding of the import of the text.

One of the "doublets" that appears in Genesis and provides an opportunity for either attacking the unity of the text (as the critics would have it) or enhancing our understanding of each narrative, is the covenant that God makes with Abraham. This covenant, which appears twice within a space of three Chapters (15, 17), includes three components:

1. The relationship with God wherein He will be Abraham's God, with all that that entails;
2. The blessing that Abraham will be a great nation with countless descendants;
3. The bequeathing of Canaan to Abraham's select seed.

We will take the opportunity given us by this apparent repetition to investigate, rigorously and carefully, those points of convergence and,

against that backdrop, the unique nature and significance of each covenant. Again, we will use "Hashem" to represent the Tetragrammaton and
"God" as translation of "Elohim."

INTRODUCTION

In both of these covenants, God commits Himself (so to speak) to give
Abraham the two great, intertwined promises: the Land and Progeny.
These promises are interdependent. There is no point to inheriting a
Land that cannot be passed on, nor is there much succor in knowing
that he will have countless descendants if they have no place to consider
home.

The covenant (we will, for now, treat both interactions as one) has
echoes throughout the Bible (see, e.g., Exodus 2:22, Leviticus 26:42, II
Kings 13:23) and, as such, has significance for the ongoing success and
weal of the Israelites. Central and critical as this covenant is, there are
some troubling aspects to the textual presentation that I would like to
address in this chapter.

Without looking into the textual details of each *B'rit* (covenant), as we
noted, one question immediately presents itself: Why was there a need
to reiterate the *B'rit* of Chapter 15 in Chapter 17? In other words, if the
major Divine commitments of Land and Progeny were already promised
in the "Covenant Between the Pieces" (Chapter 15), why was there a need
to recommit to them via the "Covenant of Circumcision" (Chapter 17)?

A second question comes on the heels of the first: Once we discern the
additional components found in the second covenant that necessitate it,
why aren't the two events integrated, or at least presented sequentially
in the Torah? If we accept chronological fidelity as a premise of the text
(Ramban's approach; see, inter alia, his comments at Exodus 18:1), we
would have to reformulate this question as follows: Why was it necessary
to introduce—and commit to—the Covenant Between the Pieces significantly earlier than the Covenant of Circumcision, such that the two
events are interrupted by the events of Chapter 16?

ANALYZING THE TWO B'RITOT

Before we can respond to our two questions of superfluity and sequence,
we ought to analyze the text of each *B'rit*, identifying those significant
differences that may hold the key to our problem. Instead of assessing each

B'rit independently, we will look at the common topics, noting how each is addressed in each *B'rit*.

THE LAND

Although the promise of the Land of Canaan is a central feature in each *B'rit*, the Land is not presented in a uniform fashion.

B'rit bein haB'tarim ("between the pieces"— Chapter 15)

> And He said to him, "I am Hashem who brought you out of Ur of the Chaldeans, to give you this land to inherit it . . ." In the same day Hashem made a covenant with Abram, saying, "To your seed have I given this land, from the river of Egypt to the great river, the river Euphrates; the Kenites, and the Kenazites, and the Kadmonites, and the Hittites, and the Perizzites, and the Rephaim, and the Amorites, and the Canaanites, and the Girgashites, and the Jebusites." (15:7, 18–21)

B'rit Milah (circumcision—Chapter 17)

> And I will establish My covenant between Me and you and your seed after you in their generations for an everlasting covenant, to be a God to you, and to your seed after you. And I will give to you, and to your seed after you, the land where you are a stranger, all the land of Canaan, for an everlasting possession; and I will be their God. (17:7–8)

EVALUATION

The salient features of the Land in *B'rit bein haB'tarim* are its boundaries and the foreign people who presently reside there, along with it being the destination towards which God brought Abraham out of Ur of the Chaldeans.

Conversely, there are no boundaries given to the Land in the *B'rit Milah,* nor is there any mention of how Abraham got there. The only explicit mention of the Land is the eternal relationship between Abraham (and his seed) and the Land: all the land of Canaan, for an everlasting possession.

We will continue to assay the significant distinctions between the *B'ritot*. Once we have covered the major themes as presented in both, we will analyze these different presentations.

THE PROGENY

The second thread that runs through all of the Abrahamic promises is *Zera* – progeny. Again, this promise is addressed in two clearly diverse manners in the two *B'ritot*.

B'rit bein haB'tarim (Chapter 15)

> And, behold, the word of Hashem came to him, saying, "This shall not be your heir; but he who shall come forth from your own bowels shall be your heir." And He brought him outside, and said, "Look now toward heaven, and count the stars, if you are able to count them;" and He said to him, "So shall your seed be." (15:4–5)

B'rit Milah (Chapter 17)

> "And I will make you exceedingly fruitful, and I will make nations of you, and kings shall come out of you."(17:6)

EVALUATION

In Chapter 15, there is no concern whatsoever given to the quality of the seed, only its vast number, like the stars in the sky. In addition, there is no direct relation to Abraham other than their being his descendants, but they could all come from one child. In other words, Abraham could have one child (son or daughter) who would, several generations down the line, be the source of many children.

In Chapter 17, each of these facets is intensified. Not only will Abraham have children, but also they will be kings and leaders of nations. In addition, he himself will be blessed and become fruitful, implying that Abraham himself will father numerous children.

THE REST OF THE FAMILY

B'rit bein haB'tarim (Chapter 15)

There is no citation because, quite simply, the rest of Abraham's family is ignored here. Although we understand why Ishmael is left out of this *B'rit* — he wasn't born yet — Sarah is likewise omitted.

B'rit Milah (Chapter 17)

> And God said to Abraham, "As for Sarai your wife, you shall not call her name Sarai, but Sarah shall her name be. And I will bless her, and give you a son also of her; and I will bless her, and she shall be a mother of nations; kings of people shall be of her." (17:15–16)

EVALUATION

This one is quite clear. Not only is Sarah included in the *B'rit Milah*, but she is also given equal billing to Abraham. Her name is changed to reflect her changed status among the nations; she will be blessed with a child and she will be blessed with being the mother of nations.

In addition, Ishmael, who we would assume to be left out of the terms of the *B'rit Milah* (besides the obligation for Abraham to circumcise him), is given a similar blessing:

> And as for Ishmael, I have heard you; Behold, I have blessed him, and will make him fruitful, and will multiply him exceedingly; twelve princes shall he father, and I will make him a great nation. (17:20)

CONTEXT

B'rit bein haB'tarim (Chapter 15)

> After these things the word of Hashem came to Abram in a vision, saying, "Fear not, Abram; I am your shield, and your reward will be great." (15:1)

B'rit Milah (Chapter 17)

> And when Abram was ninety nine years old, Hashem appeared to Abram, and said to him, "I am *El Shaddai;* walk before me, and be perfect. And I will make My covenant between Me and you, and will multiply you exceedingly." (17:1–2)

EVALUATION

The *B'rit bein haB'tarim* (and its immediate antecedent, God's appearance to Abraham presented here) comes in response to something that has frightened Abraham. Most of the *Rishonim* associate this fear with the story of the war between the kings into which Abraham intervened, saving Lot and defending the five local rulers against the four marauding kings. This is supported by the opening phrase: "After these things." (The *Rishonim* are divided as to what caused Abraham's fear: his concern that his merit had been used up as a result of his miraculous victory, that the kings would come after him for revenge, that his reputation would be soiled among the inhabitants of the Land, and so on. See the classic commentators, *ad loc.*)

B'rit Milah, conversely, doesn't come "after" anything. It takes place a full thirteen years after the birth of Ishmael, the last event mentioned in Chapter 16. The text seems to imply that this *B'rit* was made not in response to a fear of Abraham, but rather in Divine "anticipation" of the birth of Isaac. Indeed, Ishmael's blessing (of being fruitful and siring twelve princes) is only in response to Abraham's plea: "O that Ishmael might live in Your presence!" (17:18)

SUMMARY

B'rit bein haB'tarim

1. Is a response to Abraham's fear
2. Focuses only on Abraham's success
3. Promises only progeny, ignoring the quality of that seed
4. Does not concern itself with Abraham's direct relationship with that progeny
5. Presents the Land by its borders and as the location of Abraham's rescue from Ur of the Chaldeans

B'rit Milah

1. Is given in anticipation of the birth of Isaac
2. Includes Sarah as an equal beneficiary of the Divine blessing
3. Promises children who are kings and leaders of nations
4. Associates that blessing directly with Abraham, as he himself is to be fruitful (as will Ishmael)
5. Presents the Land as an *Ahuzat Olam* (everlasting possession), making no mention of the borders of the Land or the identity of its present-day inhabitants

ONE MORE SIGNIFICANT DIFFERENCE

We have assayed the thematic differences between the two *B'ritot*, not-ing how common issues are treated differently in each place. There are, however, significant linguistic differences that will help us discover the underlying difference that explains all of the above-mentioned variations. One of these differences lies in the operative word throughout this chap-ter: *B'rit*.

Although common convention relates to both settings — indeed to both chapters — as *B'ritot*, that word is used quite differently in each selection. Although the term "*B'rit bein haB'tarim*" is the traditional ap-pellation given to the covenant forged in Chapter 15, that phrase does not appear anywhere in the Bible. Indeed, the word "*B'rit*" appears only once in the entire Chapter: "*Bayom Hahu Karat Hashem B'rit Et Avraham*" ("on that day, God forged a covenant with Abram . . .") v. 18.

The key word *B'rit* is presented without the definite article and is treated as "a covenant," which is exactly what we would expect. After all, this covenant had never been made before; no one had ever been promised this Land prior to Abraham, and the earlier promises (12:7, 13:14–17) were sufficiently vague as to warrant a clear delineation of the borders of the Promised Land.

The word *B'rit* appears, in one of two forms, thirteen times in Chap-ter 17. Significantly, in the first *Parashah* (Masoretic paragraph) of that Chapter — addressed directly to and about Abraham — the word *B'rit* shows up three times, and *B'riti* (which we will discuss forthwith) shows up seven times. As we will discuss in detail in the next chapter, when a word shows up seven times within a defined literary unit, that is a strong indication that it is the *leitwort* (guide word) of that unit, setting the tone for the entire selection.

Let's consider this word *B'riti*, specifically in the context of our chapter. Here is the first occurrence of this word:

> And when Abram was ninety nine years old, God appeared to Abram, and said to him, "I am El Shaddai; walk before me, and be perfect. And I will make My covenant between Me and you, and will multiply you exceedingly." (17:1–2)

Unlike the undefined *B'rit*, which can be applied to any previously un-known pact, *B'riti* is best deconstructed as *HaB'rit Sheli*, "My covenant," which refers to an already existent agreement—the one that is known to be associated with "Me."

It would be tempting to interpret the *B'riti* of Chapter 17 in light of the *B'rit* of Chapter 15; to wit, the referent of *B'rit Milah* is the *B'rit bein haB'tarim*. This approach is, however, untenable. The *B'rit* reiterated (numerous times) in the *B'rit Milah* section has nothing to do with the ceremonial or covenantal aspects found in Chapter 15. The *B'rit* of Chapter 15 expressly and explicitly grants Abraham a particular stretch of land — a stretch that remains undefined and relatively peripheral to the agreement entered into via the *B'rit Milah* of Chapter 17.

We are, therefore, left with one final question: What is the *B'rit* that is referred to (at least seven times) in Chapter 17?

AN EARLIER PROBLEM

The unidentified *B'rit* that permeates Chapter 17 is not a new problem within Genesis. The word *B'riti*, referring to a pre-existing covenant, appears in the context of the Flood narrative. When God commands Noah to build the Ark, he states: "But I will establish *B'riti* with you; and you shall come into the ark, you, and your sons, and your wife, and your sons' wives with you." (6:18)

What covenant is the referent here? At this point, God had made no covenant with Noah — that only appears in the postdiluvian scene, where the covenant is marked with the placement of the rainbow. Even in that context, the phrasing is none too clear:

And God spoke to Noah, and to his sons with him, saying, "And I, behold, I establish My covenant with you, and with your seed after you . . . and I will establish My covenant with you; neither shall all flesh be cut off any more by the waters of the Flood . . . This is the token of the covenant which I make between Me and you and every living creature that is with you, for perpetual generations: I have set My bow in the cloud, and it shall be for a token of a covenant between Me and the earth. And it shall come to pass, when I bring clouds over the earth, and the bow is seen in the cloud, that I will remember My covenant, which is between Me and you and every living creature of all flesh; and the waters shall no more become a flood to destroy all flesh. And the bow shall be in the cloud; and I will look upon it, that I may remember the everlasting covenant between God and every living creature of all flesh that is upon the earth." And God said to Noah, "This is the token of the covenant which I have established between Me and all flesh that is upon the earth." (9:8–17)

Throughout this section, the rainbow is called an *Ot B'rit* (a sign of the covenant), but not the covenant itself. At no point are the terms of the actual covenant specified, except insofar as the consequence of that agreement is that God will never again destroy the earth with a Flood. Note, however, that the passage *begins* with the phrase: "*Et B'riti . . .*"; again, we must ask: Which covenant is being fulfilled here?

THE ORIGINAL B'RIT

If God, while speaking to Noah, refers to *B'riti*, there must have been a *B'rit* between God and Mankind before Noah. That takes us back, of course, to the first man.

The creation of Man (in the first Creation narrative, 1:1–2:3) is described as follows:

> And God created man in His own image, in the image of God created He him; male and female He created them. And God blessed them; and God said to them: "Be fruitful, and multiply, and replenish the earth, and subdue it; and have dominion over the fish of the sea, and over the fowl of the air, and over every living thing that upon the earth." (1:27–28)

Although not explicitly called a *B'rit*, the charge given Man at Creation is, indeed, a pact. Man has been given something (the earth and all "lower" creatures) and has, in kind, committed himself (or been committed) to rule over them, while caring for their continued existence.

What, then, is God's commitment here? If Man's job is to oversee the maintenance and successful growth of God's universe, what must God do? It stands to reason that God has agreed, so to speak, to continue to "support" the universe by maintaining the natural climes, proper cycles, and so on in order to allow Man to continue to flourish.

It is only when Man fails his task miserably that God "reneges" and the world of creation is regressed to primordial chaos (during the Flood—see Chapter 6 earlier in this book).

In other words, the original *B'rit*, between God and Man, involves a mutual commitment to maintain and support God's world.

FLASH FORWARD TO THE FLOOD

Now we can understand the *B'rit* to which God is referring when He commits to fulfill *B'riti* with Noah. The statement, broadly read, is understood as follows: Even though I am destroying all of Mankind, I will fulfill my original *B'rit* with you and your family.

Subsequent to the Flood, the rainbow becomes the sign of that covenant (*B'riti*), such that both parties to the agreement have a tangible and visible sign of their agreement, assuring that it will never again be threatened so sorely.

BACK TO ABRAHAM

After ten generations of Mankind's sinful behavior, God set out to start over. Ten generations after Noah, the world had sunk again — but this time, instead of destroying most of the world and saving the few righteous people, God selects the righteous individual (Abraham) who will become the teacher of Mankind. Instead of building a new world from scratch, Abraham's job will be to build a nation that will be able to teach the whole world how to worship God in truth, justice, and generosity of spirit (see Genesis 18:18–19).

Before proceeding to analyze the two *B'ritot* with Abraham, the differences between them and the need for two separate covenants, a quick overview of the first half of the "Abraham narrative" (through both covenants) is in order:

Chapter *12:* Abraham is commanded to leave his land and move towards Canaan, going through the Land and ending up in Egypt as a result of the famine. While there, he endures a difficult encounter with Pharaoh.

Chapter *13:* Upon his successful and safe return from Egypt, Abraham must separate from Lot; after Lot chooses the lush Jordan plain, God promises the Land to Abraham.

Chapter *14:* The war of the four kings against the five kings. Abraham intercedes in order to save Lot and has a curious détente with Melchizedek, the local priest, and with the king of Sodom.

Chapter *15: B'rit bein haB'tarim.*

Chapter *16:* Sarah, realizing that she likely will not bear children, suggests that her maidservant, Hagar, stand in for her as a child bearer for Abraham. When she becomes pregnant, Hagar treats her mistress lightly; in response, Sarah oppresses Hagar, who runs away. (See the harsh

assessment of Ramban and Kimhi of Sarah's behavior ad loc.) An angel
encounters Hagar, directing her to return to Sarah, suffer under her hand,
and bear the child, who is to be called Ishmael.

Chapter *17: B'rit Milah.*

Note that all of the interactions involving Abraham up until the *B'rit
bein haB'tarim* are between Abraham and outsiders: Pharaoh, his separation from Lot, the foreign kings, Melchizedek, and the king of Sodom.
What, you may ask, is missing here?

When God blessed Adam, effectively committing to ***the B'rit***, He told
him to be fruitful and multiply. Man's blessings begin at home, raising a
family and ensuring that his own moral and spiritual growth, along with
his material success, not only be passed on, but also grow and increase with
the next generation. Abraham's ultimate task, to be the next "Adam" of
the world, could not be completed as long as all of his interactions were
with outsiders. He was certainly a successful recruiter for God, but the
realization of his potential would only happen when he would transmit
the tradition of his faith to his own children.

We can now review the *B'rit bein haB'tarim* and understand its unique
thematic stylings. This agreement was not an affirmation of the original
B'rit; hence it is not introduced that way. The only concern being addressed here is Abraham's fear — a fear of retribution from the vanquished
kings, a fear that his work will be for naught, as he has no seed. In response,
God promises him that he will, indeed, have descendants. Their quality is
of no import here, because Abraham has not asked for children who will
follow his path and endorse his values — just children to inherit his gifts.

As such, *Eretz Yisra'el* (the Land of Israel) is described by its boundaries
because it operates, in the context of this *B'rit*, purely as a safe haven. Note
the central verse in Chapter 15: "I am God who brought you out of Ur of
the Chaldeans, to give you this land to inherit it." (15:7)

The emphasis here, just as it is in the verse foreshadowed here (the
opening of the Decalogue), is not the beauty or special qualities of the
Land; rather, it is the Land where God brought Abraham after saving him
from the land of the Chaldeans. Canaan's borders are the most important
feature here, because Abraham must know how far his "safe territory"
extends.

This is the *Eretz Yisra'el* embraced by many over the years, especially
in the last 150 miraculous years of national renascence. Many are drawn
home not out of an attraction to the sanctity and glory of the Land, but

rather out of an utter rejection of exile and, oft times as not, chased home by inhospitable nations.

Before Abraham can step into the shoes of Adam (and Noah) and become a partner in the original *B'rit*, he must turn to his family and attend to that dimension of his life. For the first time, in the "sandwich" chapter (Chapter 16) between the covenants, the entire narrative is devoted to the goings-on inside of Abraham's tent(s).

We now turn to Chapter 17 and understand that this is the "real" *B'rit* — *B'riti*, the commitment by God to fulfill, with Abraham, His original pact with Mankind. His entire family is blessed with the same blessing given to Man: *P'ru Ur'vu* (be fruitful and multiply) is echoed here: "*Va-Arbeh Ot'kha . . . VeHifreiti Ot'kha* (17:2,6). The Land of Israel is not merely the haven for refugees from Ur of the Chaldeans, from Egypt (or from the former Soviet Union); it is the eternal possession of a nation of kings. Everyone in Abraham's family is blessed, and this recommitment to *the B'rit* is in anticipation of the first opportunity to really fulfill it, through the birth of the promised son, Isaac.

POSTSCRIPT

One more critical feature found in the *B'rit bein haB'tarim* has no echo in the *B'rit Milah,* a difference we can readily appreciate in light of this analysis. The core prophecy of the *B'rit bein haB'tarim* is the destiny of Abraham's seed:

> Know for a certainty that your seed shall be a stranger in a land that is not theirs, and shall serve them; and they shall afflict them four hundred years; And also that nation, whom they shall serve, will I judge; and afterward shall they come out with great wealth. (15:13–14)

This promise, which has been fulfilled several times in our history (focally at the Exodus), again posits the Land of Israel not as the palace of kings, but as the haven of refugees.

We now understand the need for two covenants. When we need our Land as a refuge, when we return with shattered families and as a broken people, the *B'rit bein haB'tarim* stands as our guarantee. When, however, we are finally able to rise to the challenge to teach the entire world, to be (in the words of Chapter 17) a "father of many nations," the Land will be our eternal possession, the birthplace of royalty who will fulfill the destiny established for all of Mankind.

AFTERWORD

By aligning the common features of the "doubled story," we revealed great differences between them, differences that complemented each other. As we continue our study, we see more and more "dualistic perspectivism" inherent in the ultimate unity of God's world.

XII   FROM HEBRON TO SODOM
The Leitwort

INTRODUCTION

A significant tool of interpretation that was always recognized by the classical commentators but has become more formalized and systematized in the last century is the identification of a *leitwort* or key word (in Hebrew, *Milah Manhah*), which is an unusual word that appears within a literary unit with great frequency. Experience bears out that this word will invariably appear seven (or a multiple of seven) times within the unit. For example, the key word *Tov* (good) appears seven times within the first Creation story; the root שבת (meaning "rest") appears seven times in the passage regarding the Sabbath in Exodus 31; the word *Ben* (son) appears seven times in the opening section of the book of Samuel. In each of these cases, the *leitwort* serves to underscore the subtext of the passage. In the three examples cited here, the subtexts are: the essential goodness to God's world as He created it; the entire purpose of the framework of the Sabbath as a cessation from labor; and the exposition of the opening passages in the book of Samuel are all focused on Hannah's desire for a son.

In many cases, identifying a *leitwort* (or several — there may be more than one in a section; for instance, the final literary unit in the Torah, Moses's death, contains three key words: Moses, the Land of Israel, and the nation) only serves to confirm that which is abundantly clear in the text. In other cases, it may reveal that we are focusing on the wrong subject or event and should be paying attention elsewhere.

This chapter on the destruction of Sodom will provide a vivid example of the latter, where a careful read of the story and identification of the *leitwort* provide an unexpected and new perspective on the story. One ancillary tool that will be used here is the identification and demarcation of the literary unit, such that we can divine its parameters and identify structures within.

THE PROBLEM

The story of the destruction of Sodom, which properly encompasses Chapters 18 and 19 in Genesis, opens with a scene as famous as it is difficult. Abraham, recently self-circumcised into the covenant, is sitting at his tent-opening in the heat of the day when God appears to him. At that point, the text becomes hard to decipher. Is the appearance of God made manifest through the vision of three men coming to visit, to whom Abraham shows his storied hospitality (as Maimonides explains)? Or is God's visit interrupted by the "real world" intrusion of three strangers, who later prove to be His own agents, who come to Abraham's tent? In any case, the opening scene seems to be focused on the "glad tidings" of a miraculous birth — one year hence — of a son to Abraham and Sarah. Sarah's laughter foreshadows the name of that long-awaited son — Isaac.

Yet, the entire visitation episode is, from a broader view, entirely unnecessary. In the previous scene (Chapter 17), when Abraham was commanded to enter the covenant and to change his name as well as the name by which he called his wife (see Malbim at 17:15), he was promised a son with Sarah and that son's name was already given: "But My covenant will I establish with Isaac, whom Sarah shall bear to you at this set time in the next year." (17:21)

Not only is his name given, Abraham is also told the date of the birth; all of the information imparted by the angelic guests was already given to him. What need was there for them to visit?

Although a significant number of "detail" questions can be raised regarding the "annunciation," I'd like to direct attention to the rest of the story as it unfolds. In order to do that, we first have to clarify where this story ends.

FROM ABRAHAM'S TENT TO THE CAVE AT ZOAR

Even though the seventy-one verses that comprise Chapters 18 and 19 make up two full chapters and are conventionally broken into more than three separate readings ("*Aliyot*"), they are one paragraph in the Masoretic text. In other words, the only division that is inherent in the text — the breakdown into *Parashot* — defines this sequence of scenes, a veritable travelogue that begins and ends in the mountain country but descends to the topographical and moral abyss of Sodom, as one literary unit. As such, I would like to assay the entire unit and ask several overarching questions on the sequence.

In addition to the first question regarding the telos of the angelic visit, the famed negotiation over the fate of Sodom (which makes up the latter half of Chapter 18) is also burdened by some glaring difficulties.

Abraham presented the foundation of his argument:

> "Will You also destroy the *Tzaddik* with the wicked? . . . Be it far from You to do after this manner, to slay the *Tzaddik* with the wicked; and that the *Tzaddik* should be as the wicked, be it far from You; Shall not the Judge of all the earth do right?" (18:23–25)

(I have deliberately avoided translating *Tzaddik* for now; we will return to the meaning of this word later on.)

At that point, it is reasonable that Abraham should have pointed to the possibility of there being one *Tzaddik* in the city, for God's justice would just as surely be tarnished if one person were to be wrongly punished as if that fate were to befall fifty. Why does he begin at fifty, and only negotiate down as far as ten?

In addition, the premise of his negotiation is shaky: why would Abraham think that there were any *Tzaddikim* in Sodom? When Lot moved to that district, the text told us that "the men of Sodom were wicked and sinners against Hashem exceedingly" (13:13); why would he think that suddenly there would be any *Tzaddikim*? However we may translate the term, it doesn't jibe with "wicked and sinners."

Once we move to the next Chapter, and the furthest descent of the travelogue, we are assailed by more questions. Why did the angels enter the city of Sodom at all? If their purpose was to save Lot (and members of his family), why send two? The Midrash (quoted by Rashi ad loc.) makes much of the notion of each angel having a unique mission, so there was only need for one angel to rescue the fortunate ones. Why send two angels?

One final question in Sodom: The deal struck with God was that if there were ten *Tzaddikim* in Sodom, the city would be spared. Where did the angels — or anyone else — complete the search and find the city wanting? When they entered Lot's house and were pursued by an angry mob, there was no evidence that there weren't *Tzaddikim* who didn't participate in the attempted gang-rape of the visitors? If we posit that the angels had the omniscience of their Master, then the entire visit is unnecessary, as is God's refrain in the negotiations "If I find in Sodom…"

As we continue to follow Lot, his wife and daughters, and their angelic guide out of the city, the band of refugees is charged not to look back; when Lot's wife fails to heed the command, she becomes a pillar of salt (19:26, but see Gersonides ad loc.). Yet, in the next verses, we read that Abraham gazed at the city and watched as the smoke rose. This interjection is odd on several accounts:

- Why does the text abruptly switch its focus, for a mere three verses, from Lot on his way from Sodom to Zoar to Abraham standing on Mount Hebron?

- Why are the refugees forbidden from looking back as the city falls, with such dire consequences, while Abraham may gaze, undisturbed and unaffected?

- Verse 29 — the end of the interjection — states: "And it came to pass, when God destroyed the cities of the Plain, that God remembered Abraham, and sent Lot out of the midst of the overthrow, when He overthrew the cities in which Lot dwelt." Why is Abraham mentioned here in conjunction with Lot's salvation? If there was any need to mention Abraham's role in saving Lot (yet again, see 14:16), it should have been presented either at verse 12 when the angels reveal their plan to Lot, or after Lot is rescued and safely housed in Zoar.

The end of this long narrative takes us to the cave in Zoar, where Lot's daughters get their father drunk and, on successive nights, seduce him in order to create some progeny for themselves in their errant belief that the world has been destroyed. In concocting the plan, the elder daughter says to her sister, "Our father is old, and there is not a man on earth to come in unto us after the manner of all the earth." (v. 31)

What is the significance of his age here? It seems a gratuitous remark, considering that if, indeed, there are no men left in the world, they would need to act immediately even if their father were young.

In summary, we have seven questions regarding this series of subplots that comprise one story:

- What is the purpose of the angelic visitation to Abraham?
- What are we to make of the negotiations over Sodom?
- Why do the angels enter the city at all?
- When is the search for ten *Tzaddikim* completed — in failure — such that the fate of the city was sealed?
- Why is there a mention of Abraham's gazing at the city?

- Why is Abraham's role in saving Lot placed (awkwardly) in the middle of the description of Lot's flight to safety?
- Why does Lot's elder daughter declare "our father is old"?

Before we can solve the particulars, we need to attend to the unity, structure, and intra-connection of the components of this unit of seventy-one verses.

THE UNITY OF THE NARRATIVE

I recommend following this section with text in hand.
Although the story begins in Hebron and ends in Zoar, there is a circle that nearly becomes closed by the end of the passages. The narrative begins in the mountainous region of Judea, abruptly descends (in more ways than one) to the lowest point of human civilization, and then returns up to the mountainous area overlooking the formerly fertile plain of Sodom (see 19:30, "And Lot went up out of Zoar, and dwelt in the mountain . . ."). This is but one piece of the integrity of the unit.

A close look at the unit reveals that there are two sequences here that mirror each other in an inverted manner.

A. Birth

A: (18:1–15) The story begins with the arrival of three people (= angels), to a place (Hebron) where there will be the birth of a child, whose name (*Yitzhak*) will be a deliberate play on words (*Midrash Shem*) associated with the events related to his conception (Abraham and Sarah's laughter), and a repast (food) is served at that place.

A': (19:30–38) The story ends with the arrival of three people (Lot and his two daughters) to a place (the cave above Zoar) where there will be the birth of two children, whose names (Moab, ben-Ami) are a deliberate play on words associated with the events related to his conception (Moab = *MeAv* [from the father]; *Ben-Ami* [son of my nation]), and a repast (wine) is served there.

I would like to propose that this is why the text credits the daughter with the seemingly superfluous statement "our father is old"; it further strengthens the parallel with the annunciation at Abraham's tent, where Sarah thinks "my lord (= husband) being old . . . ." (18:12) Yet note the stark differences between the two scenes, drawn together to show us how very different they are.

Abraham receives his three visitors during the day, in the open, with a meal that consists of everything but wine, in a state of total consciousness. (According to Maimonides, this visitation was a prophecy and never took place in the real world, and there is no higher state of consciousness than prophecy.) The astounding birth of this child will be the source of blessing to the world (note 12:2 and 17:21).

The three refugees act at night, in a cave, with a meal that consists (as far as we are told) only of wine, in a state of such total unconsciousness that Lot is able to be "fooled" again the next night.

I would like to propose that this is the purpose of the angelic visit to Abraham. There is no need to inform him of that which he already knows; rather, that visit is presented to contrast it with the horrible and abominable mirror scene at the end of the narrative. The purpose of this contrast will be addressed in the last section of this chapter.

This is, in addition, the reason for the gratuitous addition of the phrase "*v'avinu zaken*" (our father is old) spoken by the older daughter — it serves to bolster the parallel with the annunciation in Hebron where Sarah accurately and pointedly reacts to the glad tidings with "my lord being old . . . ."

(I am deliberately eliding sections B and B' as they serve as "interludes" and will be highlighted last.)

C. The Fate of Sodom

C: (18:20–33) The famous negotiation over the fate of Sodom takes up the end of this chapter and, as noted earlier, is beset with several general difficulties, in addition to all of the specific issues addressed by the *Rishonim*.

In this section, there is a *leitwort* that appears seven times: *Tzaddik*. Note how cleverly this word is elided in the "lower numbers" in order to preserve the sevenfold repetition.

In Rabbinic and modern Hebrew, a *Tzaddik* is a "righteous person," that is, someone whose behavior is exemplary and whose piety is unquestioned. This is not the case in Biblical Hebrew, where the word, simply put, means "innocent." For example, the passage introducing court procedures and "lashes" states "by justifying the *Tzaddik* and condemning the wicked" (Deuteronomy 25:1), clearly meaning "innocent." When David reacts unfavorably to the confession of the murder of Ish-bosheth by Rechab and Baanah (II Samuel 4:6), he accuses them of killing an "*ish tzaddik* on his bed." He certainly does not mean to elevate Saul's remaining son to sainthood, which is irrelevant to the dialogue in any case, but to accuse them of killing an innocent man on his own bed. (i.e., not in self-defense or on the battlefield).

(This meaning is only meant when applied to humans; when God is called *Tzaddik* (e.g., Deuteronomy 32:4), the meaning there is certainly nobler than "innocent.")

What, then, was Abraham using as his argument against the destruction of Sodom? The notion that God, as "judge of the earth" (Whom Abraham had been publicizing these many years) would violate His own reputation by destroying those who were innocent along with the guilty? Why didn't he then point to the possibility of there being *one* innocent person in Sodom, thereby saving the town?

There was a history to the destruction of the place in spite of innocent people being there. Noah is told by God that "I have found you to be a *Tzaddik* before Me in this generation" (Genesis 7:1); again, the *p'shat* is that Noah is simply innocent of the crimes of the generation and, as such, does not merit their fate. His ignominious end (to which we will return further on) seems to testify to his being less than pious; but he is not deserving of the destruction rained upon the generation of the Flood.

How did God serve His justice here? He destroyed the place and rescued the innocent. He "plucked" the innocent from the doomed place and kept him (and his family) safe while destruction rained down.

As such, Abraham, who may have harbored hopes that after these many years in Sodom, his nephew and former apprentice Lot may have influenced some of the sinning citizenry to give up their evil ways, raises that very possibility with God. If there is a large group of innocent folks, justice will be better served by punishing the wicked alone and leaving the innocent in their place. The reputation of justice (as opposed to the capricious judgment accorded to the pagan gods — compare the Noah story with that of Utnapishtim in the Epic of Gilgamesh) will not be served if a town with a sizeable population innocent of the crimes leading to the "terrible cry" that is emanating from the town is utterly destroyed and its innocent residents are displaced and made into refugees.

God allows for the possibility that there are fifty innocent people there, and that He will spare the town "for their sake" (i.e., so that they not suffer the hardships mentioned above).

The negotiations end at ten because the last group of innocents that was spared totaled just under ten (Noah, his wife, his three sons and their wives, all evidently innocent as they were saved) and their place (the world) was not spared for their sake.

The word "*Tzaddik*" is the key word of this section, because it is the possibility of there existing a community of innocents that is the linchpin of Abraham's pleas.

By the way, there is another *leitwort* in this section — *Matzo* (to find). It should be clear why this word also appears exactly seven times — the entire enterprise of the Divine investigation into Sodom depends on "finding" a group of innocent people.

C': (19:1–26) In the mirror section with which Chapter 19 begins, the fate of Sodom, negotiated in section C, is sealed. The messengers of God come into Sodom with one mission — to search for innocent people. They expedite the search by entering the city and poking at its Achilles' heel. As the prophet Ezekiel points out (16:49), and as is repeated many times in Midrashic literature, the city had a reputation for not taking care of the "other" (i.e., the outsider, the destitute, etc.). In order to test the guilt of the town, they fall upon the goodwill of others, and only Lot brings them into the house. When the townsfolk surround the house, making their abominable demands on Lot regarding his guests, Lot goes out and offers them a substitute "plaything" for the night — his own two daughters. At this point, the angels pull Lot in, saving his life, and tell him that they are going to destroy the town; again, where is the search for the innocent?

We err if we think that it is possible to live in a town where such terrible things are initiated by a mob and those who refuse to participate — but continue to reside there — are considered "innocent." To be innocent, one must publicly and obviously do what is possible to stop such abominable behavior, or, at the very least, loudly and clearly protest it.

When the angels found that no member of the town was making any attempt to stop the mob, it was a clear sign that there weren't ten innocent people; there wasn't even one. (We will look at Lot's "innocence" later on.)

Whereas the first half of this pair carries the Abrahamic optimism that there may be some *Tzaddikim* in Sodom, the mirror story that takes place in Sodom bares the city's true nature. Once the mob has been stilled by the angels, the judgment of the city is final and the only obstacle in the way of its destruction is the presence of Lot and his kin.

We still have a few loose ends to tie up — and section "B" to look at.

B. *Abraham*

B: (18:16–19) This somewhat awkward interlude, following Abraham's escorting his guests towards the mountaintop overlooking the lush valley of Sodom (and seemingly being a Divine response to Abraham's hospitality and the self-same act of escorting the guests), highlights the great promise of Abraham and the "responsibility" God "feels" towards His chosen one. As this Divine "rumination" is expressed, the angels are looking down at Sodom (v. 16).

B': (19:27–29) In an even more awkward interjection, the text leaves Lot on his way up to Zoar and returns to the hills of Hebron, where Abraham is watching the destruction. God remembers Abraham and, as a result, sends Lot away from Sodom.

I believe that the unusual location of this passage is justified by what it accomplishes within the unified narrative Just as the transition from Hebron down to Sodom is broken up with a mention of Abraham's greatness, so the return move from Sodom up towards Hebron has a parallel refocusing.

The "awkwardness" of these mentions of Abraham highlights that even though the major focus of the events in these seventy-one verses is the fate of Sodom, the real "star" of these chapters is Abraham. We will comment on this in the final section of the chapter.

We can now turn our attention to Lot (and his salty wife) and the final tally of *Tzaddikim* in the city. Conventional wisdom holds that there were three or four innocents in Sodom: Lot, his two unmarried daughters and, perhaps, his wife. I would like to propose that there were none at all; I believe that this is borne out by a careful reading of the verses.

There is a clear parallel between the stories of Noah and Lot; both are spared, along with members of their family, from Divine punishment that destroys their home. Indeed, the final picture we are given of each of them is that of a drunk being shamed by his own children.

But, the parallel falls short of totality. When God turns His attention to the ark and begins to cause the waters to recede, He "remembers Noah" (8:1) and, as a result, slows the waters and begins the process that will lead to his exodus from the ark.

Why does God spare Lot? "And it came to pass, when God destroyed the cities of the Plain, that *God remembered Abraham*, and sent Lot out of the midst of the overthrow . . ." (19:29) Lot was no better than his neighbors, as is evidenced by his shameful behavior outside of his door.

He is saved not by his own innocence, but by the merit of his uncle, brother-in-law, and former patron, Abraham.

This is why none of his entourage was allowed to look at the destruction; one may only look "down" at God's justice if one is truly raised above the status of the guilty. The immediate mention of Abraham gazing at the city should be enough to underscore this point; in the parallel section (B), the angels also gaze down, further strengthening the distinction between the innocent, who may look, and the guilty who are spared through no merit of their own, who may not. (Violation of this norm turns one into the very vehicle of the punishment, in this case, salt.)

ABRAHAM

We have responded to all seven questions posed above; yet we cannot leave our gaze down at Sodom without noting the role of Abraham in this story. As noted earlier, a superficial reading of these two chapters places the focus in and about Sodom; a more careful reading leaves us with the conclusion that the real focus is Abraham. Why else would the text "jerk" us away from Lot's travels to refocus on Abraham and his prayerful gaze at the horrible destruction raining down from heaven?

Not only is Abraham's hospitality set against the terrible norms of Sodom, but the elevation of Abraham from chieftain to "prince of God" (Chapter 23) seems to take place within these Chapters. Whereas Abraham's only interactions with other leaders had been tense (e.g., in Egypt and at the détente with the king of Sodom), from here on his power and stature are raised significantly. (Compare Abimelech's invitation in Chapter 20 to Abraham's expulsion from Egypt at the end of Chapter 12.)

The many contrasts against which Abraham is shown favorably, beginning with the annunciation (against the shameful birth of Moab and Ben-Ami), continuing with his pleading for the *Tzaddikim* (against the horrible treatment of the innocent wayfarers), and concluding with his merit, which spares Lot and his daughters (who have no merit of their own) serves to underscore the august and noble nature of our first father. Is it any surprise, then, that Abraham's name appears fourteen times throughout this narrative? (Compare this to the fourteen mentions of Moses at his consecration at Sinai in Exodus 3:1–4:17, and the twenty-one mentions of Samuel at his inauguration in I Samuel 3.)

AFTERWORD

By identifying the parameters of the literary unit, we are able to discern structures that help us clarify the subtext. In addition, once we have the contours of the unit clear, we can identify those words that repeat and stress certain personalities, themes, or events such that the *leitwort* informs our understanding of the text.

AKEDAT YITZHAK
The Power of the Concordance

INTRODUCTION

Perhaps the most powerful — and certainly the most basic — tool available to the sensitive reader is the Concordance. Although as a separate volume it is barely more than a century old, it was utilized by every serious Bible scholar, including the Rabbis of the Talmud and Midrash as well as the great medieval commentators.

The Concordance identifies each occurrence of a given word everywhere in the canon, such that any difficult word can be checked against other contexts; unusual words can be linked by their infrequent appearances; and stories, poetry, legal texts, and the like can be linked via their common words or phrases.

Even a casual perusal of the Midrashic corpus or the comments of Rashi, ibn Ezra, and others demonstrates quite clearly that they operated with an "open" Bible in front of them, using verses in Job to explain difficult phrases in Genesis, verses in Proverbs to bolster a contested explanation of a phrase in Kings, and so on. For these giants, to whom the entire Bible was always an "open book," it was an assumed vehicle of interpretation that needed no justification nor demonstration of its efficacy.

In this chapter, we will utilize the Concordance to gain fresh insight into the journeys of Abraham and the nature of his wanderings.

INTRODUCTION OF THE CHALLENGE

The tragic heroism of Abraham, in which every blessing and/or Divine gift bestowed on him came on the heels of a separation from those near and dear, is well-documented and is the focus of many a serious essay — witness Rabbi J. B. Soloveitchik's "The Lonely Man of Faith" and Søren Kierkegaard's "Fear and Trembling." We will use this particular

Abrahamic heroism as the springboard for this chapter.

Whether it was his first separation, from father and homeland; his parting of the ways from Lot; the multiple isolations from Sarah; the exile of Hagar and Ishmael; or the near-collapse of the future on Mount Moriah — in all of these cases, Abraham's greatness and the Divine favor shining on him only increased with each episode of separation. Indeed, his entire life seems to have been shaped by the first Divine command given him:

> The Lord said to Abram, "Go from your country and your birthplace and your father's house to the Land that I will show you. I will make of you a great nation, and I will bless you, and make your name great, so that you will be a blessing. I will bless those who bless you, and the one who curses you I will curse; and in you all the families of the earth shall be blessed." (12:1–3)

ABRAHAM'S LIFE: AN OVERVIEW

Although we are given scant information about Abraham before he was commanded to "leave your land" (cf. Chapter XIX), a significant number of episodes that took place between the ages of 75 and 137 are related — some in painstaking detail. Here is a brief outline of the Abrahamic narratives (Chapters 12–23):

A. *"Lekh Lekha"*—"Go unto you" (12–13)
    1. Abraham's immigration (12:1–9)
        Leaving father and family
    2. Egypt (12:10–20)
        Temporary separation from Sarah #1
    3. Parting of ways from Lot (13:1–13)
    4. Divine Promise of the Land (13:14–18)
        Abraham settles in Kiryat Arba' (v. 18)
B. War of the Kings (14)
        Captivity of Lot
C. *B'rit*/Covenant *bein haB'tarim* (15)
        Future oppression of Abraham's progeny
D. Hagar episode #1 (16)
        Temporary exile of Hagar
E. *B'rit Milah*/Circumcision (17)
        Promise of Isaac—rejection of Ishmael
F. Abraham and Sodom (18–19)

1. Visitors to Abraham's tent (18:1–15)
2. Abraham's plea for Sodom (18:16–33)
3. Destruction of Sodom (19:1–29)
4. Lot and his daughters (19:30–38)
G. Abraham in Gerar (20)
    Temporary separation from Sarah #2
H. Isaac (21–22)
1. Birth of Isaac (21:1–21)
    Permanent exile of Hagar and Ishmael
2. Pact with Philistines (21:22–34)
3. *Akedah* (binding of Isaac) (22:1–19)
    Near-death of Isaac
4. Announcement of birth of Rebekah (22:20–24)
I. Purchase of the cave of Machpelah (23)
1. Death of Sarah

Each step of Abraham's life that invites God's blessing is accompanied with (or preceded by) an instance of separation from family. Why are these two emotionally charged experiences so intertwined in Abraham's life? Why must he (if he truly must) introduce another measure of isolation in order to come closer to the realization of God's blessing?

WHY IS ABRAHAM THE "WANDERING ARAMEAN"?

I would like to pose three additional questions before beginning our analysis:

1. Throughout the Abrahamic narratives, the Patriarch is described as a nomad. Even after arriving in the Land, Abraham continually moves (note, inter alia, 12:8–9, 13:3, 20:1); where do we find that God's command to Abraham implied a life of nomadic wandering?

2. As a detail of the previous question, Abraham's behavior immediately after his successful *Aliyah* (immigration to the Land of Israel) is puzzling. God commanded him to go to "the Land that I will show you," where he will realize all manner of blessings. As soon as the first hardship presents itself (famine), Abraham abandons the Land of Divine Promise for Egypt. Even if this was intended as a temporary trip (see below, *That I Will Show You*), it is still hard to reconcile this behavior with Abraham who is "My close friend" (*Ohavi*—Isaiah 41:8).

Ramban, who raises this question (Genesis 12:10), goes so far as to say that Abraham sinned in this regard, and that this sin — going down to Egypt when he should have stayed in the Land and trusted that God would take care of him —was the cause of his children's oppression in that same land.

Can we find some way to explain Abraham's seeming abandoning of the Land and apparent lack of trust in God? Can we defend him against Ramban' charge?

3. God commands Abraham to go to "the Land that I will show you"; that there "I will make of you a great nation ... and in you all the families of the earth shall be blessed." The clear implication is that all of these blessings are not only contingent on Abraham's taking leave of his family toward "the Land that I will show you"; he must also establish himself there in order to be blessed and become a source of universal blessing.

We would expect Abraham, upon his arrival in Canaan, to purchase (or conquer) some land and establish himself as a permanent citizen and landowner, so that these blessings have the opportunity to "take hold." However, Abraham never makes an attempt to acquire any piece of the Land until his beloved Sarah dies and he purchases a catacomb for burial. Why did he wait so long to "take hold" of the Land?

LEKH LEKHA AND THE AKEDAH: PARALLEL CHALLENGES

Many commentators, as early as the Midrash (Genesis Rabbah 39:9) and as recently as the Netziv, have noted that the opening command to Abraham is strikingly similar to the last Divine command given to him: "Take your son, your only son, whom you love – Isaac, and go to the land of Moriah, and offer him there as a burnt offering on one of the mountains that I shall show you." (22:2)

Compare this with: "Go from your country and your birthplace and your father's house to the Land that I will show you." The pregnant phrases that describe the painful separation, "your country, your birthplace, and your father's house" are a near-perfect parallel to "your son, your only son, whom you love." The quixotic trek to find "the mountain that I will show you" echoes the first Divinely directed journey, to "the Land that I will show you," which marked the beginning of Abraham's way.

There is yet another parallel between these two missions that "book-end" the Abrahamic narratives in the Torah. God told Abraham that as a result of his leaving kith and kin and journeying forward, he would be blessed, be a source of blessing and, through him, all of the nations of the world would be blessed.

Compare:

"... because you have done this, and have not withheld your son, your only son, I will indeed bless you, and I will make your offspring as numerous as the stars of heaven and as the sand that is on the seashore. And your offspring shall possess the gate of their enemies, and by your offspring shall all the nations of the earth gain blessing for themselves, because you have obeyed My voice." (22:16–18)

With:

"And I will make of you a great nation, and I will bless you, and make your name great, so that you will be a blessing. I will bless those who bless you, and the one who curses you I will curse; and in you all the families of the earth be blessed."

The crowning blessing in both cases is that Abraham (and Abraham's progeny) will be a source of blessing for the rest of the world. These are the only two places in the Abrahamic narratives where this blessing is expressed. (The reference in 18:18 is not directed to Abraham; it is presented as Divine "musings" about Abraham.)

There are several ways to understand these obvious and striking parallels. We could understand them as creating a literary "envelope" structure that helps define the entire Abrahamic enterprise. Alternatively, we could suggest that these two parallel missions help establish the framework for the ten "trials" of Abraham (see M. Avot 5:3 and Maimonides's commentary ad loc.).

I would like to propose that the relationship between the first *Lekh Lekha* and the final *Lekh Lekha* is more than a literary device; it is at once integrated and causal.

"THAT I WILL SHOW YOU"

In order to respond to our four questions above and to understand the relationship between the first command given to Abraham and the *Akedah*, we need to reexamine a pregnant phrase that informs *Lekh Lekha* while obscuring it.

El ha'Aretz Asher Ar'eka (To the Land that I will show you): Abraham was not told where this Land was (although he was already moving in the right direction (see 11:31 and Ramban at the end of his comments to 12:1); just that God would show him the Land.

How would Abraham know that he had reached his destination? How would Abraham know when he reached the place where he would achieve all of those grand blessings promised by God?

Two alternatives seem plausible:

1. If God revealed Himself to Abraham — at any point — that might be an indicator that he had already reached the place in question.

2. If outside factors supported his settlement there (what is referred to in the Talmud as "absorption of the Land"—see, e.g., BT Ketubot 111a; see also BT Sanhedrin 108b). In other words, if he found the economic, military, political, and social conditions in a particular spot conducive to settling there, that might be an indication that God was showing him the place to settle.

Some of the medieval commentators grapple with this issue and suggest variations of the first alternative:

R. David Kimhi (12:7): "And The Lord appeared to Abram — He appeared to him at Elon Moreh to inform him that this is the Land to which He had referred."

Ramban (12:1): ". . . to the Land that I will show you — [Abraham] was wandering from nation to nation and from kingdom to another people until he came to the Land of Canaan and [God] said to him: I will give this Land to your seed (12:7); at that point, 'the Land that I will show you' was fulfilled."

R. Abraham ibn Ezra (12:1, second explanation) adopts a similar view, as does R. Obadia Sforno (12:1), who explains: "to the Land that I will show thee — [meaning] to the place within the Land that I will show you by Divine visions. Therefore [Abraham] passed through the Land and did not set up his tent until he reached the place where God appeared to him. . . ."

There are, in sum, two variations of this notion: Once God appeared to Abraham, that demonstrated that he had reached the destination. Alternatively, when God declared "this is the Land . . . ," that was the fulfillment. Because both of these happened simultaneously, there isn't a practical difference as to when this verse reached fulfillment, only a theoretical question of which component in that vision represented the realization of that goal: the Divine appearance or His declaration which accompanied said appearance.

There is one problem with all of these approaches: In spite of God's appearing to Abraham, and promising him the Land, Abraham does not cease his wanderings. As noted earlier, Abraham seems to continue his original journey, moving from place to place, never settling down and avoiding land acquisition for many years after the Divine appearance recorded in 12:7.

WHAT WAS ABRAHAM SEEKING?

It seems clear, then, that Abraham did not sense that he had reached "the Land that I will show you " as a result of the Divine revelation documented in 12:7. What was he looking for?

Our second proposal, above, would explain a number of anomalies in the narrative.

We will review the relevant Abrahamic narratives and note how the "absorption" (*K'litah*) approach (our second proposal) gives us a broader understanding of Abraham's actions throughout the narrative.

Abraham was looking for an indication that he had reached the place where God intended him to settle, and where all of those blessings could be realized. He continued moving south (12:9), which is a continuation of the direction he had been moving in when God gave him his first command. When the famine made the Land of Canaan unlivable, he moved further south, to Egypt. There is no indication in the text that Abraham saw that "descent" as temporary; although the text states that he went down to sojourn there (*Lagur Sham*), indicating that his intention was not necessarily to settle in Egypt. It does not mean that this was not an option if Egypt would turn out to be hospitable for him.

How, then, did Abraham know that Egypt was not "the Land that I will show you"? The hostility that he encountered in his interactions with the Pharaoh, followed by his being "escorted out" of Egypt, were probably a solid indication that this was not "the place."

Although Abraham apparently tried to settle down after his return to Canaan, his wanderings continued for many years.

For the first time (that we know of), Abraham is wealthy (13:2), and we can assume that he is ready to find a spot and settle there. Tragedy strikes again — Lot's shepherds have a dispute with Abraham's shepherds. This shows Abraham that the conditions are not yet ripe for proper settlement, so he proposes the right/left split (13:9). Lot accepts and takes the Sodom valley, leaving Abraham with the hill country of the Emorites. This should be sufficient and, indeed, the long awaited word *Vayeshev* (and he settled/

dwelt) appears at the end of Chapter 13. Subsequent to becoming enriched in Egypt and separating from Lot, Abraham is now ready to settle, which he does, in the terebinths of Mamre (Kiryat Arba'/Hebron).

Just as Abraham is settling in, conditions again conspire to deprive him of the security of stable dwelling. The very next verse introduces us to the "War of the Kings," a war that seems to have affected the entire Land of Canaan (including Hebron). In addition, by virtue of Lot's prisoner-of-war status, Abraham was drawn into the fighting.

At the end of the war, an enigmatic encounter takes place between Abraham, the king of Sodom, and Melchizedek, the king of Salem (which most commentaries associate with Jerusalem). In the course of that encounter, Melchizedek blesses Abraham and then blesses the God of Abraham: "Blessed be Abram of God Most High, Maker of heaven and earth; and blessed be God the Most High, Who has delivered your enemies into your hand." (14:19–20)

At last, the great promise is starting to be realized: ". . . and I will bless you, and make your name great, so that you will be a blessing." (12:2) It was in this place (Salem/Jerusalem) where the Divine promise attached to Abraham's task to go to "the Land that I will show you "began to become actualized.

The next few Chapters describe Abraham's increasingly intense relationship with God. The Covenant *"bein haB'tarim"* (Chapter 15) and the name change and *B'rit Milah* (Chapter 17) complete the "covenant portion" of the narrative (see Chapter 10)—but at no point in either covenant is there a mention of Abraham settling down. Indeed, the intervening Chapter describes yet more instability, as Hagar's pregnancy and subsequent haughtiness lead to cruel treatment on the part of Sarah (note the Ramban at 16:6). As a result of this, Hagar flees, only to return at the behest of God (via an angel) and to bear Abraham a son, Ishmael.

The lack of "settledness" continues through the Sodom episode (Chapters 18–19). Note that even after this great destruction (more instability in the land), Abraham wanders southwest to the land of the Philistines (Chapter 20). Since (as mentioned before) there was no inherent reason for him to continue wandering, it may be that Abraham was still looking for that place; the lack of suitable conditions for "absorption" to this point indicated that he had not gotten "there" as of yet.

The upsetting incident in Gerar — echoing the near-tragedy in Egypt — is amplified by Abraham's claim that: "Because I thought: 'Surely the

fear of God is not in this place; and they will slay me for my wife's sake.'"
(20:11)

Not only is this not "the Land that I will show you," Abraham, in
his own defense to Abimelech, presents himself as someone who is still
wandering: "And it came to pass, when God caused me to wander from
my father's house, that I said to her: 'This is the kindness you must do me:
at every place to which we come, say of me: He is my brother.'" (20:13).
Abraham's behavior is consistent with his "wandering life," which is not
yet finished!

Even the miraculous birth of Isaac (21:1–5) is not enough to bring
stability to the family; the immediate aftermath of Isaac's weaning party
is the permanent exile of Hagar and Ishmael from the household.

Abraham then makes a pact with Abimelech, the Philistine king, and
conditions finally seem conducive to Abraham's settling down and realizing all of the Divine promises.

Nevertheless, we read, at the end of Chapter 21, "And Abraham resided
as an alien many days in the land of the Philistines." Abraham was still a
Ger, an alien; he still made no move to acquire land and gain permanent
status in the Land.

We finally come to the *Akedah*. Before looking at this powerful mini-
saga and its role within Abraham's life, let's remember that, following the
thesis suggested earlier, Abraham still hadn't found "the Land that I will
show you." He continues to wander, not on account of a nomadic ideology, but because his quest is not finished. His travels to Egypt, throughout
the Land (and his unwillingness to acquire land and settle down) are all
symptomatic of his lack of "arrival"; he hasn't yet fulfilled the first verse
in *Lekh Lekha*, upon which all of his success and the success of his seed
is contingent.

Suddenly, the memory of that first command is powerfully evoked by
a hauntingly similar directive: "Take your son, your only son, whom you
love – Isaac, and go to the land of Moriah, and offer him there as a burnt
offering on one of the mountains that I shall show you." (22:2)

Abraham's journey is finally at an end — God is going to show him
the long-sought-after place, "the Land that I will show you." Although we
conventionally understand "the Land that I will show you" as a reference
to all of Canaan (since any location within Canaan wouldn't properly
be considered a land; it would usually be called a *Makom* [place]), the
verse explicitly refers to *the Land of Moriah,* later identified as Jerusalem
(2 Chronicles 3:1).

Is it any wonder that Abraham arose early in the morning to begin this final journey? God was directing him to go back to the place where he had first found a partial fulfillment of the promise — where Melchizedek had blessed him years before.

"On the third day Abraham lifted up his eyes, and saw the place afar off." (22:4) The rest of the story is well-known and does not directly impact on our theory. Nevertheless, it is prudent to point out that the name of the mountain is Moriah; Abraham later refers to it as *Hashem Yeira'eh* (God will be seen), all words associated with "seeing," as in "the place that I will show."

After these many years of wandering, of trying to finally identify the place that God intended to be the locus benedicti of Abraham (and his children), it has been found, it has been named, and it has been sanctified. The same place where Abraham was first blessed (from the mouth of Melchizedek) was now the place where the Abrahamic destiny of being a blessing for all of mankind was reconfirmed and established.

AFTERMATH

We finally hear of Abraham settling down (in Beer-sheba) with no further disruptions. We hear of this, deliberately and pointedly, in the last verse of the *Akedah* story: "And Abraham returned to his young men, and they arose and went together to Beer-sheba; and Abraham lived at Beer-sheba." (22:19) We now understand why Abraham was now ready to settle down (in Beer-sheba) — indeed, the next section describes Abraham (finally) acquiring land in Machpelah.

We can now review our questions and respond:

Q: Why does every step of Abraham's life involve separation from family?
A: Because the blessing originally given involved the growth of a great nation, every one of these episodes of Abrahamic isolation was a clear indication that he had not yet reached the place — that he had to continue the process of *Lekh Lekha*, for he had not yet reached "the Land that I will show you." He had to continue the process of "Go from . . . father's house" until finding "the Land that I will show you."

Q: Why does Abraham continue to wander, even after reaching the Land?
A: Since he had not yet found "the Land that I will show you," he had to maintain the nomadic lifestyle.

Q: Why did he go down to Egypt (Ramban's question)?
A: Because the conditions in the Land were not yet propitious for his settling there, he understood this as an indication that this was not yet the place for him to be.

Q: Why did he wait until after the *Akedah* to settle down (in Beer-sheba) and to acquire land (in Hebron)?
A: It was only after the *Akedah*, when he had found the place and had had the full reconfirmation of his blessings (every one of which was repeated at that place), that he was able to "settle down" in the land and begin the process of developing the great nation that he was promised. The birth of Rebekah — the seeds of the following generations — is announced immediately after the *Akedah* saga.

We can better understand the import of the Torah's description of Abraham immediately after that piece of the Land is acquired: "And Abraham was old, well stricken in age; and the Lord had blessed Abraham in all things." (24:1)

AND FOR GOOD MEASURE . . .

". . . to the Land that I will show you: This is Mount Moriah, as it says: Go to the land of Moriah (Gen. 22:2)." (Midrash haHefetz)

AFTERWORD

Using the Concordance (whether in book, digital, or human memory form), we are able to find connections and associations between and within stories that often help us see them in relation to each other and see how one may be the resolution of the other.

XIV PURCHASE OF MACHPELAH
Historical Background and Archaeological Evidence as Tools of Interpretation

INTRODUCTION

One of the curious turns of academic research into the Biblical text since the final third of the 20th century, is the shifting role of archaeology. To many traditionally oriented students of the text, archaeology has become an adversarial science; the mere mention of its scholars and purveyors usually carries the dreaded anticipation of a deconstruction of the Biblical text. A few archaeologists — and a lot of amateurs — have used recent discoveries and, most notably, the lack thereof, to "demonstrate" the lack of historical veracity of the text. According to many students of this discipline, the patriarchal narratives never happened, the Exodus is at least "up for grabs," and — perhaps most critically as it impacts on contemporary politics — the Joshuan conquest of Israel never took place.

This is where "Biblical archaeology" is — at its most minimalist — at the beginning of the 21st century, but it was not always that way. Biblical archaeology, although it might be liberally dated to the early first millennium, properly began in the 19th century as a British response to the German schools of Biblical Criticism. In 1865, the Palestine Exploration Fund (PEF) was founded "by a group of distinguished academics and clergymen, most notably the Dean of Westminster Abbey ... to promote research into the archaeology and history, manners and customs and culture, topography, geology and natural sciences of biblical Palestine and the Levant."[23]

Archaeologists were sent to Mesopotamia and Palestine to search and dig in order to contradict the claims of the German schools and to verify the Biblical account. Although some of the archaeologists between

---

23. http://www.pef.org.uk/history/

the late 19th and mid-20th century entered the field without clear and glaring prejudices regarding the historic accuracy of the text, the general conclusion was to confirm, in whole or in part, the Biblical narrative. The modern father of Biblical archaeology, William Foxwell Albright, is reported to have said that he expected to find contradictions between what lay underground and what the text said, but the more he dug, the closer those versions became.

We turn our attention to a related series of finds that has great impact on our text.

Many important archives were found, in various archives unearthed between the late 19th century and the middle of the 20th century, among the ruins of what are now Iraq and Iran. These archives include royal documents dating back to the early second millennium BCE through the middle of the first millennium BCE. These documents were written in cuneiform, Akkadian, Sumerian, and, in some cases, Aramaic. Scholars were immediately put to work in three areas: properly identifying the letters, translating the words, and then identifying correlations between the found text and other Near Eastern texts, including the Bible.

Not surprisingly, most of what was found substantiated the Biblical narrative (if it had any bearing on it whatsoever). For instance, in the code of Hammurabi (composed and in effect at about the same time as the patriarchal narratives; i.e., the first half of the second millennium) we find that if a person kills his fellow's slave, he must pay him twenty talents of silver. In later documents, dating from the first half of the millennium (about the time of the Sinaitic revelation), the fine for such an act was thirty talents of silver (either the silver market had dropped or slaves became a greater commodity). In Genesis Chapter 37, we find that Joseph was sold to the Ishmaelites for twenty talents of silver; Sinaitic legislation, however, maintains that anyone who kills a fellow's slave has to pay thirty silver pieces. This apparent discrepancy is easily clarified by comparing the relevant Near Eastern texts, which clearly point to a valuation in the price of a slave during this period. This does substantiate that Genesis reflects awareness of this lower price — something probably inaccessible to the putative writers who the critics credit with the composition of Genesis.

In this chapter, we will demonstrate the value of using the tools provided to us by archaeologists to enlighten our understanding of the text.

THE PROBLEM

Chapter 23 is devoted to one topic: Abraham's protracted negotiations with the Hittites for the Cave of Machpelah in Kiryat Arba' (Hebron). A superficial perusal of the text gives the impression that it was the death of Sarah that motivated Abraham to purchase this plot. A more studied engagement with the text indicates that this was the appropriate time and circumstance for Abraham to finally "take hold" of a piece of the Land of Canaan, beginning the process of acquisition that was the completion of his mission.

As such, the negotiations for Machpelah were not just geared to procuring a burial plot for Sarah; they represent Abraham's first "serious" attempt to acquire land in "the Land that I will show you."

It behooves us, therefore, to review the Torah's narration of these negotiations and to try to decipher the enigmatic requests and responses presented. For purposes of analysis, the chapter is divided into sections (they do not represent verse numbers):

"And Sarah was a hundred and twenty seven years old; these were the years of the life of Sarah. And Sarah died in Kiryat Arba'; which is Hebron — in the Land of Canaan; and . . ."

a. "Abraham came to mourn for Sarah, and to weep for her.

And Abraham stood up from before his dead, and spoke to the Hittites, saying: 'I am a stranger and a sojourner with you: give me possession of a burying-place with you, that I may bury my dead out of my sight.'"

(Abraham's request for a burial plot)

b. "And the Hittites answered Abraham, saying to him: "Hear us, my lord: you are a mighty prince among us, in the choice of our tombs bury your dead; none of us shall withhold from you his tomb, that you may bury your dead.'"

(the Hittites assent to Abraham's request)

c. "And Abraham stood up, and bowed to the people of the land, to the Hittites. And he talked with them, saying: 'If your mind is that I should bury my dead out of my sight; hear me, and entreat for me to Ephron the son of Zohar. That he may give me the cave of Machpelah, which he has, which is in the end of his field; for as much money as it is worth he shall give it me as a possession of a burying place.'"

(Abraham requests a specific burial plot)

d. "And Ephron lived among the Hittites; and Ephron the Hittite answered Abraham in the hearing of the Hittites, of all who went in at the gate of his city, saying: 'No, my lord, hear me; the field I give to you, and the cave that is in it, I give it to you; in the presence of the sons of my people I give it to you; bury your dead.'"

(Ephron agrees to Abraham's request)

e. "And Abraham bowed down before the people of the land. And he spoke to Ephron in the hearing of the people of the land, saying: 'But if you will give it, I beg you, hear me; I will give you money for the field; take it from me, and I will bury my dead there.'"

(Abraham insists on paying for the land)

f. "And Ephron answered Abraham, saying to him: 'My lord, listen to me; the land is worth four hundred shekels of silver. What is that between you and me? Bury therefore your dead.'"

(Ephron seems to insist on granting the land without payment)

g. "And Abraham listened to Ephron; and Abraham weighed to Ephron the silver, which he had named in the hearing of the Hittites, four hundred shekels of silver, current money among the merchants. And the field of Ephron, which was in Machpelah, which was before Mamre, the field, and the cave which was in it, and all the trees that were in the field, that were in all the borders around, were made over to Abraham for a possession in the presence of the Hittites, before all who went in at the gate of his city. And after this, Abraham buried Sarah his wife in the cave of the field of Machpelah before Mamre; the same is Hebron in the Land of Canaan. And the field, and the cave that is in it, were made over to Abraham for a possession of a burying place by the Hittites."

(Abraham pays for it nonetheless and receives more than the cave; he acquires surrounding land, including trees, the field, etc.)

I would like to raise several questions about this narrative:

1. Why does Abraham introduce himself to the Hittites, thus beginning the negotiations as a *Ger veToshav* ("a stranger and a sojourner")?

2. What is the gist of the Hittite's salutation of Abraham: *N'si Elohim Atah b'Tokheinu* ("you are a mighty prince among us")?

3. Once Abraham has singled out one particular field (that of Ephron), Ephron's response begins with the word *Lo* ("no"); what is Ephron rejecting?

4. Ephron seems insistent on granting Abraham a burial plot; why does Abraham keep negotiating with him?

5. Following the previous question: Why does Abraham insist on paying for the land (even though the amount is exorbitant)?

"THE BEAUTY OF JAPHETH SHALL DWELL
IN THE TENTS OF SHEM"

In order to properly address these questions, we will need to devote a significant portion of our discussion to a methodological question with far-reaching implications for the study of Torah and our understanding of classical texts. Ever since the culture of the West — basking in the very real, if exaggerated, glow of the Enlightenment — developed secular theories about the history, literature, mores, and evolution of religion, there has been an atmosphere of *kulturkampf* raging between the worlds of academia and religion. Although this state of affairs has occupied much of the attention of the Protestant world (and, to a far lesser degree, the Catholic Church), nowhere has the battleground of this conflict been fiercer — or claimed more casualties—than in our own world of Torah. The alarming rate of disaffection, attrition, and assimilation throughout the world of European Jewry over the past 200 years is staggering, and the relatively rapid replacement of Torah culture, values, and ethos with those of "the West" has played no small part in this cultural and religious tragedy.

This is not to claim that the spirit of inquiry, rigorous methodological analysis, and embrace of intellectual pursuits as having inherent value are inimical to the Torah viewpoint — the very opposite is true. It is, however, both an understatement and grossly misleading to limit a description of the modern academic mien to these noble accomplishments. For the past 200 years, with increasing cynicism and dismissiveness, the world of religious faith and commitment has been relegated to the shelves occupied by other curious ancient relics of a bygone world.

Sadly, the casualties have not been limited to those who preferred Berlin to Volozhin; the world of Torah scholarship has also been affected by the demographic and sociological changes wrought by the last two centuries of secular culture. A subtle yet significant development has been the understandably (yet regrettably) negative attitude towards secular disciplines that permeates many Torah-observant circles and communities.

This is, of course, not how the masters of Torah scholarship always viewed the pursuit of secular knowledge. The classical medieval commentators, by and large, were not only doctors, but also poets, philologists, philosophers, and mathematicians. Across the spectrum (although this is not as ubiquitous in the world of Germanic as in the Iberian and Provencal worlds of medieval Torah scholarship), the great scholars of the High

Middle Ages (Maimonides, Ramban, haLevi, ibn Ezra, Sforno, Abrabanel, Meiri, etc.) utilized these disciplines to enhance their understanding of Torah and to help develop and actualize their own Torah *weltanschauung*. This attitude towards "worldly" knowledge, already evidenced throughout both Talmuds and the Midrashim (e.g., BT Pesahim 94), was a fulfillment of a Rabbinic interpretation of the blessing of Japheth: "God enlarge Japheth, and he shall dwell in the tents of Shem." (9:27)

The Rabbis explain the relationship between Japheth (Greece) and Shem (Israel) as follows: "[this means] that the words of Japhet shall be in the tents of Shem." (BT Megillah 9b) Although, in its original context, this comment was meant to explain the special consideration accorded the Greek language in Jewish law (as regards the writing of Scripture), many medievalists understood it (and other Rabbinic dicta, e.g., BT Shabbat 75a) as a charge to harness the great intellectual accomplishments of Man, be they Jewish, Greek, or Arabic in origin. The goal of this mastery was always understood not as an end in and of itself, but rather as a vehicle for enhancing one's grasp and appreciation of God's world (see, *inter alia*, Mishneh Torah *Yesodei haTorah,* Chapters 1–4) and as a valuable tool towards enhancing one's mastery of Torah and fear of Heaven.

The tenor of Torah scholarship since the Enlightenment has been, for the most part, very different than that embraced by these giants of medieval Torah scholarship. As the "academic" world has bared its anti-religious fangs, the world of religion has, understandably, backed away. The prevailing attitude (for the past several hundred years) within most circles of Torah scholarship is one of reticence regarding the embrace of secular disciplines, especially in the world of the social sciences and humanities. As mentioned, this is an understandable reaction to the terrible losses inflicted upon the Torah world by the popularity of secular culture and academics.

(It is prudent to note that our greatest Torah leaders have all made great use of the fruits of contemporary research to increase their ability to issue proper rulings on Jewish law. This is not the issue at stake here; no one challenges the value of utilizing research for practical knowledge. We are addressing the utilization of "secular" knowledge to enhance our Torah knowledge beyond the practical realm.)

Nonetheless, there is much to recommend an ideal of utilizing the positive contributions of the past several hundred years of academic growth in "the West" to enhance and cultivate a greater appreciation for, and mastery of, our holy Torah. Although many students of Torah understand the benefit of harnessing the technological advances made available to us through arduous research (note how many yeshivot have state-of-the-art web pages, Twitter accounts, YouTube channels and Facebook accounts), this is not "the beauty of Japheth dwelling in the tents of Shem"; this is simply Shem riding on Japheth's horses (or sitting in the back of Japheth's limousine). For the richness of Greece (i.e., the "academic world") to adorn the Torah, we need to wisely and carefully identify those disciplines, sources, and schools that can indeed bring more glory and understanding into the study hall. Too much of secular "wisdom" is driven by anti-religious sentiment and bias; it is hard to find a university today that does not teach purely heretical notions as anything but the new gospel.

SCIENCE AND TORAH: DIFFERENT LANGUAGES?

We will now pick up the discussion begun in Chapter III. Beginning in the last century, a significant number of great Torah scholars addressed the "new findings" of the scientific world against the backdrop of the Toraic narrative. Clearly, the most troubling challenge to the Torah's account of history was the publication of Darwin's *Origin of the Species* and the theory of evolution introduced with that work. Although some great scholars (then and now) rejected the theories of evolution, the age of the world, and the like out of hand, many have taken a more accommodating approach.

For example, R. Shmuel David Luzzato, in the introduction to his commentary on Torah, states:

> The enlightened should understand that the intent of the Torah is not to teach about natural wisdom and science, rather the Torah was given to straighten men to the path of righteousness and justice, and to fix in their minds the belief in [God's] unity and providence, for the Torah was not given to the wise alone, but to the whole nation. Just as the ideas of [Divine] providence and recompense were not explained in philosophical terms (nor should they have been), rather the Torah spoke in the language of men, likewise the creation is not recounted by the Torah in a philosophical way, like our sages have said: "It is impossible to recount the power of the creation to human beings." (Midrash Hagadol, B'resheet 1, 1)

Rav Abraham Yitzhak Hakohen Kook, first Ashkenazic (European) chief rabbi of Palestine, wrote the following:

... Regarding the claims coming out of the new research, which, for the most part, contradict the literal words of the Torah: My opinion regarding this is that ... even though none of these new ideas is indisputably true, nevertheless, we are in no way obligated to reject and challenge them; for it is not a basic principle of the Torah to relate simple facts and events which occurred. The main thing is the content; i.e. the inner explanation of things ... these things were already stated by the early commentators, especially in the Guide to the Perplexed (I:71, II:15–16) and we are, today, prepared to expand this idea further.[24]

Many other Rabbinic giants have expressed similar sentiments, and serious students of Torah have, by and large, adopted this approach to resolving apparent conflicts between the literal sense of Torah narrative and contemporary revelations emanating from the world of the ivory tower. This is, to a great extent, the motivation that drives this book and the field of study it intends to promote.

As much as those contemporary writers who long to synthesize the two worlds (generally by using the Ramban commentary on Genesis as a springboard) wish it were different, we will likely never reach the point where the university world adopts Genesis as an accurate telling of the most ancient history. Nevertheless, there are some areas where contemporary research, done by earnest (yet secular) scholars in realms closely related to Torah narratives, have ultimately substantiated the Torah's account of history. In other words, even though we would be satisfied adopting Rav Kook's approach — that we need not reject findings of the academic world that seem to contradict Torah teachings, because the main emphasis in studying Torah is the "message"— if we can enhance our understanding of the straightforward meaning of the text through these methods, we certainly will.

CAN THESE BONES LIVE?

Archaeology is a fascinating area of research that has opened up many new doors of Torah understanding and insight. This field, relatively new and, in its finest hours, painstaking and rigorous of method, has found the Middle East to be a bountiful area for research. The many digs in Israel,

---

24. *Igrot haReayah* Letter #134, dated May 6, 1908.

Jordan, Egypt, Syria, and throughout the Middle East have uncovered virtual treasure troves of evidence linking our present to our past. The most notable example, and one that deserves far more than the passing mention it will get here, is the momentous finding of the Dead Sea Scrolls in 1947 in the series of caves known as Qumran. Our understanding of the religious schisms affecting the Judean community in the last two centuries before the common era has been enhanced hundredsfold as a result of the Scrolls — and countless puzzling passages throughout Rabbinic literature have become clarified as well.

Archaeology has been able to take us even further back — there are even instances where words in the Bible that were indecipherable to the medievalists have, as a result of archaeological evidence, become clarified. For example, the word פים in 1 Samuel 13:21 was rendered by the classical commentators as any one of various types of farm implements. This translation does not fit the verse smoothly, but, because the word is a *hapax legomenon* (occurs only once in the canon), there was no contextual reference against which to clarify it.

Recent digs in central Israel have brought the פים (read "Pim," but it probably should be read "Payim"— see Tur-Sinai's comment in Ben-Yehuda's *Dictionary of the Hebrew Language*, p. 4909, no. 1) to light. It is an ancient coin (weighing roughly 8 grams of silver); this finding has allowed us to go back to our verse and understand that the text is teaching us how much the Israelites had to pay the Philistines to sharpen their tools, rather than another item in a list of implements. (See the verse in context, the traditional commentaries, and *Da'at Mikra* ad loc.)

"I AM A STRANGER AND A SOJOURNER"

Recent discoveries of Hittite law and other Near Eastern texts have uncovered a basic piece of information that sheds light on our entire narrative: In many near eastern societies, foreigners (anyone outside of the tribal family) were not allowed to purchase land. (The interested reader is directed to Genesis 34:21 — the impact of that arrangement becomes clearer in light of the evidence offered here.)

Many theories abound as to why Abraham delayed acting on God's gift of the Land, avoiding buying any piece of real estate until the death of Sarah. There is, however, a prosaic reason that becomes clear when we view the evidence of local law in Canaan at the time of the Patriarchs. As a stranger, Abraham did not have the right to buy land in Canaan, nor did the local peoples have the right to sell it to him without special dispensation.

Before going further, we can already revisit our first question and answer: Abraham introduces himself as "a stranger and a sojourner" because he is explaining why he has no land as of yet — no place to bury Sarah. It also explains why he gathers the Hittites (or their leaders — Sforno at 23:7) to begin the negotiations. After all, why didn't he go directly to Ephron, if it was his field he desired? He congregated the Hittites in order to create the possibility for a communal decision allowing this foreigner to purchase land.

We can now understand their response: "You are a lord and prince among us . . ."; in other words, with all due honor and respect, Abraham, you are not one of us. We cannot allow you to purchase land, as that will naturalize you here. You are certainly a noble man, but a *N'si Elohim* is hardly a member of the people! We will certainly *grant* you any place you wish — no one would withhold that from you — but we cannot sell it to you. This answers question #2 above.

Let's recall the rest of the negotiations, and clarify the "between-the-lines" of each side:

> And Abraham stood up, and bowed to the people of the land, to the Hittites. And he talked with them, saying: "If your mind is that I should bury my dead out of my sight; hear me, and entreat for me to Ephron the son of Zohar. That he may give me the cave of Machpelah, which he has, which is in the end of his field; for as much money as it is worth he shall give it me as a possession of a burying-place."

(Abraham is asking the members of the clan to approach Ephron, so that he should be able to sell the land to Abraham in their presence.)

> And Ephron lived among the Hittites; and Ephron the Hittite answered Abraham in the hearing of the Hittites, of all who went in at the gate of his city, saying: "No, my lord, hear me; the field I give to you, and the cave that is in it, I give it to you; in the presence of the sons of my people I give it to you; bury your dead."

(Ephron insists on granting the burial plot. As Professor Yehuda Elitzur points out, he says *Natatti, Natatti, Natatti!* ["What more do you want, I have given it to you!"]. That is the meaning of the introductory *Lo*—I will not sell it, but I will grant it. Abraham, for his part, will not bury his dead without first gaining ownership rights via a proper sale. We have now answered questions 3–5.)

> And Abraham bowed down before the people of the land. And he spoke to Ephron in the hearing of the people of the land, saying: "But if you will give it, I beg you, hear me; I will give you money for the field; take it from me, and I will bury my dead there."

(As mentioned earlier, Abraham is insistent on purchasing land — he wants an *Ahuzah* [holding which he can bequeath to his progeny] as opposed to a *Mattanah* [gift].)

> And Ephron answered Abraham, saying to him: "My lord, listen to me; the land is worth four hundred shekels of silver. What is that between you and me? Bury therefore your dead."

(Something has shifted in the dialogue here. Explanation below.)

EAST MEETS WEST

In 1927, Edward Chiera published significant findings of a joint expedition with the Iraq Museum. Nuzi is an ancient town in Mesopotamia, a district familiar to Abraham if not to Ephron.

Among the Nuzian legal documents published, we find several examples of a curious form of adoption, known as "sale-adoption." The gist of this relationship was that an outsider (non-family member) could pay to be adopted by a family member, thus circumventing the ban on selling land to outsiders. In other words, the outsider (in our case, Abraham) would pay a sum to the clan member (Ephron) to allow him into the family, thus allowing him to become a landowner among the clan members.

This legal loophole was likely not known — or utilized — by the Hittites. Abraham, however, being a Mesopotamian by birth, would have been familiar with it; indeed, it may be that his years of "sojourning" were also an attempt to find the most suitable peoples among whom to settle, and with whom to begin his acquisition of the land via this method.

In any case, it is entirely possible that this is what Abraham proposed to Ephron, and that is reflected by Ephron's response: "what is land of four hundred shekel between you and me?" meaning, instead of the *N'si*

Elohim distance implied in the original salutation, our relationship is now one of *Beini uvein'kha* "between you and me" as kin. (This would also explain the exorbitant price paid by Abraham.)

AFTERWORD

The proposal suggested in this section is not intended, in any sense, to supplant the insightful and impactful messages gleaned by the Talmudic sages and the *Rishonim* from this significant text. As Rav Kook so eloquently stated — and as is borne out by centuries of commentary by great scholars — the essence of Torah is the message; how much our own lives are more firmly guided by the Divine teachings of Torah is immeasurably more significant than our ability to utilize various academic tools to verify historicity or other "*P'shat* modes." What we have seen is that, in contradistinction to common assumptions, the world of modern research has much to offer us in our own understanding of Torah. Was a Nuzian-type "sale-adoption" the mechanism used by Abraham to "get his foot in the door" of land purchase in Canaan? We can't know for sure — but it is certainly an intriguing possibility.

"If someone tells you that there is Torah among the nations, do not believe him; but if he tells you that there is wisdom among the nations, believe him." (Lamentations Rabbah 2:13)

The glory of Japheth — the achievements of the academic world commonly associated with the western world — indeed have their place in the Study Halls of Torah.

 ISAAC IN GERAR
Mirror Narratives

INTRODUCTION

In Chapter IV, we viewed both Creation narratives as one large chiasmus, which may or may not deflect the challenges to the unity of the text, but allowed us to identify a sub-textual message about the very nature of Creation. If we were reading it correctly, we unearthed a statement about God's universe that lay *"Between the Lines"* of the text.

In this chapter, we will take the same tool to address a difficult and age-old question — albeit of a much more mundane nature — regarding relationships within the patriarchal homes.

THE DESIRED BLESSING

"And the boys grew; and Esau was a skillful hunter, a man of the field; and Jacob was a quiet man, living in tents. And Isaac loved Esau, because he ate of his venison (*ki tzayyid b'fiv*); but Rebekah loved Jacob." (Genesis 25:27–28)

Why did Isaac favor Esau (i.e., what is meant by *Ki tzayyid b'fiv*), and why did Rebekah love Jacob? The text does not directly provide any reason for her favoring the younger twin; instead of adducing an answer from isolation (i.e., information presented about each of the characters in isolation from the child or parent in question), one needs to look at what the text tells us about their interactions. A sensitive reading of the text will shed much light on the direct relationship between Isaac and Esau on the one hand, and Rebekah and Jacob on the other, which will help us to understand the "favoritism" shown each of the sons by his "allied" parent.

The one narrative in which we see direct interaction between Isaac and Rebekah and their children (and, indeed, the only place where we find any dialogue between the two parents — more on that later) is in the story of Isaac's "deathbed" blessing (or so he thought), intended for Esau but taken by Jacob at his mother's behest.

A brief outline of the section is in order:

26:33–34: Esau marries Hittite women

27:1–4: Isaac speaks with Esau

 The information (1–2)

 The implication (3–4)

27:5: Rebekah overhears Isaac's request of Esau

27:6–13: Rebekah speaks with Jacob

 The information (6–7)

 The solution (8–10)

 Jacob's concern (11–12)

 Rebekah's response (13)

27:14–17: Jacob's preparations for entering his father's tent

 The food (14)

 The clothing (15)

 The "masquerade" (16)

 Final preparations (17)

27:18–29: Jacob and Isaac

 Approach and confusion (18–26)

 Blessing (27–29)

27:30–40: Esau and Isaac

 Approach and confusion (30–38)

 Blessing (39–40)

27:41: Esau's reaction to Jacob's "theft"

27:42: Rebekah overhears Esau's plans

27:42–45: Rebekah and Jacob

 The information (42)

 The implication (43–45)

27:46: Rebekah speaks with Isaac about Jacob marrying Hittite women

It should already be clear that a number of parallels are operating in this narrative. How significant and enlightening they may be is another question, but we will use this as a starting point for our discussion.

First, a tangential issue must be addressed, the resolution of which will affect our access to this narrative (and its parallels) by properly identifying the contours of the literary unit with which we are working in order to broaden our understanding of Rebekah's favoring of her younger son.

THE CHASM OF GERAR

If we are to utilize the interactions recorded in Chapter 27 — the "blessing" narrative — to explain the parent-child alliances as presented at the beginning of the Isaac-Rebekah narrative, we will have to reckon with the apparent chronological gap that divides them.

Subsequent to mentioning the marriage of Isaac to Rebekah, the Torah immediately tells us about her long-awaited pregnancy, the attendant confusion and consternation, the prophecy that (evidently) assuaged those concerns, the birth and naming of the twins, and a quick snapshot of their maturation: "And the boys grew; and Esau was a skillful hunter, a man of the field; and Jacob was a quiet man, living in tents." (v. 27)

This is followed by the story of Esau's sale of his birthright, sealed with the meal of lentil porridge (see, inter alia, R. David Kimhi [citing his father] at 25:33). Subsequent to that, the text focuses on Isaac's attempt to descend to Egypt to escape the famine in Canaan, his sojourn in Gerar (including another wife/sister incident — see below), and his successful return to Beer-sheba where he signs a pact with Abimelech.

It is only after all of this that the "blessing narrative" unfolds, as outlined above. How, then, can we use information gleaned from the much later story of Rebekah's interaction with Jacob to shed light on the earlier report of her love for him?

PERUSING THE GERAR NARRATIVE

A quick scan of the story of Isaac and Rebekah in Gerar (Chapter 26) points us to one puzzle, which I have not seen addressed by any of the classical commentators. In order to highlight the puzzle, let's quickly review the chapter:

1. Isaac's descent (1)
2. God's revelation and blessing (2–5)
3. The wife/sister story (6–11)
4. Isaac's material success in Gerar (12–14)
5. The wells (15–22)
6. God's second revelation in Beer-sheba (23–25)
7. Abimelech proposes a pact (26–31)
8. The well (33)

Following Isaac and Rebekah's life to this point, we see them descending towards Egypt, but only getting as far as Gerar (by Divine fiat) with twin boys in tow — boys who are already old enough to have mastered the bow and arrow (Esau) and the subtleties of business acumen (Jacob). It does not stand to reason that they would have left their only seed behind, especially because they were both unattached and had not yet taken on the responsibilities of family life. So the puzzle of Chapter 26 is: Where are Jacob and Esau?

This question is more serious than it appears at first, once we consider the series of events which unfold in Gerar.

• How could Isaac "pass" Rebekah off as his sister if they had two grown children living with them there? Remember, the earlier "wife/sister" stories (both involving Abraham and Sarah; one in Egypt and the other right here in Gerar) occurred when Sarah was still childless. Following that model — and the inherent difficulty in pulling off such a ruse with children as contradictory evidence — it is hard to read the "wife/sister" story here as taking place with Esau and Jacob nearby. Parenthetically, the only classical commentator who addresses the Esau/Jacob issue in Gerar is Ramban, who states that Isaac would have "passed them off" as another woman's children (26:7). We will revisit this comment further down.

• Once Esau's "hobby" (or "lifestyle") of a hunter is established, how could he not have gotten involved in the confrontations that his father had with the Philistines over the wells? Certainly, the Rabbinic representation of Esau as a violent person and murderer (see, e.g., Genesis Bava Batra 16b) makes his non-involvement in Isaac's battles all the harder to understand.

• A third question, not directly stemming from the absence of Esau and Jacob from Gerar, but impacting upon it, takes us to the next chapter. Isaac sent Jacob away to Padan-Aram to find a wife (Isaac's perspective) and to save his own life (Rebekah's motivation). The verse that describes Jacob's exile to Haran is "And Jacob went out from Beer-sheba, and went toward Haran." (Genesis 28:10) Why does the text have to mention that he left Beer-sheba? Since that is the location where the family is located at the end of Chapter 26, we presume that that is the place from which Isaac sent Jacob. The cogent and insightful observations of commentators as to the need to mention Beer-sheba (beginning with Rashi, "the departure of the righteous man from the town leaves an impression," to R. Isaac Soloveitchik, the "Brisker Rav," who aligned the two purposes in Jacob's flight with the two phrases) notwithstanding, the verse does communicate seemingly superfluous information.

The most evident and reasonable solution to these questions is for us to reconsider the sequence of events.

We approach all biblical texts with a number of standard assumptions, including the notion that the sequence of the story is chronologically consistent, save when overriding considerations render that impossible. Ramban is the staunchest supporter of the "chronological sequencing," known as *Yesh Muq'dam uM'uhar baTorah* (see his comments at Exodus 18:1; see also the Talmud's discussion at BT Pesahim 6b); yet even he admits to occasions where the text is clearly and blatantly in violation of chronological sequencing (the clearest example is Numbers 9:1 in light of Numbers 1:1). Again, when juxtaposition, completing one biography before moving on to the next generation (see Ramban's comments at Genesis 35:28), or other similar textual concerns are present, time sequence may suffer.

The entire description of Isaac in Gerar fits the model of a younger man, unencumbered (and as-yet-unblessed) with children, whose wife is similarly unattached and can, therefore, be passed off as his sister. Esau and Jacob don't intervene in Isaac's difficulties because they haven't yet been born. Chapter 26 is the first bit of information we are given about Isaac's life as a married man, detailing his material success and diplomatic/political ascent. Now we understand the doubled phrase at the onset of Jacob's fleeing to Haran (28:10): Jacob left *from* Beer-sheba to go to Haran. The verse is difficult — a difficulty addressed by many commentators (cf. inter alia Rashi, ad loc.). If the last location mentioned is Beer-sheba, why reiterate Jacob's point of departure? With our suggested reordering of the events, we understand why the text emphasizes Jacob's point of departure. As Ramban points out (23:2), it was the family tradition to go to worship at Beer-sheba; this is what Jacob did, leaving Hebron (where the family was living) to go to Beer-sheba to pray before leaving the Land (Just as he did before leaving for Egypt—46:1).

By the way, this also fits the model established by Abraham and maintained by Isaac and Jacob. While traveling and without children, Beer-sheba was the settlement of choice; but, after having a son, all three patriarchs settled in Hebron. Why this is the case is well beyond the scope of this chapter; for our purposes, noting the pattern serves to validate our approach.

In brief: The birth of Esau and Jacob and everything that followed from that birth occurred after the events described in Chapter 26. After Isaac returned from Gerar and settled in Beer-sheba, he returned to Hebron, where he stayed the rest of his life (see 35:27). The birth of the twins was followed by Esau's marriages and the "deathbed blessing" scene. (One may challenge this on the grounds that Isaac lived 120 years after becoming a father; how could he have thought that he was near death immediately after their birth? Note that he lives many years after the "deathbed blessing" narrative and that in any case that narrative took place at least forty years after the birth of Esau and Jacob (see 26:33), making Isaac at least 100 years old.)

We also understand why Ramban insists on the boys being present in Gerar (see above, end of question 1), due to his customary allegiance to the principle of *Yesh Muq'dam uM'uhar baTorah*, any method by which the timeline can be maintained will be adopted and utilized.

THE OVERRIDING CONCERN

We have almost overcome the obstacle to using the information in Chapter 27 to explain the cryptic comment in Chapter 25. As mentioned earlier, in order to justify incorrect sequence (from a chronological perspective) in a narrative, there must be an overriding concern. What might that concern be in our case?

The death of Ishmael, reported immediately after the death of Abraham, was significant for one reason. God had promised Abraham that He would "also" bless Ishmael, making him into a great people:

> And Abraham said to God, "O that Ishmael might live in your presence!" And God said, "Sarah your wife shall bear you a son indeed; and you shall call his name Isaac; and I will establish my covenant with him for an everlasting covenant, and with his seed after him. And as for Ishmael, I have heard you; Behold, I have blessed him, and will make him fruitful, and will multiply him exceedingly; twelve princes shall he father, and I will make him a great nation. But my covenant will I establish with Isaac, whom Sarah shall bear to you at this set time in the next year." (17:18–21)

It was important to demonstrate the fulfillment of that promise immediately after Ishmael died:

> Now these are the generations of Ishmael, Abraham's son, whom Hagar the Egyptian, Sarah's maidservant, bore to Abraham; And these are the names of the sons of Ishmael, by their names, according to their generations; the first-born of Ishmael, Nebaioth; and Kedar, and Adbeel, and Mibsam, and Mishma, and Dumah, and Massa; Hadad, and Tema, Jetur, Naphish, and

Kedem; these are the sons of Ishmael, and these are their names, by their villages, and by their encampments; twelve princes according to their nations. (25:12–16)

Once Ishmael's generations were listed, confirming the fulfillment of the Divine promise, the text listed Isaac's generations. This is not an uncommon phenomenon; for instance, immediately after listing Esau's generations (Chapter 36), the text states "These are the generations of Jacob . . ." (37:2). The likely reason for this is that once we see that even the rejected member of the family (Ishmael, Esau) is blessed with a mighty nation as part of the general promise to Abraham that his seed would be as numerous as the sand by the shore and the stars in the sky, it is critical to resume the central thread of the story with the successful generations of the selected member (Isaac, Jacob) of the clan.

That being the case, why doesn't the text simply state: "These are the generations of Isaac—Esau and Jacob," move us to Gerar, and then fill in the details of their birth, their early years, and the fateful sale of Esau's birthright?

A survey of the listings of *Tol'dot* (generations) in Genesis suggests an answer. Every time there is a mention of *Tol'dot*, there is a process of rejection and selection. When the Torah lists the *Tol'dot* of Terah, for instance (11:27), we are immediately informed of the selection of Abraham (and the rejection of his brothers). When we are introduced to the *Tol'dot* of Jacob, that entire narrative is about the (aborted) selection of Joseph as Jacob's heir to the patriarchate (see Ramban at 37:3).

Hence, it was important not only to list the *Tol'dot* of Isaac, but also to present the first steps of the rejection of Esau — and the favoring of Jacob — as part of the "*Tol'dot* schema."

Now we understand why the sequence of Chapters 25–27 is not true to the chronology of events: Ishmael's *Tol'dot* could not be left "unanswered"; once Isaac's children are mentioned, the process of the selection of Jacob and the rejection of Esau must be introduced. This is the "overriding concern" that mitigates the text's usual loyalty to chronological sequence and is why the births of Jacob and Esau were recorded before the story of Isaac's descent to Gerar.

ANALYZING THE "DEATHBED BLESSING" NARRATIVE

I suggest following this section with text in hand, opened to the end of Chapter 26.

Now that we have demonstrated that the events presented in Chapter 27 follow closely on the events in Chapter 25 (i.e., that from the time that Jacob bought the birthright until the deathbed blessing was not necessarily a long time; by the way, this makes the plain sense of 27:36 much more "readable"), we can look to the information presented in Chapter 27 to aid us in understanding the enigma posed by Rebekah's favoring of Jacob, as presented in Chapter 25.

As briefly noted earlier, the section contains a number of parallels. The structure of the selection might best be represented as follows:

A: Esau marries Hittite women.
   B: Isaac speaks with Esau
      C: Rebekah overhears Isaac's request of Esau
         D: Rebekah speaks with Jacob
            E: Jacob's preparations for entering his father's tent
               F: Jacob and Isaac
            E': Esau and Isaac
         D': Esau's reaction to Jacob's "theft"
      C': Rebekah overhears Esau's plans
   B': Rebekah and Jacob
A': Rebekah speaks with Isaac about Jacob marrying Hittite women

The chiastic structure goes well beyond the general topic of each subsection:

A: Esau marries two Hittite women (thus strengthening our argument that the family resided in Hebron at the time, and not in Beer-sheba, where the most likely "locals" with whom to interact would be Philistines). They are a source of bitterness to Rebekah and Isaac — the only time that Rebekah and Isaac are presented as having one common reaction to anything. (It is tempting to think that these two verses were placed here merely to balance the entire selection and to strengthen the overall sense of parallelism. We'll leave that temptation.)

A': Rebekah speaks to Isaac — the only time in the text that either of them speaks to each other — complaining about the Hittite women.

B: Isaac speaks to Esau about his impending death and, using the transitional word *v'Atah* ("and now"), commands Esau to go bring venison. Esau obeys without question.

B': Rebekah speaks to Jacob about his impending death, and, using the transitional word *v'Atah*, commands him to run away to Laban. Jacob obeys without question.

C: Rebekah hears about Isaac's request of Esau; she introduces her report of the information with the word *Hinei* (behold).

C': Rebekah hears about Esau's plot to kill Jacob; she introduces her report of the information with the word *Hinei*.

D: Rebekah commands Jacob to bring the goats that she will prepare; Jacob expresses concern that he will bring a curse upon himself instead of a blessing.

D': Esau reacts to Jacob's "theft" of the blessing by plotting to kill him — the ultimate curse.

E: Jacob takes on the guise of Esau, bringing the food his father loves, with coarse garments and hairy arms.

E': Esau enters with the food his father loves, with coarse garments and hairy arms.

F: The nexus of the selection: Jacob's direct meeting with Isaac, when he receives the prized blessing. There is no parallel to this subsection, nor can there be (if there were, Isaac's answer to Esau in v. 38 would have been dramatically different).

"AND REBEKAH FAVORED JACOB"

For our purposes, the significant sections of the chiasmus that may shed light on Rebekah's favoring of Jacob are B and D.

In B, Isaac speaks to Esau about his death, but we hear no reaction from the loyal son, save to go a-hunting. The eerie similarity to Rebekah's command to Jacob in B' highlights the difference — Jacob flees without protest because it is his own life he is saving; it is the prudent thing to do and protesting would be of no avail. That is certainly not the case with Esau's obeisance to his father's command. The later development of the story demonstrates that his zealous exit to the hunt was motivated by his desire to attain his father's blessing, not to bring pleasure to his father or to fulfill his command.

In D, Jacob's protests to Rebekah fall into two categories, ethical and pragmatic. He is concerned that the blessing will "backfire" because his father will discover the ruse, and he is concerned that he will fail in his father's eyes. When Rebekah accepts responsibility for these potential troubles, his concerns are assuaged and he protests no further.

In D', Esau continues to whine and complain about Jacob's "theft"; nothing that his father can do will calm him down. He is, remember, the stronger one, the brother to be feared; yet he cannot be placated.

When we compare the way each of these sons responded to challenges and potential troubles, we can readily understand why Rebekah favored Jacob over Esau and why, as the prophet Malachi indicates (1:2), God Himself validated her favoritism. The mature person, worthy of God's grace and favor, accepts the obstacles that face him and understands that his own shortcomings are the ultimate cause of his external obstacles. Once he changes that which is alterable and the terrain has been leveled to the extent possible he faces his challenge head-on. His realization of his own power is, counterintuitively, the source of his humility, which allows him to look inward for the solution. That which needs to be confronted is faced and that which needs to be repaired is attended to. Once his own internal "work" has been done, he is ready to face the external challenges. The immature, impetuous Esau is unable to overcome his anger to sense which way the wind blows and to adjust accordingly. He looks for devils outside of his heart and, as such, never solves the problem that lies deep inside.

"ALAI HAYU KULANA"

We'll end with an insight, taken from Rebekah's assuaging of Jacob's concerns. (Note – this idea is far from *P'shat* and is what we like to call a "cute *vort*" – something piquant with which to end the essay.)

Rebekah states to her younger son: "*Alai Qil'lat'kha B'ni*" (Genesis 27:13; lit. "Upon me be thy curse," meaning, "I'll take responsibility for it"). The word "*Alai*" can be understood as an acrostic, standing for *Esau, Laban, and Joseph*. Those three were, indeed, the three sources of trouble for Jacob throughout his life. To wit, Rebekah is saying *Alai* (Esau, Laban, and Joseph) will be your curse, my son.

After all three of those troubles befell Jacob, he was discussing the second return of his sons to Egypt to purchase grain. His sons told him that they could not return without Benjamin. In protesting, he stated: "Joseph is not, Simeon is not, would you take Benjamin? *Alai Hayyu Kulanah*" (Genesis 42:36; literally "upon me are all these things come"). In our approach, we might suggest *Alai* (acrostically spelling out Esau,

Laban, and Joseph) were all of them! "I've already had my three tragedies — losing Benjamin just isn't in the cards. How can I send him down into the danger of Egypt? Losing him would extend beyond the curse that I was given before taking the blessing from father."

AFTERWORD

When analyzing a narrative, we need to maintain an internal, cognitive flexibility about the order of events, especially when, imagining ourselves in the narrative, significant questions arise. By re-evaluating the sequence of the text, we were able to identify a clear chiasmus bridging two chapters. This revelation helped us resolve an unexplained favoritism in the text: Rebekah's love for Jacob is mirrored by God's favoritism for Israel.

XVI JACOB'S YEARS IN HARAN
Chronologies and Chronographies

INTRODUCTION

When Jacob, fleeing Lavan, is finally caught by his pursuer who thereupon levels serious charges of theft against his son-in-law, Jacob responds:

> ... These *twenty years* have I been with you; your ewes and your she-goats have not cast their young, nor have I eaten the rams of your flocks. I did not bring to you that which was torn by beasts, I bore that loss and you required it of my hand, whether stolen by day or at night. Thus I was: in the day the drought consumed me, and the frost by night; and my sleep fled from my eyes. These *twenty years* have I been in your house: I served you *fourteen years for your two daughters*, and *six years for your flock*; and you have changed my wages ten times ...
> Genesis 31:38–41

This statement of Jacob, taken at face value, indicates that he arrived at Lavan's door twenty years earlier. This is the basis for the chronology presented in Midrash Seder Olam:[25]

> Our forefather Jacob was 63 years old when he was blessed and at that time, Ishmael died, as it says: *"Now Esau saw that Isaac had blessed Jacob ... and that Jacob hearkened to his father ... and Esau saw that the daughters of Canaan pleased not Isaac ... so Esau went unto Ishmael, and took unto the wives that he had Mahalath the daughter of Ishmael Abraham's son, the sister of*

---

25. Seder Olam, a 3rd century Midrashic work attributed to R. Yose b. Halafta, is a chronographic Midrash which frames events from Creation to the end of the 2nd Temple period in a timeline. This Midrash is used by a number of *Rishonim*, notably Rashi, in their comments on events in the Bible. For interested readers, Prof. Chaim Milikowsky of Bar-Ilan University recently published a critical edition of Seder Olam (Yad Ben-Zvi, 2013).

Nebaioth, to be his wife." There is no reason to add "the sister of Nebaioth"; why does it state "the sister of Nebaioth?" this teaches that Ishmael gave her in betrothal and he died and Nebaioth her brother married her off to Esau. Jacob spent fourteen years hiding and studying with Eber, and Eber died two years after Jacob's descent to Aram Naharaim; he left there and came to Aram Naharayim, so it turns out that when he was standing at the well he was 77 years old and he spent twenty years in Laban's house, seven before he married the matriarchs, another seven after he married them, and six years after the eleven tribes and Dena were born; so all of the tribes were born within a span of seven years except for Benjamin; each one after just seven months. He left Aram Naharayim and came to Sukkot and spent eighteen months there, as it states *And Jacob traveled to Sukkot . . .* he left Sukkot and came to Beit-El and spent six months, offering to God . . ."

In a later formulation of this Midrash, the introductory line – "why were Ishmael's years counted (i.e. why was his lifespan of 137 years recorded)? In order to associate the age of Jacob . . ." and the Midrash continues, working on the presumption that Esau's wedding had to take place immediately after the death of Ishmael (due to the unusual mention of Nebaioth), making Esau and Jacob 63 at the time.

However, the subtle challenge to the Midrash, which the Gemara explicates – leading to the contention that Jacob spent fourteen years studying with Eber – is based on this declaration of Jacob's, along with a few other chronological data given to us by the text.

THE TIME-LINE: SEDER OLAM'S CONSIDERATIONS

Rarely does the text of the Torah, even in sequential narratives such as Genesis, provide us with dates, ages, and time-spans. Ages are nearly always given at a protagonist's death, but objective dates are never given (except in the case of the Flood, with no way for us to understand *which* calendar is being referenced). Time-spans are only given when the duration of the event itself – such as the 40/150 days of the flood, the seven years of plenty – holds inherent significance to the story.

We can, however, piece together some relational times based on the data given; for instance, we know that Isaac was 37 when his mother died, since we are given her age of 90 at his birth and her age of 127 at her death. We know that Isaac was 14 years younger than Ishmael (since Abraham was 86 at the latter's birth and 100 at the former's). We also know that Esau and Jacob were 60 years younger than their father – as the text explicitly relates. Therefore, Jacob and Esau were 63 at the time of their uncle Ishmael's passing.

This Midrash, however, is also based on working backwards from Jacob's death to determine his age at the time of his arrival in Haran. We learn that he came to Egypt at the age of 130; we also know that Joseph had been in power for nine years when Jacob came down (since the seven years of plenty began immediately upon his ascendance to the position of viceroy; Jacob and the family descended to Egypt in the second or third year of the famine). We are also told that Joseph was 30 at the time of his rescue from prison and his being placed in charge of Egypt's salvation.

Hence, Joseph was 39 when Jacob came down at the age of 130; therefore, Jacob was 91 years of age when his favorite son was born. The interaction between Jacob and Lavan immediately after the birth of Joseph indicates that this was the point when the "six years for your flock" began. Dating backwards, that means that Jacob arrived in Lavan's house 14 years earlier – or when he was 77 years of age. Seder Olam begins with this as a given, but assuming that Esau's marriage to Mahalat took place when he (and Jacob, his twin brother) was 63 – and Esau married Mahalat after Jacob's flight from Hebron – what happened to the 14 intervening years? This is where the Midrashic academy of Shem and Eber plays a role – and explains Jacob's "missing years." Parenthetically, this explanation is invoked chiefly to raise another point – that those 14 years of study were not reckoned against Jacob for his failure to honor his parents during that time; as opposed to the twenty-two "post-academy" years, for which he was held liable and therefore punished, with poetic justice (*"Midah k'Neged Midah"*) by having his beloved Joseph taken from him for twenty-two years.

SEVEN CHALLENGES TO SEDER OLAM'S TIME-LINE

This bio-chronography, however, leaves us with several unsettling problems.

First of all, we know that both Isaac and Esau married (in Esau's case, for the first time) at age 40. We don't know how old Abraham was when he and Sarah wed – so all of our information about the family indicates 40 as the proper time to marry. If so, why did Jacob wait until he was nearly twice that age to even look for a wife – and pass that double-milestone before marrying (according to Seder Olam, he was 84 when he married Leah)?

Second, when Jacob and Lavan begin their "new arrangement" after the birth of Joseph, the immediate division was made of spotted etc. sheep vs. those that were not spotted – the former going to Jacob, the latter – to Lavan. In 30:33–36, we read:

(Jacob concludes his agreement:) "So shall my righteousness witness against me hereafter, when you come to look over my hire that is before you; every one that is not speckled and spotted among the goats, and dark among the sheep, that if found with me shall be counted stolen." (v. 33) And Laban said: "Behold, would it might be according to your word." (v. 34) And *he* removed that day the he-goats that were streaked and spotted, and all the she-goats that were speckled and spotted, every one that had white in it, and all the dark ones among the sheep, and gave them into the hand of *his* sons. (v. 35) And he set three days' journey between himself and Jacob. And Jacob fed the rest of Laban's flocks. (v. 36)

It would seem that the undefined pronoun "he" at the beginning of v. 35 should refer to Lavan, as he is the subject of both the previous as well as the following verse. This, however, is difficult on two counts. Why would Jacob agree to entrust his flock to his "hostile partner" – and if Jacob is to succeed (as he does forthwith) in "super-breeding" his flock, this isn't something he would be able to do if they are entrusted to Lavan and his sons. Besides this, it doesn't seem likely that Lavan has sons – at this point – who are of an age to be entrusted with such a mission. When Jacob first arrived in Haran, Rachel, the younger sister, was tending the flock; we learn why Leah was not out with the flock (she was evidently more "feminine" with "soft eyes"), but why was a girl tending the flock at all? This should have been a job for the brothers! Rather, the most straightforward read of the story is that Lavan had *only* the two daughters when Jacob arrived – and he intended to incorporate Jacob into the family as a "son." It was only with the later birth of sons and their anxiety about their inheritance that the acrimony in the household began.

That said, the indefinite pronoun "he" must refer to Jacob – and he entrusted his flock to *his* sons (i.e. Reuben, Simeon etc.). But, following Seder Olam, even his eldest son could have been no older than 6 years old at this time, since Jacob wasn't married for the first seven of the fourteen years (immediately) preceding this negotiation.

Third, if the years are as given, then Reuben is not yet 13 when the family leaves Haran – yet he and his younger brothers, not long afterwards (according to Seder Olam, within two years) engage in negotiations with Hamor and his son Sh'khem – negotiations replete with duplicity and deception – on behalf of the clan. While this is possible, it is hardly plausible that the Hivites would agree to an arrangement made by the young sons of a patriarch without the latter's explicit confirmation.

Fourth, in that same story, Simeon and Levi (who are approximately 13 and 14) together massacre all of the men of that city, ultimately killing everyone and pillaging the town. Again, not impossible – but highly unlikely.

Fifth, by the time Jacob and his family make it back to Hebron (which, per Seder Olam, is within two years of the flight from Haran), Reuben has already engaged in his sexually inappropriate relationship with Bilhah. Regardless of how we understand what took place between them, this is the action of an older son, intent on supplanting his father as head of the clan; again, hardly a likely act of a 14-year-old boy.

Sixth, why is Joseph identified, when we first meet him in the context of his unpleasant fraternal relations, as *Ben Z'kunim* of Jacob? The phrase, simply translated, means "son of his old age" – but, according to Seder Olam, Joseph must be less than a year younger than his closest sibling (Dinah) and not all that much younger than any of his brothers – why call him "son of his old age?"

The seventh and final challenge is the most compelling: How could Jacob have fathered so many children in such a compact time period? Let's look at the givens of the text:

- Jacob worked for seven years before marrying anyone
- At the beginning of his eighth year in Lavan's house, he married Leah and, a week later, Rachel. Each of these sisters brought a hand-maid (Zilpah/Bilhah) into the household.
- There were eleven children born before Joseph: ten sons and Dinah
- None of these children were twins
- There were no overlapping pregnancies:
  - It was only after Leah had four children that Rachel "presented" Bilhah, her handmaid, to Jacob in order to "be built through her."
  - Leah "presented" *her* handmaid, Zilpah, to Jacob, to continue having children for her.
  - Only after all of this did the "mandrakes" incident take place, which led to the births of Leah's last three children.
  - After all of these births, God "remembered Rachel" and Joseph was born.

- Seder Olam's time-line presumes several necessary birth details, some of which are plausible and some – not.
  - Premise 1: There were no miscarriages (especially on Leah's part) – certainly plausible.
  - Premise 2: Leah became pregnant fairly immediately after the marriage – again, certainly plausible.
  - Premise 3: Leah (and Bilhah and Zilpah) became pregnant fairly immediately after giving birth – highly implausible, especially in Leah's case.
  - Premise 4: Each pregnancy was seven months long (this is stated explicitly in Seder Olam) – again, highly implausible.

Here is a chart of how the births would have taken place in Lavan's house, per Seder Olam's presentation of those years:

CHART OF SEDER OLAM CHRONOLOGY IN LABAN'S HOUSE

Years	Who is born	Years	Who is born
1–7	None	12	Asher at 12.7
8	Reuben at 8.7	13	Issachar at 13.2, Zevulun at 13.9
9	Simon at 9.2, Levi at 9.9	14	Dena at 14.4, Joseph at 14.11
10	Judah at 10.4, Dan at 10.11	15–20	None (Jacob working for fortune)
11	Naftali at 11.5, Gad at 12.0	21–22	Sukkot/Shchem/ BeitEl

JACOB'S YEARS IN HARAN: ANOTHER APPROACH

Seder Olam's chronology rests on two necessary assumptions:
- Esau's marriage to Mahalat took place immediately after Jacob left
- The mention of Mahalat's older brother means that he married just after Ishmael died – i.e., at age 63.

Let's revisit the text. At the end of Chapter 26 (which, as we pointed out above, chiefly took place before the birth of the twins), there is a brief note about Esau marrying two women at the age of 40. As we pointed out in the previous chapter, these two verses "jump ahead" to bridge the birth-growth-sale of birthright narrative in Chapter 25 with the blessing-narrative in Chapter 27. These women, we are told, were the source of great "bitterness-of-spirit" to Isaac and Rebekah. After a break of *Parashah Petuhah*, we are informed that Isaac was old and his eyes were failing – and that leads, of course, to the story of the "stolen blessing" and Jacob's flight to Haran. It is clear that Isaac's blindness was not an indicator of an "end-of-life" scenario (though that is what he thought) even if we interpret his "old age" as 123 (when Ishmael was 137 and died), he still lived nearly 60 more years. We could, just as easily, understand Isaac's blindness as coming directly after Esau's marriages, making him 100 years old at the time. If we allow for a few years before Isaac's reaction to his daughters-in-law, we may posit Esau and Jacob at, *arguendo*, 48 years of age. Jacob's continued bachelorhood is not as surprising – considering that Esau marrying first would be the expected norm (note Lavan's comments to Jacob in 29:26). After the sour taste of Esau's marriages to local girls, it is not hard to understand why Jacob would wait a bit longer to marry. We will yet return to Esau's third marriage and the possible allusion to his being 63 at the time.

Let us presume that the theft of the blessings took place when Esau and Jacob were 48 and that, subsequently, Jacob fled to Haran at mother's behest and with father's blessing. Father's directive to marry a girl from "the old homestead" is reasonable against the background of Esau's recent marriages to locals. Jacob arrives, let us say, at age 49 and works for seven years to marry Rachel – putting him another seven years "behind" in his responsibility to raise a family. However, as a man on the run, with no immediate hope of building an estate, he wasn't in a position to marry and support a wife and children without the arrangement with Lavan. At age 56, then, he married . . . Leah! A week later, he married Rachel and, thus, began the next stage of his life as a married man. At this point, he owed Lavan seven years of work, to "pay up" for Rachel's hand, which would mean that he would be 63 years old when he would be completely free of his debt to Lavan.

Consider that, beginning at 56 (when Rachel was around 12 years old, the customary age for girls to marry throughout the known world in the Biblical period), Jacob begins to sire children at a "normal" rate – perhaps one every two years. The only wife having children during these seven years was Leah – and Judah was, perhaps, born after the seven years were up. In the meantime, the rest of the birthing sequences play out over the course of the next ten years or so – Dan and Naphtali (3 years), Gad and Asher (3 years) – which would make Rachel, still barren, over 30 years old at the time. When Reuben (by now a young adult) brings his mother the mandrakes, Rachel desires them and "sells" her night with Jacob for them. This leads to the births of Issachar, Zebulun, and Dinah – all born of Leah herself, close to her fortieth birthday.

Time passes, Rachel grows older watching Leah's children grow up with the couplets born of her own Bilhah and Leah's Zilpah, and her alienation and pain increase. At this point, God "remembers" her and she finally becomes pregnant (at the "advanced" age of around 45) and Joseph was born; Jacob, at this point, was 91.

We can now review our questions above and respond, in order:

Jacob did not delay starting a family any more than necessary; as a result of Esau's "bad" wives and then his having to flee, he was "stuck" with Lavan's offer and put off starting a family for an additional seven years.

By the time that Jacob and Lavan made their new arrangement, after the birth of Joseph, his eldest sons were young adults, certainly capable of herding Jacob's flocks.

In similar fashion, the third, fourth and fifth questions are answered. The older boys (Reuven, Simon, Levi, Judah) were young men when Jacob left, so their negotiations with Sh'khem and Hamor, the massacre of the town by Simeon and Levi, and Reuben's actions with Bilhah are all the actions of young adults.

We understand why Joseph (and, later, Benjamin) is called a *Ben Zkunim* (or *Yeled Zekunim* – son of his old age); Joseph was, indeed, quite a bit younger than his other siblings.

And, of course, we see that the births did not need happen with the implausibly tight timing presented above – the children were each brought to full term, properly nursed and raised before the mother moved to another pregnancy.

JACOB'S ACTIONS – AND HIS WORDS

If this "smoother" read of the text is indeed valid, how do we explain Jacob's behavior in Haran? To wit, he spent fourteen years working *for* Lavan, to pay off his debt of two daughters as his wives. He spent another six years working in a strained partnership *with* Lavan to build up his estate and prepare for return to Canaan. What was he doing during those intervening years? What was he doing when Naphtali was born, when Reuben found the mandrakes, when Dinah was named?

Truth to tell, there is a larger question looming behind the entire narrative of Jacob-in-Haran. He originally left for two reasons – to flee his brother's wrath (at Rebekah's urging) and to marry a daughter of Lavan (at father's directive). When he had accomplished both – after fourteen years – he should have returned forthwith to Canaan. However, he had two other things to consider: whether Esau's anger had really subsided, and whether he had more to accomplish in Haran.

Rebekah had instructed him to flee to Haran and she promised to "summon him and bring him back" when his brother's fury was spent and he no longer planned to kill his younger twin. We never hear of her summoning her son – leaving Jacob with three possible explanations. Either Esau is still mad; Rebekah has passed away; or she wants him to stay there to accomplish something more than he has thus far. None of these conclusions would motivate him to leave – if Esau is still mad, he must stay away. If his mother has passed away, he would be going back to a situation worse than the one he left – with Esau possibly still angry and his "protector" gone. If she wants him to remain and has something else for him to accomplish – that is what he must do.

I'd like to suggest that Jacob remained in Haran, either working as a herdsman for himself or for others. Note that the text "ignores" Lavan from the moment of the second wedding until the birth of Joseph – so we needn't assume that he was working in Lavan's estate the entire time. Again, he was waiting for a message from his mother that it was time to return to Canaan.

With the birth of a son by Rachel (finally), he returned to Lavan and negotiated a separation agreement whereby he would be able to take his share of the wealth that his hard work had brought to Lavan's household. From this point on, he worked with Lavan for six years, keeping their flocks separate and finding ways to have his flocks multiply in astounding ways.

What are we to make of Jacob's words, with which we began our inquiry?

... These twenty years have I been with you; your ewes and your she-goats have not cast their young, nor have I eaten the rams of your flocks. I did not bring to you that which was torn by beasts, I bore that loss and you required it of my hand, whether stolen by day or at night. Thus I was: in the day the drought consumed me, and the frost by night; and my sleep fled from my eyes. These twenty years have I been in your house: I served you fourteen years for your two daughters, and six years for your flock; and you have changed my wages ten times . . . (Genesis 31:38–41)

Note that in Jacob's speech, he makes two separate mentions of his twenty years with Lavan – *These twenty years have I been with you* at the beginning of his response and defense and *These twenty years have I been in your house: I served you fourteen years for your two daughters, and six years for your flock* at the end. Some have suggested that this means that there were two separate periods of twenty years: twenty working for/with Lavan and twenty working alongside him; this explains away much of the difficulties we encountered. However, the repeated "twenty years" might rather form an *inclusio*, not a reference to a separate time period.

The simplest way to read Jacob's words is this: As he begins his defense, he points out that there have been twenty years of working loyally for Lavan; this is Jacob pointing out his work ethic, his honesty, and his forthrightness regarding his charges. At the end, he delineates that these twenty years were broken into two (interrupted) segments – fourteen years ("for your daughters") and, much later, six years ("for your flock"). Hence, Jacob's words reflect a clear amount of years during which Jacob, in two separate stages, was working in Lavan's estate – with an unknown amount of years between them, during which Jacob was working to take care of his family.

AFTERWORD

One of the critical tools we have in our study of narrative is the ability to step back from the text and imagine the story unfolding. As we watch it before our eyes, we can see which events "make sense" and which strain credulity. If challenging, we look for textual clues that may help us out – perhaps we are reading about a miraculous occurrence which, we would expect, would be noted explicitly by the text. In lieu of that, we may have to look for another way to understand the text that helps us ground it in a reality that we, the people of the book, understand to be a part of human – and Jewish – history.

XVII JACOB'S WRESTLING MATCH
Four Approaches, Four Perspectives

The history of *Parshanut* goes back as far as the text itself, as I adumbrated in Chapter 1. We discussed the various exegetical motivations and programs of the medieval commentators (*Rishonim*), yet there is another factor which distinguishes them from each other and will set into motion a different path of interpretation. This is especially true in Genesis, although it impacts on an exegete's approach in every one of the twenty-four canonical books of the Bible.

In the first chapter, we outlined some of the general teleological differences – what each is trying to accomplish. Rashi skillfully presents a selective representation of Midrashim. Ramban offers a broad view of the passage proposing a solution as to the overall implication and message of the text. Rashbam suggests a straightforward (*P'shat*) reading of the text which side-steps (in many cases) the rabbinic tradition. Ibn Ezra puts much energy into the lexical and syntactical considerations of the text – and so on. These are, however, differences driven by what each *parshan* sees as his task and what it is he is trying to discover about the text. Rashbam, for instance, goes out of his way to justify and validate – even venerate – the vast Midrashic tradition; his programmatic statement is that he is trying to "restore the balance" by reviving the study of *p'shat*. While presenting the Midrashic tradition, Rashi, sometimes in the same concise comment, makes note of grammatical nuances or clarifies *p'shat*. None of the *Rishonim* diminish the significance of the program pursued by others – each contributes his own particular piece to the whole of traditional text interpretation.

There is, however, another divide between exegetes, one that is not born of their self-directed agenda, but rather in their perspective on the text in general – and on the particular book or passage being analyzed.

For instance, one *parshan* may read the Song of Songs as being written fundamentally as a metaphor. Such an exegete will avoid interpreting the text as a courtship, wedding scene etc. and go directly to the analogy. Contradistinctively, another commentator may take the position that, regardless of the provenance of the song, since it was written as a courtship-metaphor, the terms and context of the metaphor must first be explained and, in light of that explanation, the application to the relationship it intends to describe can be understood. A side-by-side read of Rashi, ibn Ezra, and Rashbam on almost any passage in Song of Songs will demonstrate this divide of approaches.

In this chapter, we will look at a most mysterious scene – Jacob's wrestling match with a "man" during the night – and see how four of the *Rishonim* interpret the scene and its meaning, and the philosophic-exegetical bases that (perhaps) drive their interpretations. One caveat: this survey in no way exhausts the approaches to this scene, including approaches that continue to develop in our era (as what Rashbam would refer to as *P'shatot haMit'hadshim b'Khol Yom* – "exegesis in perpetual motion").

THE TEXT   GENESIS 32:23–33

> And he rose up that night, and took his two wives, and his two handmaids, and his eleven children, and passed over the ford of the Jabbok. And he took them, and sent them over the stream, and sent over that which he had. And Jacob was left alone; and a man wrestled with him until daybreak. And when he saw that he could not defeat him, he touched the hollow of his thigh; and the hollow of Jacob's thigh was strained, as he wrestled with him. And he said: 'Let me go, for the day breaks.' And he said: 'I will not let you go, unless you first bless me.' And he said to him: 'What is your name?' And he said: 'Jacob.' And he said: 'Your name shall be called no more Jacob, but Israel; for you have striven with God and with men, and have prevailed.' And Jacob asked him, and said: 'Tell me your name.' And he said: 'Why then do you ask after my name?' And he blessed him there. And Jacob called the name of the place Peniel: 'for I have seen God face to face, and my life is preserved.' And the sun rose upon him as he passed over Peniel, and he limped upon his thigh. Therefore the children of Israel do not eat the sinew of the thigh-vein which is on the hollow of the thigh, until this

day; because he touched the hollow of Jacob's thigh, even in the sinew of
the thigh-vein.

Before assaying the passage, I'd like to share one methodological note
about the interplay between interpretation and text. It is a tried and true
maxim that the more mysterious the passage (whether in context, lexicon,
theological implications, visions and so on) – the broader the range of
interpretation we are likely to find. To take an absurdly obvious example,
there is no disagreement about Enoch being the father of Methuselah,
nor about his being the son of Jared. There is, however, much discussion
and diversity of opinion about the meaning of his disappearance from
this world at the "tender" age of 365 – was he righteous, was he a penitent
sinner, or was he a righteous man who was on the road to perdition and
God took him "early" to save him? Did he die or was he "taken alive?"
The opacity of the verse lends to all sorts of approaches. The mysterious
image of a man "taken by God" opens up the floodgates of *Parshanut*
and, as expected, the range of interpretations is as broad as the field of
interpreters.

We should, therefore, not be taken by surprise to find that each *parshan*
brings a unique perspective to the mysterious story which we are assaying
here and that each, in turn, reads the details and context, environment
and literary evocations, in light of that perspective.

THE APPROACHES

Although it would be tempting to present the *parshanim* in strict chronological order – opening up possibilities of influence and/or response – we
will begin with Maimonides. As we will discover, his approach places him
in a different sphere of interpretation than the other four. We will then
investigate two exegetes of the French school and return to the world of
Spanish Jewry and conclude with Ramban.

A: Maimonides: Genesis as "Flexible" Narrative

R. Moses b. Maimon (1138–1204, Egypt) did not compose a comprehensive commentary on the Bible. Nonetheless, his numerous programmatic
statements, chiefly found in his philosophical works, serve to anticipate
his approach to many thorny passages, as well as providing explicit examples of his exegetical method.

By way of example, Maimonides proposed that the purpose of the story of the Binding of Isaac was to teach two great philosophic-theological lessons – the extent of fear of God and the truth of prophecy. Since he sees the narratives in Genesis as essentially being presented to teach philosophical, religious, and ethical truth, he perforce reads the *Akedah* as "lesson-driven"; this precludes his adopting the approaches of Rashi or Rashbam.

Maimonides establishes his philosophically-driven approach to interpretation of the Bible text: Every text ought to be read literally unless it *cannot* – due to standing in conflict with (either another text or) that which has been demonstrated to be true through logic. Since Maimonides, for instance, demonstrated that God *cannot* be endowed with physical traits, perforce any mention of God's "arm," "eyes," etc., must be read non-literally. Hence, Maimonides expressed a willingness to reinterpret the beginning of Genesis to include the eternity of the world – if the truth of such a proposal could be properly demonstrated. Any text which, taken literally, would contradict a textual or philosophical principle, must be read in a non-literal fashion.

One of the textual premises that drives Maimonides is that presented in Numbers 12:6–8. The qualitatively superior status of Moses' prophecy in that only he may prophesize while awake is taken by Maimonides as a general principle which he then "canonizes" as the seventh of his thirteen "Articles of Faith." In addition, Maimonides reckons any human interaction with an angel as a form of prophecy – hence, excepting Moses, that interaction must be a vision occurring within a dream or trance. Therefore, Maimonides famously interprets the annunciation scene (Genesis 18) as being a vision Abraham had (i.e., Sarah never "really" laughed, nor did she mock the possibility of such a miraculous birth).

It is clear from our passage that the "man" wrestling with Jacob is a divine being. Although we could interpret Jacob's demand that he bless him as an admission of defeat, the adversary's prophetic declaration that Jacob's name will be changed implies some form of divine knowledge. In addition, the impetus for the new name – "you have striven with God and man and have prevailed" may imply that the "man" was a representative, as it were, of God. Jacob certainly believed that to be the case, as indicated by his naming the place "Peniel" because he had "seen God face to face and been spared."

Given that this interaction was with an angel and that Jacob is someone other than Moses, we would expect Maimonides to interpret the entire scene as a vision – and not having happened in the "real world." We are, therefore, not surprised to find Maimonides including this interaction among those he reckons as being visions, in other words reading Jacob's late-night interaction as not having "really" happened at all.

B: Rashi: Genesis as Polysemous Narrative

Rashi, commonly considered "the father of exegetes," has long been the subject of more analysis, super-commentary, and critique than any other commentator. His selective utilization of Midrashim along with his own observations and those of his teachers makes for a concise yet comprehensive companion to the text.

His approach to legal texts is driven by a fidelity to the *Midrash Halakhah*, representing the text as meaning that which Halakhah eventually determines it to mean. When it comes to pre-Sinaitic narrative (i.e., Genesis and the first chapters of Exodus), however, he represents a Midrashic tradition which views the text as simultaneously operating on multiple levels – an extended form of polysemy. What the patriarchs experience in "real time" is also happening "elsewhere" or "later."

For instance, when Abraham first came into the Land (12:4–9), he came to Sh'khem at Elon Moreh, then moved south to a location on the road situated between (a place that would later be called) Beit-El to the west and ha'Ai to the east. Noting the Patriarchs's arrival in Sh'khem's town (v.6), Rashi explains that he came to pray for his great-grandchildren, who would ultimately wage war there; at the mention of ha'Ai (v.8), Rashi suggests that he prayed for his descendants who would become ensnared in the sin of Akhan and be defeated at ha'Ai – hundreds of years later, when conquering the Land under Joshua's leadership.

Rashi wouldn't negate the simple narrative flow and the construction of the altars at these places as part of Abraham's own mission, yet he allows for an added layer of meaning to the text. In every case, as is to be expected from Genesis, the added layer of meaning points to the future – sometimes mediate, other times distant – even to the *eschaton*.

We expect Rashi to read our mysterious interaction and find additional layers of meaning that speak to Jacob here as well as Jacob later; that refer to Jacob in the "here" as well as Jacob "there." And we are not disappointed.

Rashi immediately quoted the Midrashic tradition that the "man" was Esau's "guardian angel." Jacob refuses to release his angelic opponent at daybreak unless the other blesses him. Rashi explains that he was demanding that Esau (through his representative angel) accede that Jacob properly earned and merited father's blessings in spite of the subterfuge in which he engaged to get them. This is, then, the gist of the angel's response – "your name will no longer be called Jacob." Rashi explains this to mean "no longer will it be said that the blessings came to you *b'Okba* – through deceit; rather, they were given to you *biS'rarah* (hence – *Yisrael*) and openly."

As is his wont in narrative – and the more mysterious the story, the more likely this is to happen – Rashi adds an extra layer of meaning which is proximate and relates directly to the protagonist or his seed, without supplanting the straightforward meaning of the text.

One note: Rashi is not alone in reading a simultaneous "real world" narrative side-by-side with allusions to the future. Among French exegetes, Radak is a noteworthy *parshan* who does much the same, including his approach to our passage.

C: Rashbam: Genesis as Literal Narrative

R. Samuel b. Meir (~1085–~1160, France), Rashi's illustrious grandson, carved out a vital niche in the world of medieval *Parshanut* by restoring an emphasis on the study of *p'shat*. He regularly "by-passed" the Midrashic tradition – even in analyzing legal texts – to pursue what he understood as the meaning of the text, in its own context and setting. There are those who suggest that much of his innovative enterprise was motivated by the *petit renaissance* of the 12th century – indeed, even Rashi, his student Joseph Kara and others who preceded him re-discovered the study of text on its own terms and popularized this "new" method and approach.

Although many exegetes presented programmatic statements about their method of interpretation, all did so at the beginning of Genesis (some added smaller introductions before each book). Rashbam, in addition to his introduction to Genesis, added a bold statement at the beginning of his commentary to chapter 37, the beginning of the Joseph narratives cycle:

> Those who admire intelligence will perceive and understand what our Rabbis taught us – *Ein Miqra Yotzei miY'dei P'shuto*. Even though the main goal of the Torah is to teach us, via allusions in the text, the lessons, rulings and laws, through superfluous language, the thirty-two hermeneutic rules of R. Eliezer son of R. Yose the Galilean and with the thirteen hermeneutic rules of R. Yishmael. The early sages, due to their piety, chiefly engaged in studying the Derashot which are the main point; as a result they were not accustomed to

the depth of P'shuto Shel Mikra. Since the Rabbis advised that we should not accustom our sons to "meditation" (Scripture) and they also said that one who engages in Mikra – this is an incomplete measure (of study), whereas one who engages in Talmud, there is no greater measure, consequently, they were not so accustomed to (studying) the literal meaning of the text, as we read in Tractate Shabbat: R. Kahana said: By the time I was eighteen years old I had studied the whole Shas, yet I did not know that a verse cannot depart from its plain meaning.until to-day. Indeed, even our Master Shlomo, my mother's father, the light of the diaspora, who explained the *Torah, Nevi'im and Ketuvim*, intended to explain *P'shuto shel Mikra*; I, Shmuel son of Meir (his son-in-law) challenged him in his presence and he acceded that if he had the opportunity he would have to write additional commentaries based on the innovative *P'shatot* that are discovered every day. Now, the intelligent ones will see what the early ones explained.

His motivation for placing this audacious declaration at this odd place becomes clear as we learn that he is about to "drop a bombshell"; going against the strong Midrashic "tradition" which is the backbone of the "Martyrology" (*Asarah Harugei Malkhut*), Rashbam interprets the text such that Josephs' brothers were *not* the ones who sold him. This assertion startles anyone familiar with the many Midrashic associations between their sale of Joseph and many of the misfortunes that befell the family (then and throughout history). Nevertheless, a straightforward and objective read of the story has the brothers – who *planned* to sell him, arriving "too late" at the pit, as he had already been sold from there by Midianite merchants.

Rashbam consistently addresses the text independently, using the philological, semantic and syntactical fields to aid his enterprise.

We return to our passage and, once again, are not surprised by the approach taken by the *parshan*. Rashbam concedes, based on the factors adduced above, that the "man" is an angel – that is about the sum of his agreement with his grandfather. As he does in other passages, he is prepared to view the behavior of the patriarchs as less than ideal and posits that Jacob's odd decision to cross the Yabbok at night was an attempt to flee Esau altogether and to avoid the reunion/confrontation. This, Rashbam contends, was a failure of faith in God's promise that "I will be with you and will guard you in all that you go, and I will return you to this Land; for I will not abandon you until I have done all that I spoke of to you."

As such, God dispatched a "man" to wrestle with Jacob – to keep him in place to prevent him from fleeing; he would be forced to stand and witness the fulfillment of God's promise that Esau would not wound him. This explains the angel's relinquishing Jacob at daybreak – he can no longer flee, so the task is complete. Jacob's limp, which Rashi reads as a "badge of honor," is, according to his grandson, a mark of punishment for his unwillingness to stand and see the Divine promise fulfilled.

Rashbam, with his characteristic independence, views this interaction against the backdrop of Jacob's anticipations and anxieties and the inner conflict between God's promises and his very real human fear of his brother.

D: Ramban: Genesis as Foundational Narrative

R. Moses b. Nahman (1174–1270, Gerona), who eventually immigrated to Palestine and spent the last few years of his life there, was a *parshan* par excellence whose commentary on Torah is considered, in many academies, to be the preeminent approach to the text.

One of the hallmarks of Ramban's commentary on Genesis – something he alludes to in his introduction to Exodus – is his viewing the book of Genesis as foundational and essential. In defending the inclusion of this book (in response to Rashi's opening comment in the name of "R. Isaac" at 1:1), Ramban reckons Genesis as "the book of creation – of the nation." All of the elements that will become part of the historical rhythm and cycles of the nation are established by the actions of our forefathers and foremothers.

For example, Ramban critiques Abraham for abandoning Canaan during the famine and going to Egypt; he adds a critique of Abraham's treatment of Sarah in that story. His conclusion is that Abraham's behavior established a pattern his descendants were destined to repeat: to go down to Egypt in response to a famine, to suffer terribly there but, ultimately, to leave with great riches.

He continues his application of this approach in explaining a seemingly mundane and arcane passage. In Chapter 26, we read of the three wells dug by Isaac in Pleshet; that the first two were the subject of dispute with the Philistines; only the third ("*Rehovot*") was dug and used without incident. Ramban explains that these three wells represent the three Sanctuaries and he aligns the disputes recorded in Isaac's interactions with the troubles that preceded the destruction of the first two *Mikdashim* – and the promise that the third will be built comfortably, without rancor or dispute.

Overall, Ramban analogizes the three patriarchs with three periods in Israel's history: Abraham corresponds to the "dawn" of our history, until the Exodus and eventual conquest of the Land; Isaac represents the period of settlement; and Jacob, the exile (and Jacob as "Israel" – the post-exilic period of redemption). This corresponds nicely with the rabbinic tradition that Abraham established the morning prayer; Isaac the afternoon prayer and Jacob the nighttime devotion (the use of night as a simile for exile is common in rabbinic literature). Israel is, then, the next dawn of redemption; his first name-change takes place at the end of the night in our passage.

Following our "anticipatory reading," we would expect Ramban to take this nighttime wrestling match as a foundational moment for some interaction between Jacob (Israel) and (Midrashic) Esau – their historic enemies. Again, as we've seen thrice so far, our exegete does not disappoint.

Ramban begins by citing a Midrash that interprets the angel's touching Jacob's thigh as his touching "all of the righteous ones that will come forth from him . . . referencing the generation of the persecution" (in Hadrian's era, c. 140). He then explains in his own words:

> This entire event was a hint for future generations that there will be a generation in the history of Jacob's seed when Esau will overpower them until they will nearly destroy them – and this was during one of the generations of the sages of Mishnah like the generation of R. Judah b. Baba and his colleagues, as they said: 'R. Hiyya b. Aba said: If someone would direct me to give up my life for the sanctity of the Holy One, Blessed is His Name, I would do so – as long as they would kill me right away, but I cannot withstand being persecuted in the generation of *shmad* . . ."

Ramban continues:

> . . . and there have been other generations (since then) where they have done similar and worse things, we have suffered it all and it has passed us by, as is hinted to by the phrase "and Jacob came *shalem* – complete."

AFTERWORD

We have investigated a small but vital and mysterious passage in the Jacob narrative. We've found that each of the four *Rishonim* whose comments we've reviewed looked at this *parashah* differently; but that wasn't the result of a different interpretation of the words or of the setting; rather, it was the result of a unique approach to the book of Genesis and *Parshanut* which then directed each of them to read this text in his own way. Whether, as Maimonides holds (as a matter of principle) it is an angelic dialogue which must be a vision; or, per Rashi, a "doubling" which affects Jacob the man now, but also in his later interactions with Esau; whether, as Rashbam would have it, this is a strategic move employed by God to chastise Jacob for his lack of faith and to keep him present to see God's fulfillment of his promise of protection; or as Ramban would have it, a glimpse into the complex relationship between the Jews (Jacob) and the Romans (Esau) over a thousand years later – each of these approaches and messages could be found in this rich text.

# XVIII JACOB'S GIFT: MINHAH L'ESAV
Genesis 32:14–16

INTRODUCTION

Upon his return from Haran, after twenty years (or significantly more – see Chapter XVI) of separation from his brother Esau, Jacob spent considerable energy preparing for their reunion. Having successfully escaped the clutches of Laban, he sent messengers ahead in advance of his return. When they returned with a report that Esau was coming towards Jacob (which Jacob understood to mean that Esau was tracking his progress) with an entourage of 400 men, Jacob, assuming it was a militia coming to attack his camp, moved into defensive mode. He prayed for salvation (invoking the promise at Beit-El) and split the camp into two to allow for partial salvation via retreat.

He then prepared a tribute to be sent to Esau. Although it is not at all clear that this tribute was a response to the advancing entourage/army, our Rabbis read this as a part of his trinary strategy: prayer, "war," and appeasement.

The description of the tribute is unusual, as Jacob sent scores of animals, a tribute we've already seen and will see again. Yet the description here is far more detailed, listing five types of animals in male/female sets (with one exception – see below) with exact numbers of each type and gender. Moreover, Jacob instructs his servants to bring the tribute in separate groups, leaving a gap between each set. He then directs each set of servants to declare that this is a tribute to "my master Esau" and that he, Jacob, is following them, having said that, he hopes to allay his anger with this tribute and then he will greet him himself.

There is evidently something more to this tribute, something buried in the details presented and in the singularity of each set of animals, each set off independently, that can inform us as to Jacob's intent and purpose, not only with this gift, but also of this momentous reunion.

Before assaying the overall "message," let's examine each of the sets of animals – but first, a word on perspective.

THE CHARACTER'S POINT OF VIEW

We, the "omniscient" reader, have a distinct advantage over the characters of whom we are reading – and that advantage, *ipso facto*, works against us. We are aware of the actions, words, goals, and intentions of all the characters in the plot, to the extent that the text makes us privy to them.

Whereas Adam is unaware of the conversation between Eve and the serpent, we hear it loud and clear. While Moses is (blissfully) ignorant of the machinations which led to the construction of the Golden Calf, we see it in full color as it enfolds. Symmetrically, Aaron does not know that Moses' time at the top of the mountain has been interrupted and that he is on his way down already aware of the people's infidelity to God. But we, the all-knowing reader, are given a "split-screen" read of this plot. In both of these examples, all of the players will eventually gain the knowledge held by the other: Adam will learn of the serpentine seduction, and Aaron and Moses will gain full knowledge of the other's doings in good time.

Perhaps a more telling example of "insular awareness" is that of Amalek in Refidim. The text presents a bifurcated narrative, alternating between the skirmish which pitted Joshua and his troops against the desert brigands, and the scene atop the hill where Moses's hands – raised or at rest – determined the soldiers' fate and success. In this case, we have no reason to think that the Amalek raiders ever learned of the "other side" of the story.

We, on the other hand, see all of it – but ironically, this revelation blinds us to nuances of the text, which speak to the insular awareness of the various characters. We are confused by the dispute between Joshua and Moses upon the latter's descent from the mountain as to whether the sounds heard from below are cries of war or not. Since the text has already encoded for us that Pharaoh's dream was presented in two parts (as opposed to two independent dreams) we are unimpressed by Joseph's startling revelation that "Pharaoh's dream is one," noting specifically his use of the singular (*halom* in lieu of *halomot*).

If we are to properly understand what Jacob was communicating to Esau via this sequence of distinct gifts, we must look at each through Esau's eyes, knowing only (to the best we can approximate) what Esav himself could conceivably know and infer. This is a critical delimiter since we never have reason to impute prophecy – and most certainly not prognostication – to a character in the text without either explicit textual backing to that effect or an action which might indicate fore-knowledge. Since we have no reason, neither within the written Torah nor within rabbinic tradition, to regard Esau as having special knowledge of the future, we will need leave any unborn consideration alone and only focus on that which Esau would know from his own life or from family traditions and lore.

THE GIFT

A: Goats – in "Twos"

The first distinct segment of the gift was goats: 200 does and 20 bucks. This should be a fairly easy one to interpret – after all, Jacob refers to this gift as a *Berakhah* – tribute, in which he hopes to "assuage his anger." The anger which Jacob assumes Esau to be carrying is that which caused the former's flight all those years ago – his theft of the Patriarch's blessing.

This theft was engineered by Rebekah's preparation of two goats, goats which Jacob "took" to his mother and subsequently, in the guise of Esau, brought to his father.

Jacob's first message was one of appeasement, an attempt to mollify his brother and, as it were, to "return" the stolen blessings. The symbolism of 2 goats is clear, and the multiples (x10, x100) underscore the sense of deep apology and regret which Jacob was communicating to his brother.

As we anticipate Esaus' reaction and understanding of the gifts, we have to keep in mind what Jacob ultimately wants out of their relation-ship (beyond survival). More critically, what does Jacob anticipate about Esau's interest in their relationship (if, indeed, Esau does not intend bodily harm)?

Looking back at the three blessings given by Isaac to his sons, the pic-ture is clear. Whereas Esau was meant to have the position of power in the family, controlling his brother and the wealth of the estate, there is no mention of Abraham or the Divine promises given him in either the blessing *intended* for Esau nor the one *given* him. In the final result, Jacob received both the blessings of power (which he "stole") and the blessing of fertility and the Land as the continuation of the promise given to Abraham (given outright).

Jacob's intent upon his return was not to work together with Esau in continuing the family's mission; at best, Esau could be a peripheral support system to the grand enterprise of calling out God's Name and growing a family that would eventually inherit the Land.

Parenthetically, this attitude, symbolized by the anthemic verse *Va-yivater Yaakov L'vado* ("and Jacob remained alone"), just before his nighttime wrestling match with the mystical "man," is one that finds expression during the 6th century BCE in the relationship of the nascent Judean community with the more settled Samaritan group. When the *Shavei Tziyon* (returnees to Zion) began reconstructing the Temple, the Samaritans insisted on participating in the construction. The Jews' response – "It is not for us and for you to build a house for our God" (Ezra 4:3) set in motion a series of events that led to the suspension of that rebuilding effort for nearly 20 years.

B: Lambs – and Rams

The second segment was 200 ewes and 20 rams. Whereas the lambs could easily be understood against the backdrop of Jacob's years with Lavan and his main source of wealth, the rams present a distinct image which must have generated an immediate association for Esau.

Perhaps the most famous ram in history is the ram of the binding of Isaac, the ram that stood in lieu of father Isaac and was slaughtered in his stead atop the mountain in Moriah. There is little question that Esau and Jacob were both familiar with this seminal piece of family lore – there is even a suggestion in the Midrash that Isaac's early blindness was caused by the "tears of angels" which seeped into his eyes as he lay on the altar built by his father, or by God's response to Isaac having gazed at Him while on the altar. According to another Midrash, God's forbidding father Isaac from leaving the Land was also the result of the *Akedah*, as Isaac had been sanctified as an offering, and may therefore never leave the holy precincts.

Jacob was subtly communicating to his brother that even though he meant to appease him and ask his forgiveness for the theft of the "power" blessing, he in no wise intended to work side-by-side to continue grandfather's mission. The Binding was a singular event, involving one father and one child; one officiant and one offering – and Jacob was claiming the mantle as proper heir to that elite position.

The chess match continues – Jacob knows that Esau could easily accept the message of the singularity of the *Akedah* without agreeing with his brother's conclusion. Esau could claim that he is the rightful heir of that position. He was Isaac's favored son, the first-born with rights of primogeniture and, after all, he was the one who had never left the Land!

Not only did he remain in the Land, imitating his father's status as *Olah Temimah*, he also remained at his father's side, loyally serving him (one would assume, given what we know about Esau).

Jacob's next move – the next segment of his gift – must be a pre-emptive response to this anticipated reaction on Esau's part.

C: Nursing Camels

Of the four main mammal types which appear in the Bible, each has a typical use which, although not exclusive to that mammal, helps define its utility and the presumed livelihood of its master. It is helpful to remember that in the Biblical period, there were four main types of livelihood in the Levant – farmer, rancher, artisan, and merchant.

Bovines are generally associated with hard work, typically plowing the fields. In an agronomic society, this is a vital task, one which will spell the difference between preparedness for the planting season or disaster. Even though we typically associate the female bovine (cows) with milk, in the era and setting of the Bible, milk was typically that of goats. In addition, the typical source of meat was lambs, rather than oxen. Hence, if someone owned bulls or cows, it typically marked them as a farmer (or a rancher who was raising them to sell to farmers). The ox is the constant example of the animal in the casuistic legal framework of the agricultural society, as presented in Exodus 21–23.

Ovines are raised for their by-products (wool from lambs, milk from goats) and for their meat – owning lambs was a sure sign of a rancher. No farmer would want lambs, as their grazing patterns would work in direct opposition to his farming needs.

Donkeys were used for local/regional travel and for cargo. Countless instances of nearby journeys undertaken by both heroes and villains alike, as well as "neutral" characters – all involve donkeys as the vehicle for either human or cargo transport. Owning a donkey revealed little about the owner.

Dromedaries, on the other hand, have a specific and somewhat exclusive use – they are valued for their ability to traverse great distances without need for water or food and, as such, are the ideal transport for long-range travel and cargo. Owning camels is a sure sign of being a merchant who trades with peoples in other regions where the natural resources provide what is locally lacking and vice-versa.

The most prominent place that camels hold in the family history (until this point) and most obvious association to be made from their appearance as a gift is the story of "how father and mother met." Abraham sent his slave with ten camels to far-off Haran, his family home (and, perhaps, his birthplace) to find a wife for Isaac. The young maiden, Rebekah, accompanied the slave back to Canaan on camelback and was atop a camel (from which she promptly fell) when Esau and Jacob's parents first saw each other.

One additional feature of this segment of the tribute is the break in the pattern of the gifts. Every other set included males and females, ostensibly as mates. The camels, contradistinctively, included thirty nursing camels – and their young. Jacob's choice to deviate from the "mating pattern" of the rest of the tribute highlights the association with Isaac and Rebekah's "courtship" – when Rebekah journeyed to Canaan, she went with her nursemaid, presumably so that when she would bear children she would have a wet-nurse available.

Jacob's message anticipates Esau's argument – to wit, Jacob has traveled the distance that mother traveled, has undergone the travails of the road and can also reckon a camel as part of his menagerie. This makes him a (more?) fit candidate to continue the family tradition, much as Abraham traveled from the same city that Rebekah later left – and that Jacob has just fled – Haran.

This argument is, however, inherently flawed, as it points to travel abroad and exile as a badge of honor and a merit which should garner credit to Jacob. This would be far more persuasive if they were tussling over the legacy of Abraham, who traveled (and, of course, owned camels). Since it is the position of Isaac, their father, that is at the core of this (possibly imagined) dispute, camels, Haran, and travel hardly rate.

It is to that next, anticipated argument that Jacob responds with the fourth segment of the gift.

D: Bovines

Again, we turn to the family history to find the significance of oxen and cows and what story might be invoked by such a gift.

In spite of the ubiquity of oxen in the farming world of the Levant, there are only two oxen mentioned until this point; the second is the ox served to Abraham's guests at the annunciation of the birth of Isaac. Though Maimonides deems this entire scene to be a vision and not having happened in "the real world," this doesn't affect the impact of the symbolism on his descendants. Just as Abraham could have related a *story* involving ox-meat, he would have related a *vision* involving serving ox-meat. However, this would hardly be considered a significant symbol; in this case, the ox does not serve as a symbol – but as lunch.

The first ox which appears in a symbolically significant context is a part of the "Covenant Between The Pieces" in Chapter 15 (see Chapter XXI). In that covenant (which, again, per Maimonides, may have completely taken place within a vision), Abraham is commanded to take "*egel meshuleshet*" – either a three-year-old calf or three calves, along with a similar goat (or goats) and ram (or rams) – and a turtle-dove and pigeon. This calf – a young bovine – is the first component mentioned in this covenant; it, along with the goat(s) and ram(s) will be cut in half and a covenant will be made "between the pieces" (*bein haB'tarim*).

What is the gist of this covenant? When the darkness descends and, with it, a great fear falls on Abraham, God speaks to him:

> You shall surely know that your seed will be strangers in a land that is not theirs and they will enslave and oppress them for four hundred years. I will judge the nation to whom they are enslaved and afterwards they will leave with great wealth. But you will come to your fathers in peace and will be buried at a good old age. And the fourth generation will return here, because (until then) the sin of the Amorites will not have been complete.

As I've noted elsewhere, Jacob had every reason to believe that, subsequent to his "oppression" at the hands of Lavan (on foreign soil) and the meteoric growth of his estate, he was the embodiment of this covenant. He had been exiled (as directed by both parents), had endured hard labor (as outlined in his complaint against Lavan), and was now returning to the Land (with his children, the *fourth generation* from Abraham) with great wealth.

This is the import of the oxen sent as the penultimate component of the tribute. Jacob was claiming that the ultimate seed of Abraham, the descendants who deserved the legacy, were those who were distilled in the crucible of the covenant – and that was only he, Jacob, not his older brother.

This stark reminder of their grandfather's covenant with God should have been the last necessary statement to claim the legacy of Abraham – but there is one more message that Jacob must communicate.

E: Donkeys

Again, we turn to the family history and to the remarkable moments which formed the identity of the fathers and, in turn, their sons.

In the most momentous scene in the family history (to this point, at least), Abraham takes Isaac up to the mountain in Moriah, intending to offer him up to God; God stays his hand, and the family and its destiny are forever changed by that remarkable moment in time.

We noted earlier that Abraham's trek to Moriah was enabled by a donkey – Abraham, Isaac, two lads and a donkey comprised the entourage. However, when the group arrived at a site from where "the place" could be seen, he instructed the lads to "remain here with the donkey." This statement is so clearly pointed, underscored by the superfluous '*im haHamor*,' that the Rabbis comment – '*am* (instead of '*im*) *haHamor*,' (to wit) a nation which is akin to a donkey (assuming the lads to be Canaanites). Be that as it may, the donkey plays the symbolic role of "left behind" here, accompanying the holy family to the periphery of the holy place – but prevented from moving further in to the holy and forever remaining "here" while the seminal event is taking place "there."

Jacob invites Esau to join the great mission of continuing Abraham's path – "to command his sons and his household after him, that they will observe the way of God, performing righteousness and justice . . ." That participation, however, is *ab initio*, limited to the role of the "donkey." Esau may join in, but must understand that such engagement will be "from the sidelines" and that he will never be invited to play a core role in spreading the Name of God.

MEASURING THE SUCCESS OF THE MESSAGE

Jacob put tremendous effort in putting together a large gift to appease his brother and cool down the anger that he anticipated emanating from Esau. The gift, *qua* gift, accomplished its purpose; the message, however, seems to have missed its mark.

When Esau finally met up with Jacob, and the expected protestations of keeping the gift were exclaimed by both sides, Esau then invited Jacob to come with him; evidently, he did not understand (or wasn't persuaded by) the import of the multi-segmented gift.

At this point, Jacob reached back to an old strategy and engaged in subterfuge, telling Esau that due to his young children and young, nursing flock, he would not be able to keep up with Esau's pace – but he promised to catch up with Esau at some "later time." From the rest of the story and history, it seems that Jacob never intended to catch up to his brother. His solitary mission, destined to be completed without his brother's help at all, would continue as he alone inherited the Land.

AFTERWORD

One of the principles of the successful study of the Bible, as we will further explore below (Chapters XIX and XXI) is to experience the narrative from the perspective of the actors. By viewing this gift – presented in such a unique fashion and described in unusual detail through the eyes of Esau – and with the awareness of how Jacob would imagine Esau seeing it – we can better understand the implicit message intended by this tribute. The success or failure of that message is not our concern, and here's where our "omniscience" as a reader prevails and we understand what Esau could not. Jacob's destiny was frozen in the moment before his fateful wrestling match – *vayivater Yaakov levado* – and Jacob remained alone.

XIX RAPE OF DINAH
Entering the Character's World, Part I

INTRODUCTION

A fundamental principle of Parshanut is that we, the reader, are far more knowledgeable than any of the characters whose lives are unfolding before us, if only because we know how every story will end. We also have access to the plans, fears, and background of all of the players, whereas each player only knows — beyond himself — what he is allowed to learn. To properly understand the text, to be properly surprised or impressed by anyone's actions, we must read the narrative from the perspective of each of the characters and understand their reactions, statements, and silences accordingly, entering, one at a time, the mindset of each character.

This principle, well-anchored in the commentaries of the *Rishonim* and successfully demonstrated within the text, has a natural extension. Not only are particular statements and actions of the persona informed by the information he brings to the scene, but his entire attitude and the matrix of experiences that is the springboard off of which he acts are, perforce, formed by his identity. If a character was raised as a nomad, he may respond to challenges by finding diplomatic ways to elude them; if, on the other hand, he is raised on the land and learns to till it, he may stand down his challengers in a much more confrontational manner. Witness how Isaac responds to Philistine malfeasance as opposed to his father's more accommodating style.

Any study of the travails of Jacob's family must be seen against the backdrop of the difference between the father and his sons and how each was raised. It is to the foreground of Sh'khem that we turn our attention, ever aware of the different worlds of our protagonists.

"CURSED BE THEIR WRATH"

Chapter 34 records what is undoubtedly one of the most violent and morally troubling chapters in Biblical history. Here is a brief recap of the events that transpired in Sh'khem:

The family of Jacob enters the city of Sh'khem and Dinah, the one sister among eleven brothers, is forcibly taken by Sh'khem, the prince of the city-state after which he is named. Sh'khem rapes her and, through the august agency of his father, Hamor, appeals to her brothers to allow her to become his proper wife. The brothers speak *b'mirmah* with Sh'khem and Hamor, and convince them that the only way for Dinah to marry Sh'khem is if the prince and all of his townsfolk become circumcised. The townsfolk are convinced to undergo this painful operation, evidently motivated by economic gain (vv. 21–24). On the third day, with all the males in pain, Simeon and Levi kill all of the males in town, after which the brothers pillage the town and take their sister back to safety. Jacob chastises them for their actions, which they defend on grounds of concern for their sister's honor.

As mentioned, this narrative is troubling on many levels. To paraphrase a contemporary writer, whereas Jacob's children had a golden opportunity to begin to fulfill their mission of teaching the world "the way of the Lord, to do righteousness and justice," (18:19) they squandered this chance and sullied their reputation in the eyes of the neighboring peoples by acting both deceitfully and violently, destroying an entire city in response to a crime committed by one citizen, albeit the prince. Abraham's protests of "will you also destroy the righteous with the wicked?" (18:23) seem to have been inverted by his elect progeny. In addition, if we look further into the Torah, we see that rape of an unmarried woman is not considered a capital crime; rather it is a case of criminal assault (along with a fixed fine, represented here by the word *mohar*). How could Simeon and Levi act in this manner?

Conventional understanding holds that Jacob's chastisement was directed against all of their actions: the deceit, the polis-cide, and the pillage of the town. We are even more confident that Jacob was violently opposed to their behavior when we read of his deathbed charge, given to them nearly fifty years later in Egypt:

Simeon and Levi are brethren; weapons of violence their kinship. Let my soul not come into their council; unto their assembly let my glory not be united;

for in their anger they slew men, and in their self-will they houghed oxen. Cursed be their anger, for it was fierce, and their wrath, for it was cruel; I will divide them in Jacob, and scatter them in Israel. (49:5–7)

If we look into the analyses of the *Rishonim*, we will find that a much more complex picture unfolds before us; indeed, a careful reading of both texts (Chapters 34 and 49) provides us with ample reason to reexamine our assessment of the behavior of Simeon and Levi in Sh'khem. Due to space limitations, we will limit our reassessment of "the tragedy in Sh'khem" to information that can be inferred from the text itself. Interested readers are encouraged to look at the comments of the *Rishonim* through Chapter 34 (notably Ramban at 34:13; note his critique of Maimonides's explanation).

"HAKH'ZONAH . . . ?"

There are several indications that Jacob was not opposed — in principle — to the decision (and its implementation) taken by Simeon and Levi. In addition, we have several textual indications that the Torah itself gives their approach the stamp of approval.

First of all, let's look at Jacob's deathbed charge to these two brothers: ". . . for in their anger they slew men, and in their self-will they houghed oxen. . . ." Although there are opinions in the Midrash that interpret this statement as a reference to Sh'khem, simple *P'shat* does not support this read. How could Jacob be referring to the death of dozens (or hundreds) of people as "they slew a man?" In addition, what is the reference to an "ox" here?

There is one statement in the Midrash that addresses this problem, but the solution offered there is hardly a critique of the brothers' behavior: "Did they only slay one man? Doesn't Scripture state: 'they slew all the males'? Rather, they were only considered by the Holy One, Blessed is He, as one person" (Genesis Rabbah 99:6). In other words, if this is a reference to the slaying of the entire male population of Sh'khem, it isn't as grievous as all that, as their lives weren't worth much in the eyes of God (see the additional proof cited in that selection of the Midrash).

Again, the straightforward reading is a reference to the killing of one man and an ox. We will soon discover who these might be.

". . . Cursed be their anger, for it was fierce, and their wrath, for it was cruel . . . ."

Note that Jacob does not curse their actions; rather, he curses their anger (or so it seems — but see the first comment of Hizkuni to 49:7). If he were morally opposed to their behavior in Sh'khem, doesn't their anger pale in significance next to the actual slaying and pillage? Why mention that here?

Indeed, one comment in the Midrash Rabbah contrasts the violent act that earned them this "curse" with their valor in Sh'khem!

> ... [Jacob] began calling out "'Simeon and Levi are brothers ...' you acted like brothers to Dinah, as it says: 'two of the sons of Jacob, Simeon and Levi, Dinah's brothers, took each man his sword ...' but you did not act like brothers to Joseph when you sold him." (Genesis Rabbah 99:7)

This Midrash can be associated with the comment in Midrash Rabbati of R. Moshe haDarshan, to wit: The *each man to his brother* mentioned in 37:19 at the sale of Joseph refers to Simeon and Levi; not coincidentally, Joseph's abduction and sale took place in the Sh'khem region.

Indeed, many commentators maintain that the entire deathbed charge of Jacob to Simeon and Levi is only a reference to their role in the sale of Joseph, who is also known as an "ox" (see D'varim 33:17).

BACK TO CHAPTER 34

Now, let's look at Jacob's words when he confronted the brothers in the immediate aftermath of the events in Sh'khem:

> And Jacob said to Simeon and Levi: "You have troubled me, to make me odious unto the inhabitants of the land, even to the Canaanites and the Perizzites; and I, being few in number, they will gather themselves together against me and smite me; and I shall be destroyed, I and my house." (34:30)

Is there moral outrage here? Is there a challenge to their religious sensitivities? Jacob's response seems to be disapproval of their strategies, to wit: "As a result of your actions, I will now have problems with the locals. We will now be attacked by the surrounding Canaanite and Perizzite peoples."

Furthermore, the Torah seems to lend support to the brothers' actions throughout the narrative. Twice within the description of the brothers' interaction with the people of Sh'khem, the phrase "*asher timei/tim'u et Dinah ahotam"* is added to the objects of the verse. In verse 13: "And the sons of Jacob answered Sh'khem and Hamor his father with guile, and spoke, ***asher timei et Dinah ahotam*** (because he had defiled Dinah their sister) . . . ." In verse 27: "The sons of Jacob came upon the slain, and spoiled the city, ***asher tim'u et Dinah ahotam*** (because they had defiled Dinah their sister)."

Why is the Torah twice repeating something that we already know? In the second instance, we could argue that the text is anticipating a severe criticism of the brothers' behavior (addressed by nearly all commentators): If Sh'khem was guilty of the rape of Dinah, why did all of the townsfolk have to die? By equating their culpability (*asher tim'u* – "because they had defiled" – in the plural, v. 27) with his own (*asher timei* – "because he had defiled " – in the singular, v. 13), we get one of two pictures of the participation of the citizens of Sh'khem in this heinous crime:

1. They all participated physically in the defilement of Dinah, either by a Sodom-like orgy or by abetting the criminal prince.

2. Since they had the wherewithal to censure and/or punish him for his behavior, and failed to do so, it is considered their crime as well. (This seems to be the assumption underlying Maimonides's approach, cited earlier).

The latter seems to be borne out by the record of the plea of Sh'khem to his townspeople to accept the conditions of the sons of Jacob:

> And Hamor and Sh'khem his son came unto the gate of their city, and spoke with the men of their city, saying: "These men are peaceable with us; therefore let them dwell in the land, and trade therein; for, behold, the land is large enough for them; let us take their daughters to us for wives, and let us give them our daughters. Only on this condition will the men consent unto us to dwell with us, to become one people, if every male among us be circumcised, as they are circumcised. Shall not their cattle and their substance and all their beasts be ours? only let us consent unto them, and they will dwell with us." And unto Hamor and unto Sh'khem his son hearkened all that went out of the gate of his city; and every male was circumcised, all that went out of the gate of his city. (vv. 20–24)

If Sh'khem was truly an autarch, would he need the people's consent — and would he have to appeal to their mercenary sensibilities — to forge this agreement?

Besides these two (seemingly superfluous) pejorative references to the citizens of Sh'khem, note how the dialogue between Jacob and his sons is presented in the Torah:

> And Jacob said to Simeon and Levi: "You have troubled me, to make me odious unto the inhabitants of the land, even to the Canaanites and the Perizzites; and I, being few in number, they will gather themselves together against me and smite me; and I shall be destroyed, I and my house." And they said: "*hakh'zonah ya'aseh et achoteinu?*" ["Should he deal with our sister as with a harlot?"] (vv. 30–31)

The Torah gives the brothers the "last word" in their dispute with their father. Furthermore, this "last word" is so terse and direct that it seems to leave Jacob "speechless"— indication that their argument held sway. The Torah seems to be giving approval to their actions, an observation strengthened by comparing the gist of Jacob's opposition with the "facts on the ground" in the subsequent narrative.

Compare:

> And Jacob said to Simeon and Levi: "You have troubled me, to make me odious unto the inhabitants of the land, even to the Canaanites and the Perizzites; and I, being few in number, they will gather themselves together against me and smite me; and I shall be destroyed, I and my house" (a pragmatic concern that the violent vengeance wreaked by the brothers will lead to a lynching of Jacob's family).

With:

> And they journeyed; and a terror of God was upon the cities that were round about them, and they did not pursue after the sons of Jacob. (35:5 — only five verses after the dispute)

The Torah is emphatically assuaging Jacob's fears — the local people did not rise up in anger against his family as a result of their actions in Sh'khem; rather, they stood in fear of them and did not even pursue them.

There is one more piece of support for the contention that Jacob was not morally opposed to the action taken by the brothers. Just before the deathbed "blessing" given in Egypt to the brothers, Jacob accepts both of Joseph's sons as members of his own family (earning them each a full portion in the Land) and then declares to Joseph: "Moreover I have given to thee one *Sh'khem* over your brothers, which I took out of the hand of the Amorite with my sword and with my bow." (48:22) This *Sh'khem* could mean portion, as Onkelos renders it. Alternatively, it may be a reference to the city of Sh'khem itself (see Rashi and Ibn Ezra, ad loc.). If so, Jacob is not only accepting of the brothers' actions, but even "adopts" their war as his own. There are several Midrashim that indicate Jacob himself participated in the war (see, e.g., Genesis Rabbah 80:13). That would certainly take us very far from our original assumptions as presented at the beginning of this chapter.

"AKHARTEM OTI"

If Jacob was not morally opposed to the slaying and pillage of the citizens of Sh'khem, catalyzed by an act of deception, we are left with three questions:

1. Why didn't he himself lead the charge against the citizenry? As is evident from numerous narratives in Genesis, Jacob was a master at knowing how to utilize deception when appropriate.

2. After the fact, why did he register opposition to their behavior, even if it was later dispelled?

3. Once we have put Jacob and his sons on the same side of this moral dilemma, how can we make sense of their conclusion? Why were Sh'khem, his father, and all of the townsfolk liable for murder and pillage?

A crime for which the Torah mandates payment to the young woman's family should certainly not warrant this sort of treatment. In addition, as noted earlier, such behavior would seem to regress the cause of the Abrahamic tradition. How do we justify their behavior?

JACOB AND HIS SONS

We will first address the dispute between Jacob and his sons regarding the proper tactics in response to the rape of Dinah; resolving this question will provide us an approach to the other two.

We have to approach any differences in attitude that surface between Jacob and his children against the backdrop of their substantially different backgrounds and experiential matrices. Jacob grew up knowing his grandfather Abraham (Isaac was 60 when Jacob was born; hence Abraham was 160 at the time, and therefore Jacob was 15 when Abraham died) and, of course, knowing his father Isaac. Conversely, Jacob's sons never knew their great-grandfather Abraham, nor did they even meet Isaac until he was quite aged and, from all textual and Midrashic evidence, quite incapacitated (see, inter alia, Rashi at 28:10).

Jacob grew up in Canaan, but had to spend the last 20 years (at least—see BT Megillah 17a, and above, Chapter XVI) "on the run." In addition, before fleeing to Aram, his life seems to be one of isolation, save his relationship with mother Rebekah. Our story (Chapter 34) rests somewhere along the continuum from exile to return — and therein lies the rub. Jacob's children, although born and raised in what proved to be an environment of enmity, had a full family support system, as well as being brought up as the children of a wealthy and powerful member of Laban's household.

In sum, Jacob was a native of the Land who had been in exile for a substantial time, and who had a clear and direct connection with Abraham and Isaac. His children were born in Aram and had never tasted the pain and loneliness of exile, and they had had no direct encounters with the first or second generations of the clan.

Jacob's response to the rape of Dinah thus has to be understood against this background. Both grandfather Abraham and father Isaac had experienced similar difficulties with local chieftains: Sarah was taken to Pharaoh's palace (Chapter 12) and to Abimelech's rooms (Chapter 20). Rebekah, although never taken from Isaac, was presented as his sister out of the same fear of the local ruler and the general lack of morality (Chapter 26).

Here, Jacob, who had not yet encountered such a threat, was faced with a hauntingly familiar scenario — with some significant differences. Dinah was not falsely presented as a sister — she really was an unmarried sister! She was taken to the house of the local ruler, just as in the cases with Abraham, but that is where the similarities end. Whereas God had intervened on behalf of Abraham both in Egypt and in Gerar, the rape of Dinah was carried out with bestial success.

Jacob had every reason to consider as follows: If his grandfather Abraham, for whom God was prepared to intervene to spare Sarah, and who was only wandering through that land, was prepared to "play the game" and not belligerently confront the locals, how much more applicable was this action in this case. After all, God has not intervened to help us here; and these are my permanent neighbors, with whom I must be able to get along. If it was important to exercise restraint in exile, as I have with

Laban and, just now, with Esau — how much more so in the Land where I intend to establish my roots.

The brothers (note that Simeon and Levi are only singled out in describing the slaying; all of the brothers participated in the cunning negotiations as well as the pillage of the city), coming from their critically distinct upbringing and experiences, viewed the situation and the appropriate response quite differently. The non-confrontational attitude that both Abraham and Isaac had adopted while traveling was only appropriate for a land you intend to leave — ultimately, if the locals think you weak, it will have no deleterious effect on your own well-being. That is not the case, they argued, in a land that you intend to settle. If the local peoples think of our daughters as "fair game," we will never gain their respect — or fear. Our lives will be a long series of attacks and oppression. It is better, goes the argument, to make our stand here and now and let everyone know that we are not to be trifled with.

We now understand why Jacob did not originally take up arms and why he was perturbed by his sons' approach. It was not a moral opposition, but rather a disapproval of their tactics that lay at the heart of his chastisement.

Both of their positions are easily seen in their respective arguments: Jacob:

And Jacob said to Simeon and Levi: "You have troubled me, to make me odious unto the inhabitants of the land, even to the Canaanites and the Perizzites; and I, being few in number, they will gather themselves together against me and smite me; and I shall be destroyed, I and my house."

The brothers:

"Should one deal with our sister as with a harlot?"

When we are talking about an individual who violates a young woman, the Torah does not consider it a capital offense; it allows for recompense and amelioration of the situation with a large fine as appropriate for a case of criminal assault. When, on the other hand, we are dealing with an attack that challenges the dignity and honor of the people of Israel, that is a different matter entirely.

The Torah not only provides support for the brothers' position in the description of the ensuing travels which were "trouble-free," but Jewish law itself also seems to lend support to this position:

Rav Yehudah stated in the name of Rav: If foreigners (i.e., enemies of Israel) besieged Israelite towns . . . with the intention of taking lives, the people are permitted to sally forth against them with their weapons and to desecrate the Sabbath on their account. Where the attack, however, was made on a town that was close to a frontier, even though they did not come with any intention of taking lives, but merely to plunder straw or stubble, the people are permitted to sally forth against them with their weapons and to desecrate the Sabbath on their account. (BT Eruvin 45a)

POSTSCRIPT

Much ink has been spilt over the analysis of the "double identity" of Jacob/ Israel. In any case, it is curious to note that throughout this narrative, our patriarch is referred to by his "exile name," Jacob. Yet, when he "adopts" the conquest of Sh'khem, he speaks as Israel:

And Israel said unto Joseph: "Behold, I die; but God will be with you, and bring you back unto the land of your fathers. Moreover I have given to you one portion over your brothers, which I took out of the hand of the Amorite with my sword and with my bow." (48:21–22)

AFTERNOTE

We began by allowing ourselves to be disconcerted by Jacob's strange and strained reactions to the events in Sh'khem and the Torah's ambiguous treatment of Simeon and Levi. By following the various threads suggested by the third component of the methodology — entering the character's world (or the characters' worlds) — we successfully clarified the different responses to the rape of Dinah taken by her brothers and her father.

KEVER RACHEL
Contemporary Assumptions and Geographic Enlightenment

INTRODUCTION

In previous chapters, we have examined the various methods of Biblical interpretation used to decipher the meaning of the text — contextual reading, looking through the eyes of the original audience, utilizing archaeological and archival finds to enhance our understanding of the background against which the narrative plays out, rigorous contrasting of parallel narratives, and so on. In this chapter, we will analyze a thorny problem that is not inherent in the text, but rather places the text against convention. Although not the only area where conventional understanding flies in the face of a straightforward reading of the text, there is something particularly challenging about squaring the geographic identification of places mentioned in the Bible with what the text tells us about these places. More difficult than place names proper is pinpointing the location of events when the coordinates given by the text are obscure or missing.

For over a thousand years (and perhaps much longer — see below) a tomb site approximately four miles south of Jerusalem, just north of Bethlehem, has been identified and revered as Rachel's Tomb. As early as the end of the 13th century, Ramban [see his comments at Genesis 35:16] records his own identification of the place, which is near present-day Bethlehem. To be sure, we have much earlier reports of Rachel's tomb being in the proximity of Bethlehem, including a passage in the New Testament dating back to the first century, and from the 4th-century Onomasticon of Eusebius as well as the anonymous "Traveler from Bordeaux." These identifications are almost assuredly based on older Jewish traditions. Painful as it may be for the many who have shed tears at this site, an examination of the several references to her burial site in the Bible put that identification in question.

We will investigate the relevant texts, which begin in Genesis 35; using references from throughout the canon, we will endeavor to reach a conclusion that harmonizes those texts that seem to be in conflict.

GENESIS OF THE PROBLEM

At the end of Genesis, Jacob is elaborating upon his deathbed request of Joseph to bury him in the Cave of Machpelah, with Abraham, Sarah, Isaac, Rebekah, and Leah. As a form of apologia, explaining why Joseph's own mother — and Jacob's beloved, Rachel — is not buried in that hallowed spot, Jacob explains:

> And as for me, when I came from Paddan, Rachel died unto me in the land of Canaan in the way, when there was still some way [*Kiv'rat Eretz*] to come unto Ephrath; and I buried her there in the way to Ephrath — the same is Bethlehem. (48:7)

It is unclear what the tone of this explanation might be — if Jacob is justifying the road-side burial without even entering the town of Bethlehem, or if the larger issue of Rachel's absence from the Cave of Machpelah is the tacit subject here. Regardless, this verse, mirrored by an earlier verse that is part of the narrative itself, seems to pinpoint (more or less) the location of Rachel's tomb:

> And they journeyed from Beth-el; and there was still some way [*Kiv'rat Eretz*] to come to Ephrath; and Rachel travailed, and she had hard labor. And it came to pass, when she was in hard labor, that the midwife said to her: "Fear not; you shall have this son also." And it came to pass, as her soul was in departing — for she died — that she called his name Ben-oni; but his father called him Benjamin. And Rachel died, and was buried in the way to Ephrath — the same is Bethlehem. And Jacob set up a pillar upon her grave; the same is the pillar of Rachel's grave unto this day. (35:16–20)

One of the critical points of interpretation is the meaning of *Kiv'rat Eretz*. Although the Midrashim have used the phrase to identify the season of Benjamin's birth — based on various agricultural allusions in that abstruse phrase— most of the classical commentators understood it to be a measure of distance (see, *inter alia*, the comment of Ramban in its entirety). Given that, the most reasonable explanation of *Kiv'rat Eretz* is a "measure of land," i.e., a linear distance. Ramban originally understood it to be a long distance (the distance walked from sunrise until mid-morning meal-time); when he arrived in Israel and found the shrine erected in the current location of "Kever Rachel," he modified his approach and interpreted the term as "a small way" (perhaps a mile or two), as Ramban testifies: "now that I have merited to arrive in Jerusalem, I have seen with my own eyes that there is less than one Roman mile from Rachel's Tomb to Bethlehem." This would seem to seal the location of Rachel's tomb in the south.

The first problems we encounter are found in two disassociated passages in later books of the Bible, passages we shall dub "the northern passages," as they point to a location north of Jerusalem (in the territory allotted to Benjamin), and far north of the present-day "Kever Rachel."

THE "NORTHERN" PASSAGES

The two key passages that seem to support the "northern theory" are found in Jeremiah 31 and I Samuel 10.

> Thus says the Lord: A voice is heard in Ramah, lamentation, and bitter weeping; Rachel weeping for her children refused to be comforted for her children, because they were not. Thus says the Lord: Refrain your voice from weeping, and your eyes from tears; for your work shall be rewarded, says the Lord; and they shall come again from the land of the enemy. And there is hope for your future, says the Lord, that your children shall come again to their own border. (Jeremiah 31:15–17)

There are several towns named Ramah, including Ramah of Binyamin and Ramah of Ephraim (home and burial place of Samuel the prophet); Ramah of Binyamin was a transit stop where the exiles were taken on their way to Babylonia (see Jeremiah 40:1). If Rachel's voice is heard in Ramah, that may imply that that is the location of her grave.

The Targum and some medieval commentators explain Ramah as "heavens," which immediately dispenses with the problem. According to those who read it as the town of Ramah (and there is no town by that name anywhere in the vicinity of the Judean Bethlehem), the challenge may still be deflected. The text states that her voice is heard "in Ramah," not "from Ramah" (i.e., wherever she is, her voice is comforting the exiles who are presently in Ramah).

This passage is the lesser of the problems for the "southern theory," as has been shown. Nonetheless, it sits much more comfortably with a burial site for Rachel near Ramah than elsewhere.

BACKGROUND TO THE SECOND "NORTHERN PASSAGE"

The book of Samuel is devoted to the establishment of the Israelite monarchy. After seven chapters describing the birth and career of Samuel, the text shifts its focus to the preparation for a king. In Chapter 8, the people, noting Samuel's advancing age and his errant sons (who would, presumably, take over his role as leader), ask him for a king. At the end of the chapter of "The Rule of the King," Samuel sends the people home, promising them a king.

At the beginning of Chapter 9, we are introduced to Saul, a Benjaminite, who lives in Gibeah. Saul, a strapping young man with a great sense of filial loyalty, is trekking through the southern section of Mount Ephraim to find his father's donkeys who have strayed. At some point, his valet suggests that they visit the local "seer" who might be able help them find the donkeys. Samuel, in the meantime, is told by God that the awaited-king will be arriving on the morrow. When Saul, seeking prophetic guidance to find his father's donkeys, meets Samuel, looking for a new leader of the people, there is a sort of dialogic dissonance; Saul does not believe Samuel's words: "Am I not a Benjaminite, of the smallest of the tribes of Israel? and my family the least of all the families of the tribe of Binyamin? Why then do you speak so to me?" (I Samuel 9:21)

After Samuel invites Saul to be seated in the place of honor at the feast, he escorts the young Benjaminite and his valet out of town, and then:

> Then Samuel took a vial of oil, and poured it upon his head, and kissed him, and said, "Is it not because the Lord has anointed you to be captain over his inheritance? When you part from me today, then you shall find two men by *K'vurat Rachel* (Rachel's Tomb) in the border of Benjamin at Zelzah; and they will say to you, 'The donkeys which you went to seek have been found; and, behold, your father has ceased to care about the donkeys, and has become anxious about you, saying, What shall I do about my son?' Then shall you go on forward from there, and you shall come to Elon Tabor, and there you shall be found by three men going up to God to Bethel, one carrying three kids, and another carrying three loaves of bread, and another carrying a skin of wine; And they will greet you, and give you two loaves of bread; which

you shall receive from their hands. After that you shall come to the Gibeah of God, where the garrisons of the Philistines are; and it shall come to pass, when you have come there to the city, that you shall meet a company of prophets coming down from the high place with a lute, and a tambourine, and a pipe, and a lyre, before them; and they shall prophesy; And the spirit of the Lord will come upon you, and you shall prophesy with them, and shall be turned into another man." (I Samuel 10:1–6)

This passage is much more challenging and is the wedge used by anyone trying to promote the "northern theory." Samuel was speaking to Saul in Ramah (in Ephraim) and telling him about three wondrous things he would experience on his way home to Gibeah. Gibeah (identified with present-day Tel el-Ful) is also in the territory of Benjamin, a few miles southeast of Ramah. If he was going to meet people at Rachel's tomb on the way home, then not only is Rachel's tomb north of Jerusalem, but we can even identify, with some accuracy and confidence, its exact location.

Now that we've seen the four passages that mention, in one form or another, the location of Rachel's tomb, and noted that two of them seem to point us south of Jerusalem while two seem to point us north, how do we decipher them in some harmonious fashion and come to a conclusion about the location?

JEREMIAH AND THE RIVER "PERATH"

Our solution begins far from the passages that are central to the Rachel narrative and, a priori, quite a distance from either proposed location for her tomb.

In Jeremiah 13, we read of a command given to the prophet:

Thus says the Lord to me, "Go and get a linen girdle, and put it upon your loins, and put it not in water." So I got a girdle according to the word of The Lord, and put it on my loins. And the word of The Lord came to me the second time, saying, "Take the girdle that you have got, which is upon your loins, and arise, go to Perath, and hide it there in a hole of the rock." So I went, and hid it in Perath, as The Lord commanded me. And it came to pass after many days, that The Lord said to me, "Arise, go to Perath, and take the girdle from there, which I commanded you to hide there." Then I went to Perath, and dug, and took the girdle from the place where I had hidden it; and, behold, the girdle was spoiled, it was good for nothing. (vv. 1–7)

The working assumption, adopted by most of the classical commentators, is that the "Perath" here is the "famous" one (i.e., the Euphrates River).

This prophecy, in which Jeremiah is commanded to fulfill an action that will serve as a symbol of what will befall the people if they do not mend their ways (see the rest of the chapter) is not unusual in that particular regard. As Ramban (Genesis 12:6) explains:

> ... know that when [divine decrees] pass from a potential decree to a symbolic act, the decree will in any case be effected. It is for this reason that the prophets often perform some act in conjunction with the prophecies, just as Jeremiah command Baruch, his student: "And it shall be, when you have made an end of reading this book, that you shall bind a stone to it, and cast it into the midst of the Perath, and you shall say: Thus shall Babylon sink..." (Jeremiah 51:63–64). Likewise in the matter of Elisha when he put his arm on the bow [held by Joash, king of Israel]: "Then Elisha said: 'Shoot!'; and he shot. And he said: 'the Lord's arrow of victory, even the arrow of victory against Aram...'" (2 Kings 13:17)

The difficulty here is one of distance and geology. Is it reasonable that Jeremiah would be commanded to travel over 700 miles to the Euphrates River in order to fulfill this symbolic action, then return home, cover that distance again to retrieve the girdle, and return a second time? In addition, the Euphrates Valley is lush and green; there are no *S'la'im* (the word for rocks used in the verse) at water's edge.

Solving the "Perath" riddle will also, incidentally, help us understand the last passage cited by Ramban, where Baruch is told to cast the book into the "Perath." We will return to the problem and its solution after a brief but critical interlude.

ANCIENT TEXTS AND MODERN MINDS

As I mentioned in the introduction to this book, much has been made of the inevitability of a clash between traditional attitudes towards the text of the Bible and academic disciplines developed and honed over the past 300 years. Popular wisdom (an oxymoron if there ever was one) holds that no one who embraces the methodology of literary analysis on the one hand, and archaeology and its sister sciences on the other hand, could honestly maintain the traditional approach to the text. Put more bluntly, the common claim is that traditionalists must bury their collective heads in the sand in order to maintain their beliefs.

Nothing could be further from the truth. Much of this claim rests on faulty assumptions about both sides of the coin. Traditional approaches to the text vary, have some measure of flexibility, and are (at least in our tradition) far from "fundamentalist." Conversely, both literary criticism and archaeology are much more speculative than is commonly believed — there is much more eisegesis (reading into the text what the reader wishes to impute) than honest exegesis (inferring from the text that which is likely the true meaning).

When it comes to archaeology, there is a general confusion as to the nature and purpose of this area of the study of the past. Although 19th-century Biblical archaeologists were charged with the mission of disproving the German critics and establishing the veracity of the Biblical narrative, it never developed into a method of proving what did and didn't take place in the ancient world: to use findings to help understand the *realia* of that world; to find urban, climactic, numismatic (and so on) clues that would help to sharpen our view of the past as we know it; or to assist us in fine-tuning our understanding of the ancient world.

Those "new archaeologists" who have recently used their shovels to try to bury the Bible have, by and large, been discounted by their colleagues (and even their students), religious and secular alike.

In the meantime, those earnest and honest students of the Bible who are motivated by a true desire to understand the text — and it should be noted that there are many secular students of the Bible who approach it with reverence and a passion for uncovering its truths — have found that both literary criticism and the wonderful developments in the areas of literary analysis as well as the marvelous "underground life" revealed by the archaeologist's spade have done so much to help us understand the Bible on its own terms. The overwhelming majority of articles in academic journals that specialize in these areas of Biblical studies focus on identifying the ancient roots of levirate marriage (the sometimes compulsory marriage of a widow to one of her husband's brothers), the socio-religious background for the piercing of a slave's ear, and so on. Significantly, many of the claims suggested by the classical commentators, often ridiculed by an earlier generation of "academicians," have been substantiated by recent finds.

What was said earlier, as noted, holds true for all of those who love and revere the text on its own terms. For those of us who, in addition, understand the text to be Divine Writ, we take the passion for truth one critical step further. We not only enjoy gaining greater understanding and perhaps revealing the meaning of heretofore mysterious passages, but we also understand it to be a religious obligation of the highest degree. What can serve the communication of God's word to the world more than the proper elucidation of the text?

This must, of course, be undertaken with a great sense of humility and trepidation — but the knowledge that we are dwarfs standing atop the shoulders of the giants of the generations, guided by our tradition (so that we won't jump to the shoulders of some other giant) and very aware of our responsibilities as interpreters of the text (so that we will not forget upon whose shoulders we stand), gives us security and comfort, as well as a constant prod to delve further, ask more probing questions, and dig deeper to understand the text.

EPHRATH = BETHLEHEM

The textual cornerstone of the "southern theory" is the proximity to Ephrath, which is Bethlehem. As a starting point, it should be noted that there is more than one town named "Bethlehem" in the Land of Israel; Zebulun inherits, among its cities, the town of Bethlehem (Joshua 19:15), and Zebulun's territory is far to the north. This is easily understood, because a town was given the name "Bethlehem" due to its location amid wheat and barley fields (*lehem* means bread). The town was the central locus for trade and processing of wheat and barley (as highlighted in the book of Ruth). Hence, any area rich in grains would likely have, at its hub, a town named "Bethlehem."

One referent is notably omitted in the two passages in Genesis; when referring to the "famous" Bethlehem, the text often clarifies its identification by appending "Yehudah" (of Judea) (see, e.g., Judges 17 and 19). Both references in Genesis note the proximity of Bethlehem to Ephrath, but leave out the more familiar Yehudah. (See Chapter X, in the final section, for an explanation of why this would be a perfectly acceptable identifier.)

Instead of beginning our search from Bethlehem, let's start from the other marker in the verse, Ephrath.

A few miles north of Jerusalem, there is a spring that was, well into the 20th century, a main source of drinking water for the city. The spring is known by the locals as *Ein-Farah*, which most Biblical geographers and cartographers identify with the city of Parah mentioned among the cities of Benjamin (Joshua 18:23). It is not unreasonable to posit that Parah or Ein-Farah was alternatively called "Ephrath" (identical root and meaning: "פרה" means "fruitful").

Modern commentators (including those traditional students of the text who embrace the findings of cartographers, archaeologists, and the like in enhancing our understanding of the text) have long held that the "Perath" where Jeremiah was commanded to hide his girdle is none other than Ein-Farah (see *Da'at Mikra* to Jeremiah 13). This spring is bounded by the type of rocks called *S'la'im* in the Bible, and the obvious word association of "Parah" with "Perath" makes the symbolism that much more accessible. Hence, when Baruch is commanded to throw the scroll into the Perath, he actually threw it into the spring at Farah. Due to the morphological association, that could serve to symbolize the fall of Babylonia, bordered by the "other" Perath.

It is likely that this area, lush and well-watered, was surrounded by healthy and abundant crops and may have served as a "Bethlehem"—indeed, among the list of the returnees to Zion who returned to the cities of Benjamin in the 6th century BCE we find: "The men of Bethlehem and Netophah, a hundred and eighty eight." (Nehemiah 7:26) Thus, it is well within reason to suppose a town named "Ephrath" built around the spring of "Parah," a town that was later renamed "Bethlehem" on account of the grain processing center that developed around there. This would explain the phrase "Ephrath, the same is Bethlehem." The convention of place identification in the Bible is to first use the ancient name and then associate it — for the contemporary audience — with the later name. For example: "And the border passed along from thence to Luz, to the side of Luz — the same is Beth-el." (Joshua 18:13) The ancient name of the town was Luz until Jacob renamed it Beth-el. (Genesis 28:19)

In sum, we have found a likely candidate for Ephrath/Bethlehem in the area just north of Jerusalem, directly in the route of Saul's return home and very near the Ramah mentioned by Jeremiah.

JACOB'S ROUTE

The theory presented above was advanced by Nogah Hareuveni *z"l*, an important contributor to the study and understanding of the Bible. Hareuveni founded *N'ot K'dumim*, an outdoor educational center for the study of the *realia* of the Bible. In his commentary on the book of Jeremiah, Hareuveni addressed the problematic Ramah association in

Jeremiah and recalled, in a sort of nostalgic pastorale, a walk through the land of Benjamin before 1948 when he encountered the spring at Farah and was struck by the possible solution outlined in the previous section.

In promoting his theory, the author has to address another challenge from *realia*. The ancient road from Sh'khem to Hebron, which passes directly through Beth-El (today the Arab village of Beitin), remains atop the crest of the mountains in a fairly straight north-south line. That road also passes directly through Bethlehem of Judea. At the time of Benjamin's birth and Rachel's death, Jacob was moving, with his family, servants, and livestock, south from Beth-el towards Hebron (cf. Genesis 35:27). If we accept the southern theory, we understand the location — it's right on the route to Hebron. If, however, we buy into the "northern theory," what are Jacob and his camp doing several miles east — and downhill — from the main road?

Hareuveni argues that *realia* actually supports his contention. Jacob was not traveling alone; he had children, a pregnant wife, and lots of livestock. As Jacob himself said to Esau:

> And he said to him, "My lord knows that the children are tender, and the flocks and herds with young are with me; and if men should overdrive them one day, all the flock will die. Let my lord, I beg you, pass over before his servant; and I will lead on slowly, according to the pace of the cattle that goes before me and the children . . ." (33:13–14)

It would not be practical to march the camp directly on the hilltop route without finding a suitable spot for his beloved wife to give birth. Here, a few miles off the road, was the well-known spring of Farah, surrounded by its grape arbors and lush fields. Jacob undoubtedly left the road to bring his camp to Farah for this momentous event — the birth of his only son to be born in the Land, and the only one to be a "son of Israel" (the rest were all "sons of Jacob"—*B'nei Ya'akov*).

The text, however, testifies that she gave birth some distance from Farah — *Kiv'rat Aretz* — and herein lies the final mystery to be unraveled by Hareuveni's claim.

KUBUR BANI ISRA'IL

Approximately three miles west-northwest of Farah there were five identical stone structures, measuring about fifty feet by ten feet. ("Were" because one of them was taken down to make way for the bypass road – Route 60 – around Ramallah erected in the late 1980s.) These structures serve no obvious purpose — commerce, abode, or worship — and have always been called *Kubur Bani Isra'il* by the locals. I visited the site in 2001 — it is right off of the bypass road – and noted that it rests on the incline down towards Farah. For many years, archaeologists and students of the Land have wondered what to make of these structures and why the indigenous population (whose traditions of place names have been a critical key in unlocking the identification of Biblical sites) insisted that this was *Kubur Bani Isra'il* (i.e., *Kiv'rot B'nei Yisra'el,* the Graves of the Children of Israel). Prof. Yoel Elitzur (whose defense of the contemporary location of *Kever Rachel* is shared below) told me that while leading a tour of the site, an elderly Arab came by and when asked the name, he replied *"Kubur Bani Isra'il."* When asked the meaning of the name, he shrugged and said: "My grandfather called it by that name, his grandfather called it by that name. . . ."

Hareuveni's theory is like an onion; each mystery that unravels opens another, which in turn makes itself accessible. He suggests that *Kubur Bani Isra'il* is none other than the tombstone of *Kever Rachel*, which later generations of Jews used as a burial site.

According to this version of the "northern theory," not only do all of the verses fall into place — using our new, surprising, "northern" Bethlehem/Ephrath — but the identity of these odd structures suddenly becomes clear.

THE MIDRASHIC EVIDENCE

A number of Midrashim support the "northern theory":

1. "Why did our father Jacob see fit to bury Rachel on the road to Ephrath? He saw, through Divine inspiration, that the exiles will eventually pass by there; therefore, he buried her there so that she should beg God's compassion for them, as it says: 'A voice is heard in Ramah . . . .'" (Genesis Rabbah 82:10) The author of this Midrash seems to accept as a fait accompli that Rachel is buried somewhere north of Jerusalem, as that is the route taken by the exiles on their way to Babylonia, as noted earlier. We will return to this Midrash in our defense of the "southern theory."

2. Rabbi Meir states, "[Rachel] died in her son's territory [i.e., the territory of Benjamin]" (Sifri B'rakhah #11). Remember, from the earliest passage in Genesis, that Rachel gave birth, died, and was buried all in one

spot. If she died in what would later become Benjaminite land, then she was buried there. (That means that not only was Benjamin the only son to be born in Canaan, but he also was born in the territory that would be named after him and inherited by his descendants.) This suggestion of R. Meir augurs well for our "northern theory." We will yet return to this passage, as well as the Midrash about Rachel's placement as a sentinel for the departing exiles.

ELITZUR'S SOLUTION: LITERARY ANALYSIS PROVIDES GEOGRAPHICAL ACCURACY

Prof. Yoel Elitzur points out several difficulties in the "signs" given to Saul, the resolution of which not only maintains the popular location of *Kever Rachel*, but also provides added insight into the significance of that special place. The rest of this section is a synopsis of Prof. Elitzur's article.

There is one particular textual problem in the geographic marker used for the first "sign." "When you part from me today, then you shall find two men by *K'vurat Rachel* in the border of Benjamin at Zelzah." If the location of *Kever Rachel* was known at the time, why add the other geographic landmarks (the border of Benjamin, Zelzah)? If, conversely, the location of *Kever Rachel* was not well-known at the time (or to Saul), why incorporate it at all?

Several general problems emanate from these six verses. Many commentaries have understood them to be "wonders," in the sense presented above (to wit, three such odd things will happen exactly as the prophet foretold, thus fortifying his prophecy about the monarchy). This is difficult on several accounts: The word "*Ot*" (sign), as opposed to "*Mophet*" (wonder), generally means "indicator" (i.e., a wondrous event that has an inherent or symbolic connection to the event it purports to confirm). The signs are not presented as ancillary to Samuel's anointing of Saul; they flow directly from his declaration and seem to be a part of the consecration of the new king.

The overabundance of details (geographical and other) that are found in this foretelling of Saul's walk home is highly unusual and does not fit the common style of the Biblical narrative.

In order to understand the literary structure of the three signs, we will first analyze the last two, and then return to our point of departure, *Kever Rachel.*

Here again is the key passage:

> Then Samuel took a vial of oil, and poured it upon his head, and kissed him, and said, "Is it not because the Lord has anointed you to be captain over his inheritance? When you part from me today, then you shall find two men by *K'vurat Rachel* (Rachel's Tomb) in the border of Benjamin at Zelzah; and they will say to you, 'The donkeys which you went to seek have been found; and, behold, your father has ceased to care about the donkeys, and has become anxious about you, saying, What shall I do about my son?' Then shall you go on forward from there, and you shall come to Elon Tabor, and there you shall be found by three men going up to God to Bethel, one carrying three kids, and another carrying three loaves of bread, and another carrying a skin of wine; And they will greet you, and give you two loaves of bread; which you shall receive from their hands. After that you shall come to the Gibeah of God, where the garrisons of the Philistines are; and it shall come to pass, when you have come there to the city, that you shall meet a company of prophets coming down from the high place with a lute, and a tambourine, and a pipe, and a lyre, before them; and they shall prophesy; And the spirit of the Lord will come upon you, and you shall prophesy with them, and shall be turned into another man." (I Samuel 10:1–6)

Each sign shares some components:
1. Location (Elon Tabor, Gibeah)
2. Number of people (3, group)
3. Description of people (going up to Beth-el one with . . . and one with . . . and one with . . . , coming down from the altar with a lute and a tambourine and a pipe and a lyre)
4. Interaction with them (and they will greet you, and give you two loaves of bread; which you shall receive from their hands, And the spirit of God will come upon you, and you shall prophesy with them)

We would expect the first sign to follow this pattern, but it seems to deviate. Instead of there being a brief notation about the location where Saul would meet them, there is an overwhelming amount of information in that regard (by *K'vurat Rachel* in the border of Benjamin at Zelzah);

yet there is no description given of these men, unlike the pilgrims and prophets described in the second and third "*Otot*" (signs), respectively.

Without fully solving the "component imbalance" of the first sign (which we will do forthwith), a pattern begins to emerge that demonstrates the significance of these signs and their sequence. Note that each sign is introduced by Saul's progress: "When you part from me today . . . then shall you go on forward from there . . . after that you shall come to . . . ."

First he meets two, then three, then a whole group of people.

First "you shall find," then "you shall be found," and then "you shall encounter."

First "they will say to you" (Saul is passive), then "you shall receive from their hands" (Saul is active), then "you shall prophesy with them" (total joining).

We now see that we are not dealing with "*Moph'tim*" (wonders), but rather with signs that are indicative of the spiritual ascendance and progress of Saul. We also understand that the signs are part of the anointing of Saul. Saul grows from a "donkey-seeker" to a man imbued with God's spirit. The final phrase, "and [you] shall be turned into another man," is not part of the third sign; rather, it is the goal and summation of the entire process.

BACK TO KEVER RACHEL: SOLVING THE FIRST SIGN

As noted above, the first sign seems to deviate from the pattern of details found in the other two. There is too much geographic detail (and, in any case, the mention of *Kever Rachel* seems to be of no help or else should be sufficient) and no description of the two people he will meet there.

The Tosefta in Sotah provides an answer that seems, prima facie, to be a "weak" defense of the southern theory:

> . . . rather, [Samuel] said to him: Now, as I am speaking to you, they are at K'vurat Rachel. You are walking and they are coming and you will find them at the border of Benjamin at Zelzah. (Tosefta Sotah 11:7)

Having concluded our literary analysis, we see that this statement is not merely a defense of the popular location of *Kever Rachel*; it is also an astute observation about the three signs. The mention of *K'vurat Rachel* in the first sign is not a "geographic marker"; rather, it is the description of the two men, as follows:

Sign	Number	Location	Description	Interaction
I	2	Zelzah	At *K'vurat Rachel*	They will tell you . . .
2	3	Elon Tavor	Ascending to Beit-El	You will take from them
3	Group	Giv'ah	Descending from the altar	You will join them

The current presence of these men at *K'vurat Rachel* is not a way for him to find them, for they won't be there (south of Jerusalem) when Saul meets them; rather, they will be coming north, from *K'vurat Rachel*, and Saul will meet them at Zelzah.

We can now place the final piece into the puzzle of the signs of Saul: The progression is not only in number of people met, not only in the level of Saul's interaction with them, but also in the quality of the spiritual experience in which they are engaged. The final, ultimate experience is prophecy; a pilgrimage to a Sanctuary is also a spiritual experience, although one that falls short of prophecy. The visit to *Kever Rachel*, while not on a par with a visit to an altar, also has religious and spiritual implications and dimensions.

We now understand the great attention paid to detail in these verses; each component serves to fill out the sequential growth of Saul, until his spirit is captivated by prophecy.

Kever Rachel is, as indicated in Genesis, a few miles north of Bethlehem; the challenge verse from Jeremiah was rather easily answered. The more difficult challenge, from the prophecy of Saul's return home, was not only resolved, but we gained a deeper appreciation of the relationship between the three signs given Saul and his development into the first King of Israel.

POSTSCRIPT

As noted earlier, two Midrashim seem to support the "northern theory": R. Meir's statement that Rachel was buried in her son's territory, and the Midrash that explains Jacob's decision to bury Rachel on the road as motivated by his desire that she act as a sentinel for the exiles who would pass by.

Each of these, maintains Elitzur, can be understood as support for the "southern theory", as follows:

R. Meir's statement, when examined closely, is not an attempt to "re-locate" *Kever Rachel* north of Jerusalem; rather, it is an "expansion" of Benjamin's borders to include the area of Bethlehem. The dispute in the Sifri is not about the location of *Kever Rachel*; it is about the location (in which tribe's territory) of the Temple.

The second Midrash would seem to present a problem; as noted earlier, the exiles to Babylonia were taken northward from Jerusalem.

The authors of the Midrash who flourished in the shadow of the de-struction of the Second Temple often utilized verses referring to the first exile and destruction (586 BCE) as references to the persecutions of their own times. See, *inter alia*, the Introductions of Lamentations Rabbah.

Jerome, the early Church father and historian, in his commentary to Jeremiah 31, writes that after the quashing of the rebellion associated with Bar-Kosiba, the captives were taken by order of Hadrian to the great fair north of Hebron, where they were sold as slaves. Perhaps the Midrash in question is alluding to this tragedy, for indeed, they passed by *Kever Rachel* on the way to being sold into slavery.

How remarkable is it, then, that the *P'sikta* (2:3) has a slightly different version of our Midrash:

> I buried her there. Why? It was known to Jacob, that ultimately the Temple would be destroyed and his children would go into exile, and they would go to the Patriarchs [in Hebron] begging them to pray for them, and they won't help them. Once they will be on the road, they will come and embrace Kever Rachel and she will stand and beg God's compassion. . . .

AFTERWORD

One of the critical tools of interpretation is to know that which we know and to admit ignorance where appropriate — and we need not be afraid of where that admission may lead us. Our commitment to the covenant at Sinai does not waver even when we call into question a contemporary geographical identification; the engagement and involvement of trying to discover the harmonious resolution between conflicting reports led us north and south, to an archaeological mystery and topographical solution on the one hand and to a literary solution on the other.

XXI JOSEPH'S DREAMS
Entering the Character's World, Part II

INTRODUCTION

Our next two forays "Between The Lines" will take segments of a well-known story and reevaluate what we know about them, what we think we know about them, and what the text really tells us.

There are three stories in the *Parashot* that cover the life of Joseph:

1. **Descent**: (Chapters 37–41) Joseph's descent into the pit, his descent to Egypt and, ultimately, his descent into the Egyptian prison.

2. **Ascent**: (Chapters 42–44) His ascent to vice-regent of Egypt.

3. **Reunification** (Chapters 45–50) Joseph's reunification with his brothers and his father.

The most well-known stories regarding Joseph are found in the first part of the biography — his dreams and his successful interpretation of dreams. Yet there are a number of assumptions made by the casual reader and absorbed into exegesis that miss some major turning points in the story and that shroud significant developments within the characters presented to us. We will first read the lines, then read between them, and discover that much of what we thought we knew about Joseph, his father, and his brothers needs to be reevaluated.

As I've pointed out several times in earlier chapters, to properly understand the text, to be properly surprised or impressed by anyone's actions, we must read the narrative from the point of view of each of the characters – to the extent that the text, context, and external information allow. This will allow us to solve a mystery surrounding the story of Joseph, the Dream Interpreter.

These Chapters (comprising the weekly Torah portion of "*Parashat VaYeshev*") make up the first story of the Joseph cycle. They are "book-ended" with stories about dreams, both stories featuring Joseph as the central character. At the end of this story, we are told about Joseph's suc-

cess in the prison of the court of Egypt and of his insightful explanation
of the dreams of two of his fellow prisoners:

> And they dreamed a dream both of them, each man his dream, in one night,
> each man according to the interpretation of his dream, the butler and the
> baker of the king of Egypt, who were bound in the prison. And Joseph came
> in unto them in the morning, and saw them, and, behold, they were sad. And
> he asked Pharaoh's officers that were with him in the ward of his master's
> house, saying: "Wherefore look ye so sad to-day?" And they said unto him:
> "We have dreamed a dream, and there is none that can interpret it." And
> Joseph said unto them: "Do not interpretations belong to God? Tell them
> to me now." (40:5–8)

Joseph is confident about his ability to explain their dreams, and that
confidence is quickly validated, as each of his explanations is played out
in Pharaoh's court. The butler is restored to his position and the baker is
hanged. (40:21–22)

Where did Joseph get this confidence; indeed, where did he get the
ability to interpret dreams? The earlier dream sequence involving Joseph
in the beginning of this story (Chapter 37) posits Joseph not as a dream
interpreter, but rather as the dreamer. His brothers and father are the ones
who make inferences from his dreams – but he just reports them. When
did he learn how to explain dreams?

This question carries extra significance in light of the later story of
Joseph's redemption from prison. The butler finally remembers Joseph
and reports his successful dream interpetation abilities to Pharaoh. This
leads to Joseph's rise to greatness as a result of his explanation of Pharaoh's
dreams.

DREAMS AND REACTIONS

Methodological note: The reader is often surprised to find that he or she is
far wiser than any of the actors about whom he or she is reading, yet this is
a point repeated many times in the text. For instance, when Joseph and his
brothers meet in the next story (Chapters 41–44), we know who is who,
yet the brothers are ignorant of the true identity of the regent of Egypt.
Joseph is ignorant, as well, of the goings-on back in Canaan, although we
have been following that drama avidly and intimately.

The astute reader of Biblical narrative must always keep in mind what each of the actors knows so far as can be discerned from the text. Strange and surprising behavior can often be explained with this as background; conversely, conventional reactions suddenly loom as odd and disturbing when we factor in the essential compartmentilization of each character.

In order to understand Joseph's ability to interpret the dreams of the butler and baker — and then those of Pharaoh — let's look back at the first dream sequence at the beginning of the cycle:

> And Joseph dreamed a dream, and he told it to his brothers; and they hated him yet the more. And he said unto them: "Hear now this dream which I have dreamed: for, behold, we were binding sheaves in the field, and, lo, my sheaf arose, and also stood upright; and, behold, your sheaves came round about, and bowed down to my sheaf." And his brothers said to him: "Will you indeed reign over us? or will you indeed have dominion over us?" And they hated him yet the more for his dreams, and for his words. And he dreamed yet another dream, and told it to his brethren, and said: "Behold, I have dreamed yet another dream: and, behold, the sun and the moon and eleven stars bowed down to me." And he told it to his father, and to his brethren; and his father rebuked him, and said unto him: "What is this dream that you have dreamed? Shall I and your mother and your brothers indeed come to bow down to you to the earth?" And his brethren envied him; but his father kept the matter in mind. (37:5–11)

Joseph had two dreams: the dream of the sheaves and the dream of the stars. An in-depth study of the differences between these dreams—surely a worthy enterprise—will be taken up in a later volume. We do note, nevertheless, several significant differences in the reaction of his family members to the dreams. Resolving two questions about these reactions and one (seemingly) ancillary issue will help us understand Joseph's later confidence and ability as a dream interpreter:

1. Why did Joseph tell his brothers about his dreams? He already had a tempestuous relationship with them and, surely, relating these dreams would do nothing to reverse that trend.

2. When he told them that he had had the first dream (the dream of the sheaves) before informing them of the content, they hated him more than before (37:5). After he related the content of the dream, his brothers accused Joseph of plotting — or at least contemplating — a "takeover" of the family. After he related the second dream (the dream of the stars), they

had no reaction. Note that the dream of the stars is much more impactful than the dream of the sheaves in two ways:

a. Not only are the stars (brothers?) bowing down (akin to the blessing given to Jacob—27:29), but the sun (father?) and moon (mother?) are also bowing.
b. Unlike the first dream, where their sheaves bowed to his sheaf, the second dream had the stars, sun, and moon bowing to Joseph himself.

Nevertheless, the brothers remained silent in response to hearing this dream, although they were jealous. (37:11) Note that he related this dream twice; to his brothers and, later, to his father in their presence. Why didn't they react to the second dream either time?

3. The father, on the other hand, reacted to the second dream in the same fashion as the brothers' reaction to the first dream — yet he "kept the matter in mind" (i.e., he waited to see if it would be fulfilled). Why did Jacob simultaneously castigate his son for this "egocentric" dream, indicating a dismissive attitude towards it, while waiting to see if it would come to pass?

JACOB AND HIS BEN Z'KUNIM

Solving one other difficulty at the beginning of the Joseph narratives will set us on the path to a solution. As we are introduced to Joseph and the special relationship he had with his father, we are told: "Now Israel loved Joseph more than any of his other sons, *ki ven z'kunim hu lo* [because he was the son of his old age] . . . ." (37:3)

The commentators provide several opinions about the key phrase *ben z'kunim hu lo*. Rashi understands it as our translation indicates—since Joseph was born to Jacob when he was old, the father felt a special affection for him. Ramban challenges this interpretation on two points:

1. Joseph was apparently born not much later than Issachar and Zebulun.
2. The verse states that Jacob "loved Joseph more than *any* of his other sons"; the implication is that Jacob loved him more than Benjamin, who was born much later and when Jacob was much older.

The 2nd-century Aramaic translation known as "Onkelos" translates *ben z'kunim* as "wise child." Ramban points out the difficulty with this translation: The verse states *ki ven z'kunim hu lo*—he was a *ben z'kunim* to him (to Jacob). If *ben z'kunim* is rendered "wise child," then there is no need for the possessive *lo* afterwards. Clearly, the *ben z'kunim* position was not an objective description, rather it was relational to Jacob.

Ramban then offers his own explanation:

> The custom of elders was to take one of their younger sons as a servant, and he would lean on him at all times, never separating from him. He would be called "the son of his old age" (*ben z'kunav*) since he would serve him in his old age ... this is what they [the Rabbis] intended when they stated (Genesis Rabbah 84:8) "Everything that [Jacob] learned from Shem and Eber he passed on to [Joseph]," i.e., he transmitted to him the wisdom and secret teachings. ...

Following Ramban's explanation, Joseph had every reason to see himself as the heir of the Abraham-Isaac-Jacob tradition. As the closest and most favored recipient of Jacob's wisdom and tradition, Joseph understood that he was destined to experience some of the same events that befell his father — and to have a similar relationship with God. (See Rashi at 37:2, "... everything that happened to Jacob [also] happened to Joseph ...")

JACOB: THE FIRST DREAMER

Among our Patriarchs and Matriarchs, the only one who we are told had a dream was Jacob. Jacob dreamt not once, but twice – on his way out of the Land (28:12–15) and when being beckoned back (31:10–13).

It is interesting to note that the only other two dreams recorded in Genesis before Joseph were nearly identical occasions. God appeared to Abimelech (20:3–7) to warn him to return Abraham's wife to her husband. God then appeared to Laban (31:24) to warn him not to attack Jacob. These two dreams are not of a category with Jacob's or with the three remaining couplets of dreams — Joseph's, Pharaoh's stewards', or Pharaoh's. Those dreams contained a message about the future of the individual or his nation, not a divine intercession on behalf of the righteous.

It is reasonable to posit that Jacob related his dreams, their meanings, and their outcomes to Joseph. The favorite son, heir apparent to the tradition, had every reason to believe that if he dreamt a dream where the "message" of the dream was obvious, that he should regard it as prophecy and the word of God — just as his father experienced.

DREAMS AND VISIONS

We can now look through the first dream sequence and understand the different reactions of the brothers and Jacob, and what Joseph learned from them.

> And Joseph dreamed a dream, and he told it to his brothers; and they hated him yet the more. And he said unto them: "Hear now this dream which I have dreamed: for, behold, we were binding sheaves in the field, and, lo, my sheaf arose, and also stood upright; and, behold, your sheaves came round about, and bowed down to my sheaf." And his brothers said to him: "Will you indeed reign over us? or will you indeed have dominion over us?" And they hated him yet the more for his dreams, and for his words. And he dreamed yet another dream, and told it to his brethren, and said: "Behold, I have dreamed yet another dream: and, behold, the sun and the moon and eleven stars bowed down to me." And he told it to his father, and to his brethren; and his father rebuked him, and said unto him: "What is this dream that you have dreamed? Shall I and your mother and your brothers indeed come to bow down to you to the earth?" And his brethren envied him; but his father kept the matter in mind. (37:5–11)

It is clear from the preceding verses of this section that Joseph was engaged in a power struggle of sorts within the structure of the family (see Rashi and Ramban at 37:2). Joseph then experienced a dream with an obvious implication for that struggle and its (seemingly divinely mandated) outcome. He told the dream to his brothers, and they hated him even more just for telling them! He must have been confused by this (unless he wasn't aware of it), for why would they not be interested in hearing the word of God, especially as it affects them so directly?

When he relates the dream of the sheaves (only to his brothers—his father does not hear of it), they understand its implication and berate him for it. What did they find so offensive about his vision?

The verses do not indicate that the brothers disbelieved his dream, but that they were offended by it. The brothers had a piece of information that was not yet known to Joseph: Although their father Jacob is a prophet, and his dreams are indeed visions from God, that is no longer the case with the next generation. A dream may not necessarily be a vision; it may be the expression of subconscious desires and repressed urges (as conventional psychology maintains). The Talmud (BT Berakhot 56a) records two incidents where the local (non-Jewish) governor challenged one of our Sages to predict the content of his dreams on the coming night. In each case, the Sage described a detailed and horrific dream, which so preoccupied the governor that he dreamt about it that night.

An important distinction between a vision dream and a subconcious-based dream is in interpretation. If the dream is truly a prophecy, its meaning should be fairly evident, as it is not generated by the person's own subconcious. We need not be privy to the psychological makeup of the dreamer to understand the message. A conventional dream, as we are all aware, may take a great deal of sophistication to understand, although that is not always the case.

The brothers were not offended by the dream; rather, they were offended by the apparent cause of this dream. They believed that Joseph must be thinking about his takeover of the family so much that these thoughts had entered his dreams. Their derision and hatred is now clear — but why did they keep silent at the second dream?

Evidently, there was a tradition in the house of Jacob that although a single dream may be caused by internal thoughts and ruminations, if that same dream (or the same "message" clothed in alternate symbolism) occurs twice, it is no longer a happenstance — it is truly God's word. We find this approach explicitly stated by Joseph when he explains Pharaoh's doubled dream: "And for that the dream was doubled unto Pharaoh twice, it is because the thing is established by God, and God will shortly bring it to pass." (41:32)

When Joseph reported his second dream to his brothers, they did not "increase their hatred" at either the report of the dream or at the retelling of its content. The fact of the second dream — and its similar implication — was no longer reason for hatred, but rather for concern and jealousy.

Jacob, however, had heard nothing about the first dream. That is why he, upon hearing about Joseph's second dream, responded in an almost identical fashion as the brothers did to the first dream: "What is this dream you had? Will your mother and I and your brothers actually come and bow down to the ground before you?" (37:10)

At this point, Jacob surely expected his other sons to have a similar reaction, but they were silent. (As we see from the incident in Sh'khem [Chapter 34], these sons were not shy about speaking up in their father's presence; their silence here is telling.) After his rebuke, the Torah tells us that "his brothers were jealous of him, but his father kept the matter in mind." Jacob must have been surprised by the brothers' silence, and must

have figured that this dream was not the first one Joseph had shared. That
clued him in that there may be more to this dream than he first thought,
and therefore he "kept the matter in mind" (i.e., he waited to see if it
would be fulfilled).

Joseph learned a powerful lesson from this encounter: Even if a dream
is "just a dream" and not prophecy, this is only true when it is an isolated
incident. When the dream is repeated, this is a sign from God and must
be understood in that way.

We can now return to Joseph in the Egyptian prison and explain his
response to the butler and baker. When he learned that they had both
experienced significant and terrifying dreams in the same night, he understood that these were more than dreams. He reasoned that just like a
dream that occurs twice to the same person is more than a dream, similarly,
if two men sharing a fate have impactful dreams on the same night, their
dreams must be divine messages. His response, "Do not interpretations
belong to God? Tell them to me now," (40:8) is not presumptuous. He
was telling them that their dreams were more than "just dreams"—they
were in the province of God and, as such, would not need sophisticated
interpretation (as is the case with a subconscious-based dream). The
dreams would be fairly easy to understand, as indeed they were. Joseph
earned his reputation as an interpreter of dreams — and his ultimate
freedom and final rise to power —not by interpreting dreams at all! He
earned it by remembering the lesson from his father's house — that the
"doubled dream" is a mark of prophecy — and by applying it intelligently
years later in the Egyptian dungeon.

AFTERNOTE

Much of what may seem new in this explanation was achieved simply by
applying the first component of our methodology — always keeping an
eye on each actor as an independent character. What did Joseph know?
What did his father know? What did the brothers know? It is clear from
the odd reactions at the beginning of the story that there is a subtle shift
going on "Between The Lines" of what we are told; we only discover
the reason for that in Joseph's explicit words to Pharaoh regarding the
significance of a "doubled dream."

XXII JOSEPH'S BROTHERS
Asking the Right Question

INTRODUCTION

Another vital principle of *Parshanut* is to pay close attention to the larger scheme of things within the narrative. It is all too easy (and common) to be caught up in the solution of "local" problems (i.e., the meaning of words and phrases, inferences to be drawn from them, etc.) and to miss the larger issues that need to be addressed. We will continue looking at the Joseph story, take a step back, and ask a "global" question that will be answered only after attending, carefully and rigorously, to the nuances of the text.

JOSEPH'S BROTHERS IN EGYPT

The story of the encounter between Joseph and his brothers in Egypt is well known; however, a closer look at the text reveals some seemingly strange behavior on the part of the brothers. I would like to begin by posing two questions. Through a careful look at some of the events that led up to the stand of the brothers in Joseph's quarters, we will not only answer these questions, but also gain a clearer understanding of the debate between Joseph and his brothers.

> Now Jacob saw that there was corn in Egypt, and Jacob said unto his sons: "Why do you look one upon another?" And he said: "Behold, I have heard that there is corn in Egypt. Go down to that place, and buy for us from there, that we may live, and not die." And Joseph's ten brothers went down to buy corn from Egypt. (42:1–3)

Why did Jacob send nearly all of his sons down to Egypt? From everything we have ever heard about this family — going back to Abraham's first "ascent"— it is a wealthy family. This family (from Abraham to Isaac to Jacob to his twelve sons) has plenty of cattle, sheep, and slaves (but see ibn Ezra's treatment of Isaac's wealth at Genesis 25:34 and Ramban's critique ad loc.). Because Jacob was concerned that the way to Egypt was dangerous (which is why he didn't send Benjamin — see 42:4), why did he send *any* of his sons? Why not send some of the servants of the household or, at least, one or two sons with some slaves to carry back the grain?

When Joseph's brothers came down to Egypt, they were brought to the great viceroy (their brother) who was reputed to have great powers of clairvoyance (see 44:5, 15). The viceroy accused them — three or four times — of being spies (42:9–16). Finally, he agreed to allow them to come back to buy more grain (and to free their brother, Simeon), only if they would return with the younger brother of whom they spoke. (How the return with Benjamin would prove their honesty is not made clear by the text.)

The brothers knew that the viceroy was wrong about their being spies! As they averred, time and again, they were only interested in purchasing grain. Since the supposedly clairvoyant viceroy was so "off-base" about their motivations, how would he know if the "Benjamin" they brought back was really a younger brother? Why didn't the brothers find some young man, dress him up like a Canaanite (see Joshua, Chapter 9), and give him enough information to play the role of Benjamin? The viceroy—whose reputed powers of insight were obviously "smoke and mirrors"—would never know the difference between this "shill" and the real Benjamin! Why put their father through the heartbreak of sending Benjamin — and delay their next trip to the Egyptian grain center — when they could have avoided all of it with this ruse?

JOSEPH'S BROTHERS IN CANAAN

Before addressing these questions, let's look back at the events at the beginning of the Joseph cycle. There are two more questions I would like to ask about the brothers and their associations and location.

At the beginning of the Joseph story, we are told that Joseph had a special relationship with the four sons of Jacob's concubines. (Jacob's children were born of four different mothers: Reuben, Simeon, Levi, Judah, Issachar, and Zebulun shared Leah as a mother; Joseph and Benjamin were Rachel's sons; Gad and Asher were born to Zilpah, Leah's handmaid; and Dan and Naphtali were born to Bilhah, Rachel's handmaid.)

These are the generations of Jacob. Joseph, being seventeen years old, was feeding the flock with his brethren, being still a lad even with the sons of Bilhah, and with the sons of Zilpah, his father's wives; and Joseph brought evil report of them unto their father. (37:2)

Why did Joseph associate with the sons of the concubines? Rashi explains that the sons of Leah degraded him and so he built an alliance with the "lesser" sons of Zilpah and Bilhah. (See, however, Ramban's response ad loc.)

Furthermore, since Jacob lived in and around Hebron (see 37:1, 14), why were his sons shepherding his flock in the vicinity of Sh'khem, approximately sixty miles to the north? (37:12) The mountain range that extends from south of Hebron northwards to Sh'khem includes plenty of good grazing land — why was his flock so far away?

In sum, we have posed two "local" questions about the brothers' behavior on their descent into Egypt and two more going back to the original presentation of the family dynamic.

ONE LAST QUESTION

Within the spirit of "spreading the net far and wide" I would like to address a seemingly unrelated question about a verse in Deuteronomy. Deuteronomy represents Moses's farewell address, presented to the Israelites in the plains of Moab during the fortieth year after the Exodus (Deuteronomy 1:1–5). In the second chapter, Moses describes the military and political history of the surrounding lands, including that of Seir (southwest Jordan):

> And the Horites formerly dwelled in Seir, but the children of Esau succeeded them and they destroyed them from before them, and dwelt in their stead; as Israel did to the land of his possession, which the Lord gave to them.
> (Deuteronomy 2:12)

This verse challenges our traditional approach to Revelation and to the Mosaic authorship of the Torah. Moses is describing what had happened in Seir to the Israelites, and is relying on an event they knew well to illustrate it. How could the Joshuan conquest — which was a year in the future — serve as an illustrative model for them?

The devotees of the schools of Higher Biblical Criticism (see Chapter III) have a field day with this verse. Various traditionally oriented solutions (e.g., S'forno, Hizkuni), usually associated with the conquest of the lands on the East Bank of the Jordan (which had already happened), have been proposed, but they are all relatively weak because that land was never considered "*The* Land." This is a troubling verse that awaits a comfortable and traditional resolution.

THE FOURTH GENERATION

To solve this larger problem, which has a strong element of the polemic associated with it, we will need to step further back from the trees and survey the forest of Jacob's behavior upon his return home.

I have already pointed out that we, the reader, are somewhat wiser than any of the human characters in the Bible by virtue of our "prescience"; that foreknowledge is often an obstacle to proper understanding, as will be demonstrated below.

A careful reading of the activities of Jacob and his children, beginning after the successful reunion with Esau, reveals that this family had already begun realizing the promise given to their great-grandfather (Abraham), grandfather (Isaac), and father. Abraham was promised that his descendants — who would return after four generations — would inherit the Land (15:16). The divine promise to Abraham of the Land was not an immediate gift; rather, it was a commitment that the Land would eventually become the property of his descendants. By virtue of Isaac never having left the Land (see Genesis 26:1–4), God's promise to him was, similarly, one of potential and not to be actualized in his life. (Note that throughout their lifetimes, both Abraham and Isaac are considered "sojourners" or "strangers," and never settle anywhere within the Land. Note especially Abraham's self-description in his negotiations with Ephron [Genesis 23:4].) Jacob was given a similar promise on his way out of the Land (28:13), but from the wording in God's promise to him upon his return (35:12), it seems that the time had come for the promise to be realized. This is why Jacob requested to be freed from Laban immediately when Joseph — the fourth generation from Abraham (see below for explanation as to why none of the older sons would be considered a fourth generation)— was born (30:25). He had every reason to believe that the "Covenant between the Pieces" made with Abraham (Chapter 15) was about to become fully realized. Since we, the all-knowing reader, are fully familiar with the way the Covenant was actualized (servitude and Exodus), we barely give a thought to how Jacob would have thought about it — the pitfall of knowing too much.

Excluding Abraham's purchase of a (necessary) burial plot, Jacob was the first of our ancestors to actively try to settle the Land. Immediately after his successful rapprochement with Esau, he purchased land in Sh'khem (33:19). As a result of the Sh'khem-Dinah episode, Simeon and Levi, two of Leah's sons, conquered the town of Sh'khem (34:25).

We then come to an anomaly in Chapter 37. When the brothers (how many of them?) debate what to do with Joseph, Reuben speaks up and implores them not to kill him (37:22). It is reasonable that Judah, who later spoke up about the possible profit to be made from the sale of Joseph (v. 26), was not present when Reuben made his plea, or else why didn't Judah speak up then? Although the text is not clear about Judah's presence, Reuben certainly "disappeared" while Joseph was in the pit (v. 29: "And Reuben returned to the pit; and, behold, Joseph was not in the pit . . ."). Where did Reuben go?

In the next chapter, we read about Judah's "separate" life away from his brothers. There is a serious chronological problem with this story. If it took place immediately after the sale of Joseph (which is one way to read 38:1—see Rashi), we have seemingly irreconcilable information, as follows:

The text clearly tells us that no more than twenty-two years passed from the sale of Joseph until the reunion with his brothers. (Joseph was at least 17 when sold; he was 30 when brought before Pharaoh; there were 7 years of plenty and then, after 2 years of famine, the brothers were reunited.) In Chapter 38, Judah began a business relationship with a local Canaanite man, married a local woman, and had three sons with her (and the third son was significantly younger than the second — see 38:11). The oldest son married Tamar and died, the second son refused to fulfill his obligation to his dead brother and died, and the youngest son finally grew up (see 38:14). Tamar had relations with Judah and gave birth to Peretz and Zerach. In Genesis 46:12, we are told that the *children* of Peretz were among the group that came down to Egypt — no more than twenty-two years after the sale of Joseph! It boggles the imagination to suppose that Judah would marry and have children, marry those children off, then have his own children with Tamar and that those children would marry and have their own children – all within twenty-two years.

For this reason, Gersonides (among others) concludes that the Judah story occurred concurrently with the events in Chapter 37. In other words, while the brothers were still tending their father's flock as young men (early 20s), they (or at least Judah) were also entering into independent business relationships.

We know that Simeon and Levi had already conquered the city of Sh'khem, and that Judah's business took him to Chezib, near the "seam" between Philistine and Judean territory of later years (see 38:5). If Reuben was able to be away from the brothers (to tend to his own affairs) while they were in Dotan (near Sh'khem) and return to them, he must have also had some land and/or business in the north.

The picture that emerges is quite clear. The children of Leah were beginning to settle the Land, mostly in the north. Because of this, they shepherded their father's flock (evidently in rotation) near their own holdings in Sh'khem. Before going further, we can provide a clear and reasonable explanation for the enigmatic and troubling verse in Deuteronomy (2:12):

> And in Seir dwelt the Horites aforetime, but the children of Esau succeeded them; and they destroyed them from before them, and dwelt in their stead; as Israel did unto the land of his possession, which the Lord gave unto them. (Note the mention of Esau, Jacob's brother.)

The first conquest of the Land that God gave us was initiated not by Israel the Nation, but by Israel the man (Jacob). During the life of Jacob, he and his children (sons of Leah) began purchasing and/or conquering land in Canaan in order to fulfill the promise given to their family. Moses's illustration is indeed one from a familiar past, and is therefore instructive and enlightening.

THE SONS OF ZILPAH AND BILHAH

Why, then, is Joseph described as associating with the children of the concubines? Why aren't they also spreading out, building their families and their estates?

In order to understand this, we have to look at the different visions for the family held by Jacob and Joseph. Jacob clearly believed that the sons were not to be treated equally or seen as a unit; witness his request to return to Canaan upon the birth of Joseph, his allowing/encouraging only the children of Leah to build their own fortunes, and the special treatment he accorded to Joseph and Benjamin.

Jacob had every reason to adopt this approach. In his family, only one son (Abraham, Isaac, Jacob) was the torch-bearer of the tradition, while the other sons (Nahor, Ishmael, Esau) were rejected and given other destinies and legacies. Jacob reasoned that he would also have to choose one son who would be the next patriarch, and that the other sons would be given separate inheritances. The sons of Leah, being the children of a proper wife, were given the opportunity to conquer and settle the Land, because it was promised to their father and his children. The sons of Rachel — who would be the true heirs — would directly inherit Jacob's holdings. The children of the concubines, coming from "second-class" wives, would not inherit anything; rather, they would remain workers for the estate of Jacob, just as he worked for his father-in-law. Jacob's vision, based on his family's experience, includes no "Israelite Nation," just "Children of Israel."

This is why Joseph associated with the sons of Zilpah and Bilhah; as Jacob's workers, they would naturally stay close to home. Joseph was also close to home as he stood to inherit Jacob's holdings.

Joseph had a different perspective on the destiny of the family. His dream of the sheaves (Genesis 37:7) carried two messages that were offensive to his brothers, one explicit and the other implicit. Explicitly, the dream indicated that Joseph would be their ruler. Implicit in this vision is a united family/nation with one king. Following the vision of Jacob, there could never be a ruler over the brothers because they would not comprise a political unit that could be governed. Joseph's dream implied that they would eventually be united and share a common destiny.

THE BROTHERS IN EGYPT

Returning with the brothers to Egypt, let's look at the family's status and fortune. At the beginning of Chapter 42, we are told that Jacob asked all of his sons (except Benjamin) to go down to Egypt, "that we may live, and not die." Clearly, two major changes had taken place as a result of the famine. First, the sons had moved back to their father's house (or extended household), such that he could address them all at one time. Second, they were in danger of starvation. Their fortunes must have been lost (since they were shepherds, it stands to reason that the famine hit them especially hard), causing them to move back to the "empty nest"—and they likely had no slaves left to send. This was the first (of many) cycles of conquest and loss of the Land.

When the brothers came before Joseph, we are told that:

And Joseph knew his brothers, but they did not know him. And Joseph remembered the dreams which he dreamed of them, and said to them: "You are spies; to see the nakedness of the land have you come." (42:8–9)

What was it about his dreams that caused him to accuse them of being spies? What connection is there between the dreams he dreamt twenty-two years earlier and the presence of his brothers in his court?

When he saw Gad and Asher standing side by side with Reuben and Simeon, he understood that one of two changes had taken place in his family. Either Jacob had been persuaded that the Josephian vision of "The Israelite Nation" was correct and had unified his sons and convinced them that they had a common destiny (but, if so, where was Benjamin?). Or, the only other reasonable conclusion, they had lost their fortunes and had been drawn back together.

Here is where Joseph's brilliance and insight came into play. A person who has never known wealth is not enraged and made jealous by exposure to opulence. On the other hand, someone who had wealth and power — and lost it — has great difficulty in accepting the other's fortune with equanimity. Joseph knew that the brothers would feel jealous of his wealth and that of Egypt, and might be contemplating military action, at least internally, if not as an outright conspiracy.

When Joseph accused them of being spies, that charge must have hit a resonant chord inside of their minds and hearts. This *Tzaphnat Pa'ane'ach* (Joseph) must really be insightful to read our minds so adroitly! When he then took Simeon (one of the two "activist" brothers — see 34:25) from them, they must have been convinced that his "second sight" was legitimate and worthy of consideration. When he demanded that Benjamin be brought down, they had no choice but to fully comply, as this viceroy could see their thoughts, read their minds, and properly identify Benjamin as "the young brother of whom you spoke."

AFTERNOTE

What we've discovered in this chapter was achieved by applying the second rule of interpretation: In spite of our concern with detail, *stepping back and asking the global questions*. By noting the oddness in the behavior of Jacob's family, both in Canaan and in Egypt, we were able to read between the lines to follow the fortunes of the family.

XXIII JACOB'S BLESSING OF JOSEPH
Intra-Biblical Parshanut

INTRODUCTION

We are accustomed to thinking of commentary as existing outside of the text. Whether it be the homiletics of the Midrash, the linguistic concerns raised by ibn Ezra, the narrative subtext brought to light by R. David Kimhi, or the ethical instructions derived by Gersonides, commentary is separate from the text. This, of course, is the subtext of our entire work: identifying the roots of the commentary within the text itself.

Nonetheless, there are clear examples of internal commentary, where the text comments upon itself. Although it is easy to find examples of this within late Biblical literature (the greatest example being Chronicles, chiefly seen as a commentary on Samuel and Kings), there are even examples within the Torah.

Although it is harder to identify commentary within one book, there are numerous texts that are opaque "on location" but are explicable by finding a parallel text that reveals much.

In this chapter, we will assay a challenging text from the end of Genesis, and identify a "mirror text" earlier in the book. We will then use that earlier text to clear up some of the difficulties in the latter text.

JACOB'S BLESSING OF JOSEPH

One of the most famous deathbed scenes in our literature involves Jacob's blessing of Joseph and his sons:

"They are the sons God has given me here," Joseph said to his father. Then Israel said, "Bring them to me so I may bless them." Now Israel's eyes were failing because of old age, and he could hardly see. So Joseph brought his sons close to him, and his father kissed them and embraced them. Israel said to Joseph, "I

did not expect to see your face; and here God has let me see your children also."
Then Joseph removed them from his father's knees, and he bowed himself
with his face to the earth. And Joseph took both of them, Ephraim on his right
toward Israel's left hand and Manasseh on his left toward Israel's right hand,
and brought them close to him. But Israel reached out his right hand and put
it on Ephraim's head, though he was the younger, and crossing his arms, he
put his left hand on Manasseh's head, since Manasseh was the firstborn. Then
he blessed Joseph and said, "May the God before whom my fathers Abraham
and Isaac walked, the God who has been my shepherd all my life to this day,
the angel who has delivered me from all harm, may he bless these boys. May
they be called by my name and the names of my fathers Abraham and Isaac,
and may they increase greatly upon the earth." (Genesis 48:9–16)

This famous deathbed scene is etched into our consciousness and is re-
played in Jewish homes every Friday night when we bless our children:
"May God make you as Ephraim and as Manasseh." (ibid., v. 20)

Upon close inspection, there are a few anomalies regarding this narrative, which are worthy of our attention:

- Why did Jacob embrace and kiss his grandchildren before blessing
  them? We don't find him doing this with his own children in the
  subsequent blessing scene (Chapter 49).
- Why does it matter which hand is used to bless the "more deserving"
  child?
- If Jacob wanted to raise the position of Ephraim over that of Manasseh,
  why didn't he insist that they switch positions; why cross his hands?
  (This question is exacerbated by the end of verse 14 — he crossed his
  arms because Manasseh was the firstborn: Why is Manasseh being
  the firstborn a reason for crossing his arms?)
- Why did Jacob prefer Ephraim to Manasseh, giving him the greater
  (right-handed) blessing? When challenged by Joseph, his response
  was: "I know it, my son, I know it; he also shall become a people, and
  he also shall be great; Nevertheless, his younger brother will be greater
  than he, and his descendants will become a multitude of nations" (v.
  19); however, this response is enigmatic and puzzling. If Jacob had
  indicated that Ephraim was more worthy, more saintly, or otherwise
  more deserving, we could understand. His answer indicates anything
  but that; it seems that Jacob has elected to "go with the winner" and
  support the son who is destined for greatness. What can we make of
  his response and his thinking?

- What was the blessing with which Jacob blessed his grandchildren while he had his hands on their heads? The text indicates that as he placed his hands on their heads, he blessed Joseph (regarding their well-being) — but not them!

FLASHBACK: ISAAC'S BLESSING

Even a cursory reading of our text quickly brings to mind another blessing scene in Genesis, which we assayed earlier: Isaac blessing Jacob in the guise of Esau, followed by the actual blessing received by Esau.

In both scenes, the one who bestows the blessing (Isaac, Jacob) suffers from poor eyesight, he embraces the recipient(s) of the blessing, and the text of the blessing is not mentioned in the text (see 27:23 and v. 27 carefully). More accurately, each scene includes two blessings (v. 23 and 27; 48:15 and 20), neither of which is explicitly presented in the text.

There are several questions to be asked about the narrative in Chapter 27 (in addition to the parallel questions we have already raised from Chapter 48), the resolution of which will help us understand Jacob's behavior with his grandsons:

- Why was Rebekah so concerned that Jacob get that particular blessing, even at the risk of his being cursed instead?
- What is the relationship, if any, between Jacob's purchase of the *b'khorah* (right of the firstborn) at the end of Chapter 25 and his deceptive taking of the blessing in Chapter 27?
- To paraphrase Esau's question (27:38), did Isaac have only one blessing to bestow? Why couldn't their father have repeated the same blessing — or given one of equal worth — to Esau?

THE B'KHORAH: WHERE DID IT GO?

I'd like to ask one more question before beginning to decipher our text.

As we see from Jacob's gift of a double portion (Ephraim and Manasseh) of land to Joseph, he was given the financial benefits of the *b'khorah* (see Deuteronomy 21:17). The verse in 1 Chronicles states:

> And the sons of Reuben the first-born of Israel — for he was the first-born; but, because he defiled his father's bed, his birthright was given to the sons of Joseph the son of Israel, yet not so that he was to be reckoned in the genealogy

as first-born. For Judah prevailed among his brethren, and of him came he who is the prince; but the birthright was Joseph's. (5:1)

Besides the financial benefits of the *b'khorah* (double inheritance), there seems to be a second component inherent in the *b'khorah* — political power. The verse indicates that although the financial rights of Reuben's *b'khorah* were bestowed to Joseph, the political component was given to Judah, who became prominent among his brothers. The Midrash (Aggadat B'resheet #83) adds a third dimension to the *b'khorah* — *Kehunah* (priesthood). (This is further demonstrated by the "switch" of these rights and responsibilities to the Levites [Numbers 3:41], where it is clear that representation at worship was the duty of the firstborn; see also *Onkelos* at Genesis 49:3.)

In other words, until Sinai, the firstborn in a family would inherit three rights:

• Double inheritance
• Political control over the family
• Representation of the family at sacrificial rites

On his deathbed, Jacob gave the financial-*b'khorah* to Joseph and the political-*b'khorah* to Judah, but who received the worship-*b'khorah*?

KEHUNAH: THE LEGACY OF EVERY FAMILY

The families of Abraham and Isaac did not follow the ideal pattern for Jewish family life; in each case, only one son was chosen to carry on the tradition of the family and the rest were sent away. The conventional understanding is that the first proper family within our tradition was that of Jacob; twelve sons, all included and all maintainers of the tradition. We therefore expect the firstborn (Reuben) to be accorded the usual rights appropriate for that position, and are surprised to see them taken away from him.

I'd like to propose another way of understanding Jacob's family. Just as Abraham and Isaac's job was to raise one son to follow in their respective footsteps, similarly Jacob had the responsibility to raise twelve sons to build upon the tradition he received. In other words, he was not raising one family, with the eldest occupying the conventional position of *b'khor*; he was raising twelve families, each of which would have their own *b'khor*. (Although Reuben is called the *b'khor* of Jacob (e.g., 35:23), this may be referring to simple birth order, not to position within the family.) This explains how Jacob "transferred" the *b'khorah* to Joseph, something that is forbidden in Deuteronomy (see 21:17 again). He wasn't eliminating a *b'khor*, he was simply appointing the family headed by the financial wizard among the sons as "chief financial officer" of his estate (Canaan). In the same way, he appointed Judah, who had earned the allegiance of his brothers, as the family that would rule over the other families — but only with regard to those issues that affect all twelve as a unit. Within each family, the *b'khor* would hold both financial and political rule. Regarding the *Kehunah* — the spiritual *b'khorah* — that remained within each of the sons of Israel and became the responsibility of each of their firstborn sons.

s'mikhah: embrace and transmission

R. Obadia Sforno (48:18), in explaining the importance of the right hand in Jacob's blessing, states:

> Since "laying of the hands" (*s'mikhah*) with the hand focuses the spirit toward the object upon which it is placed, as he placed his hands upon him [referring to Moses's *s'mikhah* of Joshua — Numbers 27:23] and the right hand is [generally] stronger than the left, therefore the *s'mikhah* of the right [hand] will focus more than the *s'mikhah* of the left.

S'mikhah is a law that first appears in the beginning of Leviticus: "*v'Samakh Yado* [And he shall lay his hand] upon the head of the burnt-offering." (1:4) The requirement of *s'mikhah* is such that in the case of any private offering, immediately prior to slaughtering the animal, the owner of the offering must lay his hands on the animal with all of his strength. In his explanation of the meaning behind animal offerings, Ramban (Leviticus 1:9) suggests that the person bringing the offering should view himself as if he were on the altar. The catharsis of offerings is achieved when the owner experiences his own sacrifice vicariously through the offering. *S'mikhah*, performed immediately before the offering is slaughtered, is the process by which the owner transmits his energy into the animal in order that the offering truly represent him on the altar.

(On the point of *s'mikhah* with all of one's strength: Think of how powerfully we hug a close friend or loved one at times of great sadness or joy, and compare it to how we hug a casual acquaintance when the occasion calls for it.)

There is another *s'mikhah* in the legal corpus besides that preceding an offering. As Sforno points out, when Moses was preparing to transmit the mantle of leadership to Joshua, he performed *s'mikhah* on Joshua, laying his hands on Joshua's head. Following Sforno's reasoning, Moses was transmitting his energy/self to Joshua, investing him with (at least) a connection to Moses's experience atop Sinai. Through the 1400 years when *s'mikhah* was operative[26] (see BT Sanhedrin 14a), each recipient of *s'mikhah* was given a piece of the experience of Moses at Sinai, along with all of the others in the intervening chain. Each recipient had a direct link to the Revelation at Sinai and to the fount from which the Oral Law springs.

THREE TYPES OF BLESSINGS

Before Sinai, there were three types of blessings bestowed by people:

- The conventional well-wishing blessing (e.g., Genesis 47:7, 10).
- The designation-blessing (e.g., Chapter 49, where Jacob gave his children a blessing, which was, essentially, his last will and testament). This designation-blessing was an assignment of duties, properties, and the like within the family.
- The conferral-blessing, which was the model for the post-Sinaitic *s'mikhah*. Unlike a well-wishing blessing, in which the person who is most deserving gets the finest "wish," this blessing is a real conferral of power and strength to the recipient. Since this conferral-blessing was a highly charged emotional experience, reflecting a deep connection between the two parties involved, in order for it to be effective, the bestower had to first have a direct connection to the recipient. Sforno (Genesis 48:10) explains that Jacob requested that Joseph bring his sons close in order to embrace them. The embrace was intended to create the proper emotional and spiritual connection between them to make the conferral-blessing effective.

We can now address those questions we asked about the Isaac-Jacob-Esau scenario:

Rebekah was aware that Jacob had purchased the rights of the first-born

---

26. The transmission of authority via *s'mikhah* was ceased during the Hadrianic persecutions; according to the report in the Babylonian Talmud, R. Judah b. Bava was the last sage to confer authority on a subsequent generation. See BT Avodah Zarah 8b.

(*b'khorah*) from Esau, meaning that he would be "in charge" of the family affairs, both financial and political. (Isaac was evidently unaware of the sale — see 27:19.) The person in charge is in the greatest need of support and strength; there are always those who would overthrow him and he has nowhere to go but down. The "underdog," in contrast, can only move up. Rebekah was so concerned that Jacob should receive Isaac's strength and power through the conferral-blessing that she was willing to risk the possibility of a curse.

When Jacob approached Isaac, his father embraced him (27:22), attended to his voice (ibid.), and "blessed" him. (This is apparently a conferral-blessing, as there are no blessing words provided here.) Isaac then ate and drank of the venison brought by Jacob, embraced him again, smelled his clothes, and "blessed" him again (vv. 25–27). Note that Isaac connected with Jacob using all four available senses. Subsequent to these blessings, which I am theorizing are both occasions of *s'mikhah*, Isaac stated:

> May God give you of the dew of heaven, and of the fatness of the earth, and plenty of grain and wine. Let peoples serve you, and nations bow down to you. Be lord over your brothers, and may your mother's sons bow down to you. Cursed be everyone who curses you, and blessed be everyone who blesses you. (27:28–29)

These words are not the blessing, as he has already blessed Jacob. Rather, these words represent a verbal version of the strength he has given his son; to wit, he is affirming in words that which he has already transferred by hand. Not only has he transmitted the ability to receive God's bounty, but also the strength to rule over his brother!

There is a textual hint to this idea. In 27:37, Isaac declares: "Behold, I have made him lord over you and have given all of his brothers to him as slaves – and with grain and wine *s'makhtiv* (I have sustained him) . . ."; Note that Isaac himself states that he has performed a type of *s'mikhah* on Jacob!

It is no wonder, then, that Isaac is "out of blessings" when the real Esau shows up! How can he give the same ruling strength to two people? The best that he can do is to give Esau the strength that ". . . when you break loose, you shall break his yoke from your neck." (v. 40)

EPHRAIM AND MANASSEH (REDUX)

We can now go back to the scene at Jacob's bedside and understand it in a new light:

* And Joseph said unto his father: "They are my sons, whom God has given me here," Then Israel said: "Bring them, to me so I may bless them." (48:9) Jacob wanted to confer the strength of leadership on Joseph's family.

* "Now Israel's eyes were failing because of old age, and he could hardly see. So Joseph brought his sons close to him, and his father kissed them, and embraced them."(v. 10) In order to confer this strength, he had to first connect with these two sons of Joseph, which he did by embracing them.

* "Israel said to Joseph, 'I did not expect to see your face; and here God has let me see your children also.' Then Joseph removed them from his father's knees, and he bowed himself with his face to the earth." (vv. 11–12) Here we see that the original embrace (v. 10) was merely a preparation for the blessing, not the blessing itself.

* "And Joseph took both of them, Ephraim on his right toward Israel's left hand and Manasseh on his left toward Israel's right hand, and brought them close to him. But Israel reached out his right hand and put it on Ephraim's head, though he was the younger, and crossing his arms, he put his left hand on Manasseh's head, since Manasseh was the first-born." (vv. 13–14) Since Manasseh was the firstborn, he would always maintain that status and would be the spiritual leader of that family. Manasseh's position in the family necessitated that he not be switched to the left side, so in order for Jacob to give Ephraim the "stronger" blessing, he had to cross his arms.

* "And he blessed Joseph, and said: 'The God before whom my fathers Abraham and Isaac did walk, the God who has been my shepherd all my life to this day, the angel who has delivered me from all harm may he bless these boys. May they be called by my name and the names of my fathers Abraham and Isaac, and may they increase greatly upon the earth.'" (vv. 15–16) Note that here he is *blessing Joseph, not Joseph's sons*; this is a well-wishing blessing, not the gist of the conferral-blessing given to Ephraim and Manasseh.

* "And when Joseph saw that his father laid his right hand on the head of Ephraim, it displeased him; so he took his father's hand, to remove it from Ephraim's head to Manasseh's head. Joseph said to his father, 'Not so, my father! Since this one is the firstborn, put your right hand on his

head.' And his father refused, and said: 'I know it, my son, I know it; he also shall become a people, and he also shall be great; Nevertheless his younger brother shall be greater than he, and his offspring shall become a multitude of nations.'" (vv. 17–19) This (previously) enigmatic response is now clear. Jacob is not "favoring the winner"; he is giving the greatest strength (his right hand, following Sforno's explanation) to the son who will need it most — whose progeny will be more numerous and widespread.

* "And he blessed them that day, saying: 'By you Israel will invoke blessings, saying, 'God make you like Ephraim and like Manasseh.' " So he put Ephraim ahead of Manasseh." (v. 20) Again, as in the Isaac-Jacob story, a second embrace leads to a second conferral-blessing. Jacob then verbalizes a consequence of the blessing: that these two boys will be the model of all blessings. This is, however, not the essence of the blessing, which is the conferral of power.

POSTSCRIPT

The Midrash Tanhuma indicates that "his younger brother shall be greater than he" refers to Joshua, who will come from the tribe of Ephraim and will conquer the Land. Interesting, is it not, that this *s'mikhah* was a forerunner to the first "official" *s'mikhah* given — as Moses lay his hands on the head of Joshua and conferred upon him the mantle of leadership.

AFTERWORD

Often, to quote the Rabbinic maxim, "words of Torah are poor in one place and rich in another." By finding parallel and associated passages, we are able to shed light on each of them, as they inform each other and us to discover what lies between the lines.

AD KI YAVO SHILO
The Riddle of Judah's Blessing Genesis 49:8–12

יהודה אתה יודוך אחיך ידך בערף איביך ישתחוו לך בני אביך:
גור אריה יהודה מטרף בני עלית כרע רבץ כאריה וכלביא מי יקימנו:
לא יסור שבט מיהודה ומחקק מבין רגליו **עד כי יבא שילה [שילו]** ולו יקהת עמים:
אסרי לגפן עירה ולשרקה בני אתנו כבס ביין לבשו ובדם ענבים סותה סותו:
חכלילי עינים מיין ולבן שנים מחלב:

INTRODUCTION

These five verses, comprising Jacob's deathbed "blessing" of Judah, have long been the focus of many a scholarly study; both the intimations of royalty alluded to in the middle verse as well as the geographic and agricultural markers seemingly identified in the final verse have been discussed, analyzed, utilized and, exegetically (as well as homiletically) interpreted by both classical as well as modern scholars.

I'd like to focus our attention on the curious mention of שילה (*qeri* שילו) in the middle verse. I will present a brief survey of the scholarship until this point and then suggest an alternative understanding of the mention of שילה here – a suggestion that will be premised on several larger points about the history (and *ur*-history) of the Israelites as well as an observation about the socio-political makeup of the people during the key periods which impact on this blessing: Jacobite settlement, enslavement-Exodus, and conquest-settlement of the Land.

- עד כי יבא שילה – A SURVEY OF THE SCHOLARSHIP

The mention of שילה is, broadly speaking, interpreted in two ways; the first, adopted by a few of the classical commentators, is as the name of the town in the territory of Ephraim that would later house the Tabernacle (Joshua 18:1, 1 Samuel 1–4, Jeremiah 7:12). The second is, briefly put –

not that town; i.e. a range of interpretations that read שילה as something besides a toponym.

We will briefly survey the range of approaches that read שילה as something besides the toponym. Every one of these interpretations is anchored in Midrashic literature. Citations follow the synopsis of each commentator below.

The Rabbis (BT Sanhedrin 98b) suggest that שילה may be a name – but a proper name, that borne by the Messiah.

Saadiah Gaon suggests that שילה is a poetic form of שלו – i.e., "that which is his," alluding to monarchic rule. (Gen. R. 98:8, 99:8). (LXX [the Septuagint] seems to have the same read). Onkelos seems to combine the suggestion from Sanhedrin with this, interpreting it as "until Messiah will come, to whom the monarchy belongs."

Rashi, after citing that interpretation, quotes the Midrash, supporting its contention from Psalm 76:12, that שילה is a compound of שי לו – gifts will be brought to him (gifts here understood as tribute). (*Pesikta Zutra* Gen. 49)

R. Abraham ibn Ezra proposes four different interpretations – underscoring the challenge of interpreting this verse. He first quotes the שלו ("that which is his") take – already mentioned by Saadiah and Rashi; he then suggests two variations on the word both meaning "child" or "offspring" (שליא or שליל) and, for his final take, he cites those who interpret it about the city of Shiloh. We will return to this interpretation. (*Peskita Zutra*, ibid.)

Other commentators, including R. Joseph Bekhor Shor, Radak and Gersonides, either adopt one of these approaches or read שילה as the place-name – with surprisingly creative and varied twists – as outlined below.

R. Obadiah Seforno does add a new etymological wrinkle: he proposes that שילה is a compound of two words – שלו (as in "bottom") and שלום – that the Judean descendant will have endless (bottomless) peace in his day. This is, as far as I can tell, unattested in any earlier work and is apparently Seforno's innovation.

- עד כי יבא שילה – "UNTIL HE COMES TO SHILOH"

Although nowhere in Rabbinic literature is the verse explicitly interpreted as referring to a particular place – the town of Shiloh – an interpretive tradition exists which supports this read.

It is no surprise that the first commentator to suggest that שילה refers to the town is ibn Ezra (although he indicates that "some interpret it as," he doesn't tell us who these commentators are); he then assumes that it means "until Shiloh is destroyed" – כי יבא being read as בא השמש (the setting of the sun), i.e., that Judah's time will not come until Shiloh's time is over. He supports this from the verses at the end of the historiosophic Psalm 78. The difficulty with this explanation is that the promise of Judean rule is given as lasting *until* שילה (in this case, until its destruction) and not commencing at that point. In other words, שילה is an end-point for Judean rule, not a beginning, as ibn Ezra would have us read it.

Rashbam, again to no one's surprise, adopts the "straightforward meaning" of the verse (as referring to the town) and addresses our challenge admirably. He understands that Judah will indeed rule *until* coming to Shiloh; he explains this as referring to Rehob'am (Solomon's son), when he came to the city of Sh'khem (Rashbam: it is near Shiloh) to be crowned as the third Judean monarch. At that point, the people demanded that he lower taxes, he took the (bad) advice of his boyhood chums and threatened to raise taxes even more, at which point, the people rebelled and that was, for all intents and purposes, the end of the united Judean empire. All of this is explicit in the text of I Kings 12.

The difficulties with this approach (from a traditional perspective) are, essentially, two: The lack of any mention of שילה as a significant location anywhere in the Patriarchal narratives makes the sudden interjection of this locus a bit jarring. Secondly, as Rashbam himself accedes, Shiloh is *near* Sh'khem, but is *not* Sh'khem. We might be tempted to defend Rashbam by asking us to consider Jacob's prophecy as approximate – as we find in the case of many Divinely given prognostications (see BT Berakhot 55a). This is difficult, however, as Sh'khem was a well-known and centrally located town that played a great role in Jacob's settlement period (Gen. 34; see the allusion at Gen. 48:22) and he would hardly have "missed" it by a few miles and mentioned Shiloh in its stead.

R. Hizqiyah b. Manoah ("Hizquni," c. 1250–1310, France) paraphrases Rashbam's comment and adds a helpful piece which addresses the problem we raised above – that the kingdom will belong to Judah until such time as it is torn away by the directive of the prophet, Ahiyyah, who hailed from Shiloh (hence, "Ahiyyah haShiloni" 1 Kings 11:29). Ahiyyah is the prophet who encountered Jeroboam and anointed him, tearing the garment into twelve symbolic pieces and announcing the Divine punishment of the cessation of the majority of the nation from Judah's rule (ibid., v. 30).

Another innovative approach to the mention of Shiloh here was advanced by R. Hertz Homburg (1749–1841) in his "Hakorem."[27] The reference to Shiloh is aimed at Samuel the prophet, born of his mother's fervent prayers at Shiloh (1 Samuel 1) and who would be the prophet to anoint a king from the house of Judah (hence, the nations "gathering" is a reference to the tribes gathering at Ramah to demand that Samuel "give us a king" [1 Sam. 8:4–5]).

- אשר יקרא אתכם באחרית הימים

Earlier in this essay I suggested that the vast range of comments on our verse can be divided into those that see שילה as the name of the town (or a reference to events taking place there) and everybody else (with a spectrum of interpretations and meanings). I would like to propose that there is another binary division that may make more sense in assessing the exegetical history of this passage: between those who see Jacob's prophecy as "long-range" (i.e. alluding to Messianic times) and those who view it as "short-range" – in other words, relating to either the Exodus and subsequent conquest or to the later (by approximately 400 years) division of the kingdom at Sh'khem.

In and of itself, the premise raises a thorny problem – why are we to assume that Jacob's words here were prophetic at all? He opens the session by informing his sons that he wants to tell them "what will befall you at the end of days" – but nothing in his words seems to speak to any apocalyptic scenario; indeed, his first two addresses (to Reuben and to Simeon and Levi together) address these sons' wayward behavior, Jacob's disapproval, and his subsequent acts to remove or limit their power. Jacob's words to Zebulon, Dan, Gad, and Asher seem to be futuristic, but may be supporting the particular talents each of these sons has demonstrated in their lives; Zebulon as (potentially seafaring) merchant, Dan and Gad as fighters, and Asher as provider of precious goods. The blessings to both Naphtali and Issachar seem to be directed towards their own abilities – as fleet of foot and diligent at work, respectively. His blessing to Benjamin, again, seems to have no meaning (nor realization) as a prophecy aimed at near or distant future. Indeed, the only other long blessing goes to Joseph – and that is descriptive of his attractiveness, travails, and ultimate position among his brothers.

---

27. vol. 1; pub. Wien, 1861

Therefore, we might want to reexamine the blessing given to Judah in this context and read it as descriptive and directive – and not prophetic – and to then interpret our passage along those lines.

- לכו נא אל מקומי אשר בשילו

Before proposing a solution to the riddle of "Shiloh" in our verse, I'd like to suggest that the significance of that Ephraimite town itself needs to be explored.

The establishment of the sanctuary and tabernacle at Shiloh is noted in Joshua 18:1. Before that point, with the exception (it will be argued) of our verse, Shiloh is not yet mentioned – nowhere else in the Five Books, and only as a border marker ("*Ta'anat Shiloh*") in Joshua 16:6. No reason is given for the establishment of the "place that God will choose to make His name dwell" at Shiloh; perhaps a proper explanation of our verse will also provide the rationale for Joshua's selection.

We often think of the relationship between the nation and the Land – and specific *loci* in the Land – as beginning primarily with the conquest under the leadership of Joshua. Of course we are all aware that Jacob "renamed" Luz to Bethel, that all of the patriarchs lived in both Hebron and Beersheba. Yet we don't typically associate settlement and identification with particular areas in the Land with the period of the "Avot."

Yet a simple read of Genesis presents a different picture. Abraham built an altar in Sh'khem (Gen. 12:6–7), and built altars and called out in God's Name on the north-south route between Bethel (to the west) and Ha'ai (to the east) (ibid., v. 8). As has been frequently suggested, settlement in the Jacobite period, between the return from Haran to the descent to Egypt, is clear, is regional, and has great impact on the future settlement to take place when their descendants return home.

In all of that narrative, the heartland of the Patriarchal settlement and enterprise was in the mountain region from Sh'khem to the north to Hebron to the south; Judah's "leaving his brothers" (Gen. 38:1) involved his going to Timnah (a future city of Judah!), which is down the slopes of the Judean mountains ("Shephelat Yehudah"); Simeon and Levi conquer Sh'khem and, as is evidenced by their herding father's flock in that area (far from Jacob's home in Hebron), have their own financial interests in that area.

As such, the perspective of the sons of Jacob – and of that Patriarch himself – was likely that they were beginning the process of settlement, continuing the mission of their great-grandfather Abraham; all of them operating in the orbit of Abraham's original path, southward from Sh'khem along the mountain road.

The small town of Shiloh is situated on the road south from Sh'khem, north of the well-known and much larger Bethel/Luz. Abraham almost assuredly passed by (or through) the site that would become Shiloh. I'd like to propose that Jacob selected Shiloh as the place where his sons' descendants would build an altar to call out in God's Name, to continue the mission that is the raison-d'etre for – and justifies – the conquest and settlement of the Land.

That said, what is the ultimate purpose of this shrine? Put differently – how are the sons of Jacob and their descendants to relate to this place and, in parallel, to each other?

The overall impression of Jacob's deathbed blessing is that each of the sons and his progeny has a specific location, task, economy, and role to play within the body politic. In other words, Jacob's vision is not that of a single nation, rather of a federation of tribes who are unified by their allegiance to the mission to be a blessing to the world, to the privileged task of bringing God's Name to humanity and, thereby, to be a source of blessing for all of mankind. In other words, the goal is not to reside together but to operate in concert to continue the national destiny. What is it that holds the center? In a politically-defined society, it is the seats of power; in an economically-defined society, it is the vaults of wealth; in a spiritually-oriented society, it is the Tabernacle.

The vision was to establish a national "hub" at Shiloh, picking up off of the mission and the path taken by Abraham, its first commander, and to have all of the families of Jacob view it as the hub of their national wheel, the center that defines the perimeter.

● עד כי יבא שילה – SHILOH AS END-POINT

If we accept the foregoing, that Jacob's intent in these blessings is to guide the family's structure and direction, the Judean passage fits elegantly. Jacob began by "demoting" the first three brothers, Reuben for one reason (the Bilhah episode) and Simeon and Levi for a common reason (likely the massacre at Sh'khem) from the mantle of leadership of the clan – as it stood at that time.

Judah had proven himself to be the leader of the brothers, both in his persuasive words to the brothers in the matter of the sale of Joseph,

and his success in convincing father to allow Benjamin to come down to
Egypt with him. That the brothers saw Judah as their leader is evidenced
by their response to the former event (both of these crises, parenthetically,
are points where Reuben abjectly failed, not only as leader but also as
brother). Father's esteem for his fourth son is seen by his choosing Judah
to lead the way and prepare Goshen for his arrival. (Gen. 46:28)

Jacob names Judah as head of the family after his death – since "your
brothers acknowledge you." He is then described – as Jacob describes
Issachar, Naphtali, Dan and Benjamin – using an image from the animal
world. Judah is the lion of the family, the ferocious leader to whom all
show obeisance.

Now to our verse:

לא יסור שבט מיהודה – the scepter of leadership shall not depart from
Judah. In other words – Judah is not only the leader while father is alive
– father is willing him the leadership of the family after his death to hold,
as it were, the scepter of rule.

ומחוקק מבין רגליו – in spite of Shadal's claim that kings would hold a
scepter at their feet, the simple read of this refers to "fruit of the loins."
Given that Jacob has been promised that God will bring him back up
to the Land (Gen. 46:4), at which time the families of his children will
disperse to their own economies and regions, he is extending Judah's rule
over the brothers to his progeny – until such time as the notion of a single
leader among the brothers becomes passé.

עד כי יבא שילה – this is to be Judah's position until the national spiritual
hub is established at Shiloh; the inauguration of a solid foundation of the
Tabernacle demonstrates that the "era of the tent of dwelling" is over and
the people will have turned a new page to an era of tribal identity oriented
towards a common middle. Jacob is simultaneously willing his sons to
establish that national hub at Shiloh – as per above – but at the same time
directing them that once that has become a "fact on the ground," there
is no need for a single leader among the brothers. It will be time for each
tribe to find their own leaders and council of elders – as happens after
the establishment of Shiloh.

ולו יקהת עמים – the עמים here are the tribes as we find, for instance,
in Deut. 33:3 (see Rashi, ibn Ezra, and Ramban, ad loc.) and ibid, v. 19.
When the tribes gather at שילה to dedicate the משכן, that will be the point
at which Judah's reign will cease and each tribe will rule over himself, as
we find during the period of the Judges, until David came and united
the tribes into one nation, a restoration of the Egyptian-Joshua model.

The final two verses of Judah's blessing confirm this read. The mixture of red and white, wine and goat's milk, speaks directly to the territory we know as Judah's territory – a territory in which his descendants will remain, looking northwards towards that great national center which keeps Judah in the south, Asher in the north, Reuben and Gad on the east bank, and Ephraim and Manasseh in the heartland unified in their national quest to fulfill the mission of Abraham.

We have assayed the various approaches to the riddle of "Shiloh" in Jacob's blessing. Suggesting that it is a reference to the Ephraimite town, I proposed that we read it in its context – not as a "far-range" (Messianic/apocalyptic) nor even as a "close-range" (settlement period) prophecy, rather as a directive to set up the national-spiritual center in Shiloh along the Abrahamic route. The brothers are to obey the leadership of Judah and his children until such time as they arrive in the Land, establish that national center, and then disperse to their intended tribal settings, glued together by the common history of the Patriarchs and the Exodus, and by the common destiny of realizing the great goal of the Divine mission given to Abraham.

AFTERWORD

Stepping back from the semantic field for a moment and viewing this directive/prophecy within a historic context – where Jacob was and what he reasonably anticipated of his descendants – we were able to gain a fresh perspective, specifically towards the import of Shiloh within the next few stages of Israelite history. Doing so, we re-assessed the key preposition "*Ad*" and interpreted Jacob's words as directed towards the return and not beyond, at which point they may be living in a tribal federation.

It is to the other possibility, that they would, one day, form a united people and look to a single sovereign, that the rest of Jacob's blessings are directed, as we will see in the next chapter.

JACOB'S DEATHBED BLESSINGS
Deciphering Structure to Decode Meaning
Genesis 49:1–28

INTRODUCTION

As I've noted elsewhere, the graphic and literary structure of a particular passage or set of passages in the Bible is deliberate and may often be instructive towards understanding the underlying theme or message. This is true for parallelisms (chiefly in poetry), for chiastic structures (both within verses and across broad sections), as well as "paragraph" breaks in the text.

A word about paragraphs. A written Torah has no punctuation or vocalization. These are all provided by an oral tradition that, beginning in the 6th century, was represented by newly created vowel and trope markings. Yet, there is one graphic marker in the written text which helps us to recognize divisions – the *Parashah* (literally "paragraph). There are two types of division that are currently in use – the *parashah petuhah* (lit. "open paragraph") which begins on a new line, and the *parashah setumah* (lit. "closed paragraph") which begins after a space of nine letters' worth on the same line. Clearly, a *parashah petuhah* represents a greater divisor, hence a more distinct topic from the one prior, whereas a *parashah setumah* represents a passage which is more closely aligned with the one previous. We will observe the use of both types of *parashot* in our passage to help our understanding of the momentous scene of Jacob's deathbed blessings.

THE TEXT

There are two series of "blessings" in the Five Books which address the tribes – the one given by Moses at the end of his life and the one given by father Jacob, to his sons, on his deathbed in Egypt. Much has been written about the correlation between these two invocations: each has an introductory passage, in both cases Simeon (the son and the tribe) are given "short shrift," both begin with Reuben but are hardly laudatory and so on. In this chapter, we will steer clear of the comparison – we will leave that for our forthcoming volume on Deuteronomy – and will focus on Jacob's blessing. By identifying difficulties and unexpected turns in the sequence and content, we will suggest what our ancestor was communicating and decreeing with his final words.

In the previous chapter, I proposed a solution to one line in the blessing given to Judah; in Chapters XX and XXII, I suggested that these blessings may have been directed towards territorial assignment in the Land, and in Chapter XXIII, we discussed the general meaning of paternal blessings in the Bible. When needed, we will revisit these ideas – briefly – as we will take the long view at this dramatic scene.

Note that the sons' "blessings" are broken up as separate *parashot*, however with inconsistent dividers. Simeon/Levi begins a new *parashah petuhah* as does Judah; whereas Zebulun, Issachar, Dan, and Gad are only divided by a *parashah setumah* beginning nine spaces later. Asher begins a new *parashah petuhah*, but the next one is the final son – Benjamin. In addition to this graphic inconsistency, the blessing to Dan is followed up with a three-word verse (v. 18) which may or may not be associated with him – "I have waited your salvation, O God."

א וַיִּקְרָא יַעֲקֹב אֶל בָּנָיו וַיֹּאמֶר הֵאָסְפוּ וְאַגִּידָה לָכֶם אֵת אֲשֶׁר יִקְרָא אֶתְכֶם בְּאַחֲרִית הַיָּמִים: (ב) הִקָּבְצוּ וְשִׁמְעוּ בְּנֵי יַעֲקֹב וְשִׁמְעוּ אֶל יִשְׂרָאֵל אֲבִיכֶם: ג **רְאוּבֵן** בְּכֹרִי אַתָּה כֹּחִי וְרֵאשִׁית אוֹנִי יֶתֶר שְׂאֵת וְיֶתֶר עָז: (ד) פַּחַז כַּמַּיִם אַל תּוֹתַר כִּי עָלִיתָ מִשְׁכְּבֵי אָבִיךָ אָז חִלַּלְתָּ יְצוּעִי עָלָה: ה **שִׁמְעוֹן וְלֵוִי** אַחִים כְּלֵי חָמָס מְכֵרֹתֵיהֶם: (ו) בְּסֹדָם אַל תָּבֹא נַפְשִׁי בִּקְהָלָם אַל תֵּחַד כְּבֹדִי כִּי בְאַפָּם הָרְגוּ אִישׁ וּבִרְצֹנָם עִקְּרוּ שׁוֹר: (ז) אָרוּר אַפָּם כִּי עָז וְעֶבְרָתָם כִּי קָשָׁתָה אֲחַלְּקֵם בְּיַעֲקֹב וַאֲפִיצֵם בְּיִשְׂרָאֵל:

ח **יְהוּדָה** אַתָּה יוֹדוּךָ אַחֶיךָ יָדְךָ בְּעֹרֶף אֹיְבֶיךָ יִשְׁתַּחֲווּ לְךָ בְּנֵי אָבִיךָ: (ט) גּוּר אַרְיֵה יְהוּדָה מִטֶּרֶף בְּנִי עָלִיתָ כָּרַע רָבַץ כְּאַרְיֵה וּכְלָבִיא מִי יְקִימֶנּוּ: (י) לֹא יָסוּר שֵׁבֶט מִיהוּדָה וּמְחֹקֵק מִבֵּין רַגְלָיו עַד כִּי יָבֹא שִׁילֹה וְלוֹ יִקְּהַת עַמִּים: (יא) אֹסְרִי לַגֶּפֶן עִירֹה וְלַשֹּׂרֵקָה בְּנִי אֲתֹנוֹ כִּבֵּס בַּיַּיִן לְבֻשׁוֹ וּבְדַם עֲנָבִים סוּתֹה: (יב) חַכְלִילִי עֵינַיִם מִיָּיִן וּלְבֶן שִׁנַּיִם מֵחָלָב:

יג **זְבוּלֻן** לְחוֹף יַמִּים יִשְׁכֹּן וְהוּא לְחוֹף אֳנִיֹּת וְיַרְכָתוֹ עַל צִידֹן:　　יד **יִשָּׂשכָר** חֲמֹר גָּרֶם רֹבֵץ בֵּין הַמִּשְׁפְּתָיִם: (טו) וַיַּרְא מְנֻחָה כִּי טוֹב וְאֶת הָאָרֶץ כִּי נָעֵמָה וַיֵּט שִׁכְמוֹ לִסְבֹּל וַיְהִי לְמַס עֹבֵד:　　טז **דָּן** יָדִין עַמּוֹ כְּאַחַד שִׁבְטֵי יִשְׂרָאֵל: (יז) יְהִי דָן נָחָשׁ עֲלֵי דֶרֶךְ שְׁפִיפֹן עֲלֵי אֹרַח הַנֹּשֵׁךְ עִקְּבֵי סוּס וַיִּפֹּל רֹכְבוֹ אָחוֹר: (יח) לִישׁוּעָתְךָ קִוִּיתִי ה':　　יט **גָּד** גְּדוּד יְגוּדֶנּוּ וְהוּא יָגֻד עָקֵב: כ מֵ**אָשֵׁר** שְׁמֵנָה לַחְמוֹ וְהוּא יִתֵּן מַעֲדַנֵּי מֶלֶךְ: (כא) **נַפְתָּלִי** אַיָּלָה שְׁלֻחָה הַנֹּתֵן אִמְרֵי שָׁפֶר: (כב) בֵּן פֹּרָת **יוֹסֵף** בֵּן פֹּרָת עֲלֵי עָיִן בָּנוֹת צָעֲדָה עֲלֵי שׁוּר: (כג) וַיְמָרֲרֻהוּ וָרֹבּוּ וַיִּשְׂטְמֻהוּ בַּעֲלֵי חִצִּים: (כד) וַתֵּשֶׁב בְּאֵיתָן קַשְׁתּוֹ וַיָּפֹזּוּ זְרֹעֵי יָדָיו מִידֵי אֲבִיר יַעֲקֹב מִשָּׁם רֹעֶה אֶבֶן יִשְׂרָאֵל:

(כה) מֵאֵל אָבִיךָ וְיַעְזְרֶךָּ וְאֵת שַׁדַּי וִיבָרְכֶךָּ בִּרְכֹת שָׁמַיִם מֵעָל בִּרְכֹת תְּהוֹם רֹבֶצֶת תָּחַת בִּרְכֹת
שָׁדַיִם וָרָחַם: (כו) בִּרְכֹת אָבִיךָ גָּבְרוּ עַל בִּרְכֹת הוֹרַי עַד תַּאֲוַת גִּבְעֹת עוֹלָם תִּהְיֶיןָ לְרֹאשׁ יוֹסֵף
וּלְקָדְקֹד נְזִיר אֶחָיו:
כז בִּנְיָמִין זְאֵב יִטְרָף בַּבֹּקֶר יֹאכַל עַד וְלָעֶרֶב יְחַלֵּק שָׁלָל: (כח) כָּל אֵלֶּה שִׁבְטֵי יִשְׂרָאֵל שְׁנֵים
עָשָׂר וְזֹאת אֲשֶׁר דִּבֶּר לָהֶם אֲבִיהֶם וַיְבָרֶךְ אוֹתָם אִישׁ אֲשֶׁר כְּבִרְכָתוֹ בֵּרַךְ אֹתָם:

And Jacob called to his sons, and said, "Gather yourselves together, that I may tell you that which shall befall you in the last days. Gather yourselves together, and hear, you sons of Jacob; and listen to Israel your father.

Reuben, you are my firstborn, my might, and the beginning of my strength, the excellency of dignity, and the excellency of power; Unstable as water, you shall not excel; because you went up to your father's bed; then defiled you it; he went up to my couch.

Simeon and Levi are brothers; instruments of cruelty are their swords. O my soul, do not come into their council; to their assembly, let my honor not be united; for in their anger they slew a man, and in their wanton will they lamed an ox. Cursed be their anger, for it was fierce; and their wrath, for it was cruel; I will divide them in Jacob, and scatter them in Israel.

Judah, you are he whom your brothers shall praise; your hand shall be in the neck of your enemies; your father's children shall bow down in your presence. Judah is a lion's whelp; from the prey, my son, you are gone up; he stooped down, he couched as a lion, and as an old lion; who shall rouse him up? The staff shall not depart from **Judah**, nor the scepter from between his feet, until Shiloh come; and to him shall the obedience of the people be. Binding his foal to the vine, and his ass's colt to the choice vine; he washed his garments in wine, and his clothes in the blood of grapes; His eyes shall be red with wine, and his teeth white with milk.

Zebulun shall live at the haven of the sea; and he shall be for a haven of ships; and his border shall be to Sidon.

Issachar is a strong ass couching down between two burdens; And he saw that resting was good, and that the land was pleasant; and bowed his shoulder to bear, and became a servant to tribute.

Dan shall judge his people, as one of the tribes of Israel. **Dan** shall be a serpent by the way, an adder in the path, that bites the horse heels, so that his rider shall fall backward. *I have waited for your salvation, O Lord.*

Gad, a troop shall overcome him; but he shall overcome at the last.

Out of **Asher** his bread shall be fat, and he shall yield royal dainties.

Naphtali is a hind let loose; he gives goodly words.

Joseph is a fruitful bough, a fruitful bough by a well; whose branches run over the wall; The archers fiercely attacked him, and shot at him, and hated him; But his bow abode in strength, and the arms of his hands were made strong by the hands of the mighty God of Jacob; from there is the shepherd, the stone of Israel; By the God of your father, who shall help you; and by the Almighty, who shall bless you with blessings of heaven above, blessings of the deep that lies under, blessings of the breasts, and of the womb; The blessings of your father have prevailed above the blessings of my progenitors to the utmost bound of the everlasting hills; they shall be on the head of **Joseph**, and on the crown of the head of him who was separate from his brothers.

Benjamin is a ravenous wolf; in the morning he shall devour the prey, and at night he shall divide the booty.

All these are the twelve tribes of Israel; and this is it what their father spoke to them, and blessed them; every one according to his blessing he blessed them.

THE SURPRISING SEQUENCE

What are we to make of this passage? What is Jacob trying to impart to his sons? If we read this as a "well-wishing" blessing, we would be hard-pressed to explain the harsh admonitions administered to the eldest three sons. If, on the other hand, this is an allotment of tasks and territories among the twelve sons, the sequence – not to mention the content – is puzzling.

If Jacob intended to mete out his will, as it were, in birth order – that doesn't remain consistent after the first four sons. Zebulun and Issachar are reversed from birth order, and the four sons of the handmaids are presented in an order that is hard to figure – not by birth (should be Dan, Naftali, Gad and Asher) nor by "houses" (should be Gad, Asher, followed by Dan and Naftali).

Finally – why is Joseph presented next to last? Joseph was Jacob's favorite son; he should have either been first or, if addressed at the end to create a crescendo, should have been the absolute last. In addition, if Jacob were saving his finest and most generous blessings for the end, why is Judah addressed near the beginning?

THE BACKGROUND: STRUGGLES FOR LEADERSHIP OF THE CLAN

The final third of Genesis highlights an ongoing tension between three brothers – not necessarily in face-to-face conflict, but tension nonetheless, over leadership of the family. Reuben (the firstborn) and Judah experience three more or less direct confrontations, whereas Joseph's moves happen in apposition to the entire clan.

Reuben makes several attempts to demonstrate his leadership; in each case, Judah's parallel attempt meets with relative success. The first attempt is his abortive move with Bilhah, which results of his being stripped of the rights of primogeniture. In a somewhat parallel scenario, Judah has questionable and problematic relations with his daughter-in-law, Tamar – and, as a result of his public confession, survives the ordeal with no diminution of his station.

Reuben's second attempt is when the brothers, herding father's sheep near Dotan, declare their intent to kill the approaching Joseph. Reuben convinces them to throw Joseph into the pit, allowing him to die on his own (from thirst? starvation? the elements? presumed predators?) that they not kill him with their own hands. His intent, revealed to us by the text, is to come back later, pull the younger brother out of the pit and bring him back to father. But here, again, he fails, since by the time he returns to the pit, Joseph has been taken out by the Midianites and sold to the Ishmaelites. Judah, on the other hand, is the one who recommends the sale of their brother as a slave. Whether or not that plan ever came to fruition, it was Judah who the brothers heeded and it was his plan that ultimately played out – whether by their hand or by the hands of Midianite merchants.

The third conflict was when the brothers returned, sans Simeon, to Canaan, telling father that they would not be welcomed back in Egypt without Benjamin. Reuben reacted to father's reticence immediately, offering his own two sons as pledges for the young Benjamin's safe return. Jacob refused and, again, Reuben's position as eldest proved to be without "teeth." Judah, biding his time, waited until the food ran out and then offered *himself* as a pledge for Benjamin's safe return.

Judah's ascendance over Reuben is recognized by Jacob by the wisdom and patience of Judah's appeal to him regarding entrusting Benjamin to his care. Even more impressive was the loyalty Judah's brothers felt towards him over their eldest brother. This ascendance played out while Joseph's rise to power away from the family was firmly solidified with his being named viceroy of Egypt.

After seventeen years in Egypt, Jacob was prepared to discharge his instructions for the family. As pointed out in the previous chapter, Jacob anticipated his progeny returning to Canaan and establishing themselves there as a nation. His last act was to direct them towards successful leadership and self-government.

JACOB'S ULTIMATE GOAL: ESTABLISHING A FRAMEWORK OF LEADERSHIP

Anticipating their return to the homeland as conquerors, as sovereigns, necessitates a framework for leadership. Jacob begins by addressing his eldest sons and explaining, via his stern admonitions, why they will not play a central role in that leadership.

One prefatory note regarding tribal assignments is in order. Reuben, Jacob's eldest, will not himself return to Canaan, and neither will his sons nor grandsons. It will be several generations before the family returns as a small nation; as it turns out, it is a few more generations and they are a large nation. Why, then, would we expect traits or personal history of Reuben (for example) to have an impact on his eponymous tribe?

This is a question that wouldn't be asked in the Biblical period and is the product of modern, chiefly Western thinking. With the "liberation" from family and ethnic castes, citizens of the western world generally feel the opportunity – indeed, the right – to pursue any profession, way of life, and value system which they find to be personally meaningful. Without takings sides on the issue, suffice it to say that this mode of existentialist thinking was absolutely foreign to Biblical man. Life was only within the clan, within the family, and within the legacy of that tribal group. As such, when Reuben was type-cast with specific shades of personality and ability, that type became the assigned position of his progeny.

Reuben, as pointed out above, exhibited impatience as well as an inability to gauge the reaction of his intended audience – brothers and father. His impetuosity, especially in the Bilhah affair, cost him the reins of leadership. Jacob recognized that his own elevation as heir to the mission and legacy of Abraham and Isaac was in no small part due to his ability to bide his time and take the long view, in contrast with his impetuous and immature elder brother, Esau.

The family, grown to clan and then to small nation, will return to the Land and claim its inheritance. This claim will undoubtedly be challenged by others – including the current residents. A leader will perforce need to have a strong military presence to deter and, if needed, to engage those who would challenge the family's hegemony over Canaan. Given the family's history, the most likely candidates to lead the military establishment are Simeon and Levi (see Chapter 19 above). Yet, just like Reuben, their actions were undisciplined, operating outside of the proper channels of authority and consensus so necessary for a successful military. Had they consulted with each other, sought the counsel of their father, and followed his directions, their "violence" would have been able to be utilized within a leadership model. But unchecked, "loose cannons" are cursed and, instead of standing shoulder to shoulder as an army, are dispersed.

Judah is the leader – his brothers look up to him and he has their allegiance, as well as the trust of their father. His behavior, especially in the Joseph-Benjamin affair, demonstrated his worthiness as future monarch.

The rest of the brothers' assignments – save for two – are all related to the anticipated monarchy of Judah. The king and his government will require diplomats and traders, interacting peacefully and productively with neighboring countries. He will also need a proper, disciplined and loyal military, as well as a strong and diligent work force, along with all of the trappings of royalty. A review of the description of Solomon's court, consistently referred to in rabbinic literature as the pinnacle of Israelite sovereignty, bears this out. The military is barely mentioned, as "And Judah and Israel dwelt safely, every man under his vine and under his fig-tree, from Dan even to Beer-sheba, all the days of Solomon." This was a period of tranquility, as promised to his father. The great wealth described in Chapters 9 and 10 of 1 Kings, the navy he established as well as the tremendous building projects he undertook, all speak to a comprehensive monarchy. Zebulun serves as the naval connection with neighboring nations; Issachar represents a diligent work force, Dan and Gad are presented as disciplined and organized militia; Asher provides the luxuries associated with a monarch, and Naftali serves as the over-land diplomatic agent.

Before moving ahead to see how the two sons of Rachel fare in Jacob's will, I'd like to suggest that the unusual sequencing of the brothers, raised above, is designed to create an elegant structure, highlighting the monarch and his 4 basic needs: military, diplomatic, commercial and pomp. Note that Jacob presented the first ten sons in eight groups, combining Simeon and Levi and drawing Dan and Gad together via a clever textual bridge.

The chart below demonstrates how these eight correlate – the first four passages are matched, passage for passage, by those on the left.

Reuben is the impetuous elder who lost his position due to his inability to delay gratification. Opposite him sits the reliable "donkey," Issachar, who puts his shoulder to the grindstone, accepting the burden of slow, methodical work to complete the task

Simeon and Levi are the undisciplined loose cannons whose violence, in Jacob's estimation, endangered the entire clan. Dan and Gad, on the other hand, are disciplined (Gad operates as a "troop") and are strategists (Dan knows how to set up an ambush). This also explains why Jacob utters the three-word interjection – "לישועתך קויתי ה'" ("I wait for your salvation, O Lord") between these two. This is a cry most obviously associated with a battle, anticipating and praying for Divine salvation. The phrase, situated as the tail of Dan's passage, serves to tie Gad (whose passage follows immediately afterwards) to Dan, both presented in the context of battle.

The Gadites were considered to be courageous fighters – and were fit to settle on the East Bank to serve as a buffer against both Ammon and Moav as well as Aram in the north, as well as joining Reuben and one Manassite family as the vanguard at the conquest of the Land. Dan, on the other hand, went far out of their defined land to conquer Laish/Leshem in the north in a strategically reconnoitered and well-planned (although ethically problematic) attack.

Judah is the king – and Asher who symmetrically corresponds with him, is the only brother who has the explicit word "king" in his directive. His job is to furnish all of the glory of the kingdom; is it any surprise that Solomon's houses are built by the king of Tyre and Tyrian carpenters – all hailing from the territory adjacent to that of Asher?

Judah also has two diplomatic and commercial fleets – Zebulun's navy and Naftali's "runners." Whether we look at Zebulun as chiefly concerned with mercantile sailing and Naftali as a government agent or we are willing to imagine a greater crossover, both serve as a similar purpose. Both Zebulun and Naftali, symmetrically twinned in Jacob's structure, serve as the link between the Judean-Solomonic monarchy and the nations which surround it.

This chart outlines how the two halves of Jacob's presentation to his ten non-Rachelite sons correspond with each other.

THE STRUCTURE OF JACOB'S BLESSINGS (מבנה ברכת יעקב)

מלכות בית לאה

יִשָּׂשכָר חֲמֹר גָּרֶם רֹבֵץ בֵּין הַמִּשְׁפְּתָיִם: וַיַּרְא מְנֻחָה כִּי טוֹב וְאֶת הָאָרֶץ כִּי נָעֵמָה וַיֵּט שִׁכְמוֹ לִסְבֹּל וַיְהִי לְמַס עֹבֵד:	רְאוּבֵן בְּכֹרִי אַתָּה כֹּחִי וְרֵאשִׁית אוֹנִי יֶתֶר שְׂאֵת וְיֶתֶר עָז: פַּחַז כַּמַּיִם אַל תּוֹתַר כִּי עָלִיתָ מִשְׁכְּבֵי אָבִיךָ אָז חִלַּלְתָּ יְצוּעִי עָלָה:	*Impetuosity vs. Diligence*
דָּן יָדִין עַמּוֹ כְּאַחַד שִׁבְטֵי יִשְׂרָאֵל: יְהִי דָן נָחָשׁ עֲלֵי דֶרֶךְ שְׁפִיפֹן עֲלֵי אֹרַח הַנֹּשֵׁךְ עִקְּבֵי סוּס וַיִּפֹּל רֹכְבוֹ אָחוֹר: **לִישׁוּעָתְךָ קִוִּיתִי ה': גָּד גְּדוּד יְגוּדֶנּוּ וְהוּא יָגֻד עָקֵב:**	שִׁמְעוֹן וְלֵוִי אַחִים כְּלֵי חָמָס מְכֵרֹתֵיהֶם: בְּסֹדָם אַל תָּבֹא נַפְשִׁי בִּקְהָלָם אַל תֵּחַד כְּבֹדִי כִּי בְאַפָּם הָרְגוּ אִישׁ וּבִרְצֹנָם עִקְּרוּ שׁוֹר: אָרוּר אַפָּם כִּי עָז וְעֶבְרָתָם כִּי קָשָׁתָה אֲחַלְּקֵם בְּיַעֲקֹב וַאֲפִיצֵם בְּיִשְׂרָאֵל:	*Schooled militia vs. uncontrolled vigilantes*
מֵאָשֵׁר שְׁמֵנָה לַחְמוֹ וְהוּא יִתֵּן מַעֲדַנֵּי מֶלֶךְ:	יְהוּדָה אַתָּה יוֹדוּךָ אַחֶיךָ יָדְךָ בְּעֹרֶף אֹיְבֶיךָ יִשְׁתַּחֲווּ לְךָ בְּנֵי אָבִיךָ: גּוּר אַרְיֵה יְהוּדָה מִטֶּרֶף בְּנִי עָלִיתָ כָּרַע רָבַץ כְּאַרְיֵה וּכְלָבִיא מִי יְקִימֶנּוּ: לֹא יָסוּר שֵׁבֶט מִיהוּדָה וּמְחֹקֵק מִבֵּין רַגְלָיו עַד כִּי יָבֹא שִׁילֹה וְלוֹ יִקְּהַת עַמִּים: אֹסְרִי לַגֶּפֶן עִירֹה וְלַשֹּׂרֵקָה בְּנִי אֲתֹנוֹ כִּבֵּס בַּיַּיִן לְבֻשׁוֹ וּבְדַם עֲנָבִים סוּתֹה: חַכְלִילִי עֵינַיִם מִיָּיִן וּלְבֶן שִׁנַּיִם מֵחָלָב:	*Royalty and its trappings*
נַפְתָּלִי אַיָּלָה שְׁלֻחָה הַנֹּתֵן אִמְרֵי שָׁפֶר:	זְבוּלֻן לְחוֹף יַמִּים יִשְׁכֹּן וְהוּא לְחוֹף אֳנִיּוֹת וְיַרְכָתוֹ עַל צִידֹן:	*Diplomacy and commerce – by sea and by land*

Notes

- Alone among the brothers, Judah's name appears multiple times in his passage – with the wordplay *Yodukha*, a total of four times.
- Dan and Gad's names, including the Midrashic word play (מדרש שמות), appear seven times in their section – indicating a complete set.

JACOB'S IMMEDIATE GOAL: CONFIRMING THE CURRENT LEADERSHIP

All that said, the ideal of returning to the Land as conquering sovereigns is still at least a few generations away. In the meantime, the family will be growing in the exile of Egypt under the protective aegis of Joseph. Joseph, who would have likely been Jacob's own choice as head of the family, is relegated to the role of "governor for exile" as he does not have the allegiance of his brothers – although they clearly fear him. Joseph has one support system – and that is Benjamin, his full brother who is depicted as his military right-arm. Note that Joseph's name appears twice in his blessing – in contrast to Judah, whose name (with the *Midrash Shem – Yodukha)* appears four times.

There are two models set up by Jacob – the ideal, permanent model which employs most of the non-Rachelite sons (and even finds room for the "dispatched" ones) and the immediate, exile-mode leadership headed by Joseph and peopled entirely by Rachelites.

We are surprised to find that when monarchy is finally established in Israel, the first king selected is – Saul the Benjaminite from the Rachelite clans. Curiously, the first impression the text gives us of Saul – and the first impression he makes on the people – is his height and good looks. This echoes Jacob's blessing here to Joseph. The phrase "whose branches run over the wall" is alternately translated "the girls go up to the top of the wall (to gaze at his beauty)."

I'd like to suggest that because the original request/demand of the people for a king – "place a king over us to lead us like the nations" – was an evocation of an exile mentality, of a desire to be "like the nations" – that they were first given a Joseph-type king; it was only after that failed enterprise that evidently the people were ready for a proper monarchy, a Judean king with the full government, proper military, etc. Whereas Saul impressed others with his good looks and height but did not command the loyalty of all of the people, David was immediately beloved by all of the army and by all members of Saul's court. This may be the model for the rabbinic notion of a Josephite Messiah (*"Mashiach ben Joseph"*) who is destined to come before the "real" Messiah of the House of David (*"Mashiach ben David"*).[28]

---

28. cf. BT Sukkah 52a

AFTERWORD

We have examined Jacob's deathbed blessing without going into much analysis of the particular verses with their difficult and equivocal implications. By asking the questions we've learned to ask – about structure, setting, and context – and taking the recent history of the family into account as well as what we know to be Jacob's anticipations about the family's future, we've suggested that the entire passage be divided between the non-Rachelites and Rachel's sons. Once we saw that division and realized that there were two models of leadership being launched here by father Jacob – one immediate and simple, and the other far more intricate and accomplished, we assayed the first, ideal kingdom and saw that Jacob had addressed each of his sons, explaining to them their role and why that role was significant – or why they lost their rights to serve in that critical contributory role in the kingdom that will ultimately be created.

There is yet much more to analyze here, including the specific alignment of son to task – for instance, why was Dan considered the military strategist and why Zebulun the merchant marine – but that is beyond the scope of this chapter.

Jacob set out to create two models. The first stood for us in Egypt until the worm turned and the masters became slaves; that was reestablished in the Land in anticipation of the "real" monarchy, which was finally given to David and his progeny forever.

A SURVEY OF THE GREAT EXEGETES

OVER THE PAST 1200 YEARS, MANY GREAT SCHOLARS, FROM all corners of the Diaspora, have contributed to our understanding and appreciation of the Biblical text. Some have focused their attentions on the philological, others on the contextual, etc., as outlined in Chapter 1 of this book.

This appendix is not even close to being exhaustive; it merely highlights a few of the most outstanding contributors to the study of the Bible, especially those whose observations and methodologies have been utilized in this work. Each is listed with the essential data – era and country of origin – as well as the major contribution made to the study of Bible in general and the book of Genesis in particular. Where possible, original publication information is provided along with the most recent publication, especially in those cases where a critical work has illuminated the work of the exegete.

- The Geonim (850–1000)
  - **Rasag** Saadiah al-Fayyumi (Ben Joseph) Gaon (882–942). Born in Faiyum, Egypt, named as Gaon (head of the academy) of Pumbedita (Baghdad), Sa'adiah devoted much of his energies to defending the rabbinate understanding of the text and traditional interpretation. Sa'adiah's *Tafsir* is the earliest systematic commentary on the Biblical text of which we are aware.
    - *Tafsir Critical Edition* printed in Torat Hayyim, Mossad Harav Kook (Jerusalem 1993), annotated by Yosef Kafih.

- The Rishonim (1000–1500)
  - **Rashi**: Solomon ben Isaac (1040–1105) Born in Troyes, France. Rashi, commonly considered the greatest of the Biblical (and Talmudic) commentators, generally followed Rabbinic interpretation, including homiletic and exegetical, in his commentary.

- Commentary on Bible, printed in all standard Hebrew Bibles with commentary. First publication date: (Reggio, Feb., 1475). Critical edition printed in Torat Hayyim, Mossad Harav Kook (Jerusalem 1993), annotated by Dr. C. Chavel. Available in numerous English translations.
- **Ibn Ezra** Ibn Ezra, Abraham (1089–1164). Ibn Ezra, an itinerant scholar and "roving commentator," was born in Toledo and later moved to Cordova. He spent much of his later life (after 1140) traveling and spent time in most of the regions where Jews lived throughout Christian Europe, including Provence and Northern France. He brought many of the Spanish and Islamic influences to these areas. Chiefly known as a *pashtan*, ibn Ezra was a philologist as well as an accomplished astronomer and astrologer, sciences which he integrated into his commentary.
    - Commentaries on Pentateuch 1st ed., Naples, 1488; Critical edition printed in Torat Hayyim, Mossad Harav Kook (Jerusalem 1993), annotated by A. Weiser.
- **Rashbam** Samuel b. Meir (c. 1080–85–c. 1174) a maternal grandson of Rashi, studied "at his knee" and contributed to the great exegete's commentary. He is known as a *pashtan*, preferring the straightforward meaning of the text to traditional rabbinic homilies and heremeneutics. His comments at the beginning of Genesis 37 are particularly telling in telegraphing his exegetical approach.
    - Commentary on Pentateuch First Edition Berlin, 1705. Critical edition printed in Torat Hayyim, Mossad Harav Kook (Jerusalem 1993), annotated by D. Rosen.
- **R. Yosef Bekhor Shor** Joseph b. Isaac (12th century). A student of R. Tam (Rashbam's younger brother). An innovative exegete, he is also considered a *pashtan* and presents numerous insights into the text which deviate from Midrashic tradition
    - Commentary on Pentateuch. His commentary was published in segments in various journals until Joseph Gad published it in its entirety (1956–60). Critical edition – Perushe Rabi Yosef **Bekhor Shor** al ha-Torah / annotated by Yehoshafat Nevo. (Jerusalem 1994)
- **Rambam** Maimonides (1135–1204) born in Cordova, Maimonides lived most of his life in Fostat, Egypt and served as the doctor of the Sultan. Recognized as the greatest Jewish scholar since Talmudic times, Rambam had a prodigious literary output; although he

never published a systematic commentary on the Bible, his Guide for the Perplexed utilizes many Biblical sources and a unique interpretive approach can be discerned therein.

- Guide for the Perplexed. First published in Hebrew (translated from the Arabic by ibn Tibbon) sometime before 1480 in Italy. Classic translation into English: The guide for the perplexed / by Moses Maimonides; translated from the original Arabic text by M. Friedländer. (New York, 1956)

- **Radak** David Kimhi (1160?–1235?) Radak was a lexicographer and grammarian whose works on Hebrew language were used widely by many of the *Rishonim*. He was also a controversialist, engaging in disputations with Christians over the import of Biblical texts; some of his commentaries have an overtly polemic tone (e.g., Psalm 2).
  - Commentary on Genesis. First edition ed. A. Ginzburg, published in Presburg, 1842. Critical edition printed in Torat Hayyim, Mossad Harav Kook (Jerusalem 1993), annotated by M.L. Katzenellenbogen.

- **Hizkuni** Hezekiah b. Manoah (mid-13th century, France). Hezekiah composed a commentary on the Pentateuch, based chiefly on Rashi but utilizing numerous other commentaries; although he has innovative insights from time to time, he is generally seen as an anthology of earlier approaches to the text.
  - Commentary on Pentateuch First published in Venice 1524. Critical edition printed in Torat Hayyim, Mossad Harav Kook (Jerusalem 1993), annotated by Dr. C. Chavel.

- **Ramban** Nachmanides (Moses b. Nahman, also known as RaM-BaN —an acronym of Rabbi Moses Ben Nahman; 1194–1270)
  - Commentary on Pentateuch. Critical edition printed in Torat Hayyim, Mossad Harav Kook (Jerusalem 1993), annotated Dr. C. Chavel. Available in English translation: Commentary on the Torah [by] Ramban (Nachmanides). Translated and annotated with index by Charles B. Chavel. New York, Shilo Pub. House [1971–76]

- **Ralbag** Levi b. Gershom (1288–1344, Bagnols, France). A philosopher, physician and mathematician, Ralbag introduced a novel style with his commentary wherein after explaining the *p'shat***, he presents the ethical utility and lessons of the text. Ralbag was concerned with reconciling the text with established philosophical principles and generally followed the neo-Aristotelian thinking outlined by Rambam in the Guide.

- Commentary on Pentateuch. First published in Venice 1547. Critical edition published by Mosad harav Kook (Jerusalem, 1992–2000), annotated by Jacob L. Levi.
- **Sforno** Obadiah b. Jacob Seforno (c. 1470–c. 1550, Italy).
  - Commentary on Pentateuch. First published in Venice, 1567. Critical edition printed in Torat Hayyim, Mossad Harav Kook (Jerusalem 1993), annotated by Abraham Darom and Zev Gottlieb.
- **Abravanel** Abravanel, Isaac B. Judah (1437–1508, Portugal, Spain). A member of a distinguished family, Abravanel, philosopher and exegete, served as finance minister in the court of Portugal and in the court of Ferdinand and Isabella until the expulsion of Jews from the Iberian Peninsula in 1492. He introduced an innovative style to his commentary, presenting a series of questions on the passage and then, via his own interpretation (oft-times innovative), answering the questions.
  - Commentary on Pentateuch. First published in Venice in 1579.

- The Aharonim (1500–1900)
  - **Hirsch, Samson (ben) Raphael** (1808–1888, Frankfurt-am-Main). Hirsch was the progenitor of the school that advocated some accommodation and integration with modern culture as advanced in the age of the Enlightenment. Among his many writings, his commentary on the Torah (written in German) is likely the most well-known.
    - Commentary on Pentateuch (German). Published in Frankfurt, 1867; English translation published in London, 1963, translated by Isaac Levy.
  - **Hoffman, David Zvi** (1843–1921, Germany). Student at the Hildesheimer Seminary in Eisenstadt, he was eventually appointed as the rector of the Seminary in Berlin in 1899. He was a founding member of the Agudat Yisrael while a staunch Zionist; he was also a polemicist against reform and those who espouse the documentary hypothesis*; much of his commentary is devoted to a defense of the traditional reading of the Bible.

- Commentary on Leviticus (German – Berlin, 1904; Hebrew translation, Jerusalem 1976)
- **Shadal** Luzzatto, Samuel David (1800–1865; Italy) Shadal was a philosopher, exegete and translator, firmly rooted in the Italian Jewish tradition. He was, philosophically, a follower of Maimonidean rationalism.
    - Commentary on Pentateuch. First published 1871–76 in Italy.
- **Netziv** Napthali Zevi Yehudah Berlin, (1817–1893). Head of the Academy in Volozhin, his literary activity included a commentary on the Sheiltot of R. Aha and a commentary on the Midrash Halakhah** on Numbers-Deuteronomy.
    - Commentary on Pentateuch (*Ha'amek Davar*), originally published as *Bi'ur ha'Amek*, Wilna 1879–80.
- **Malbim**, Meir Loeb ben Jehiel Michael (1809–1879, Ukraine), rabbi, preacher, and biblical exegete. The name Malbim is an acronym formed from Meir Loeb ben Jehiel Michael. Born in Volochisk (Volhynia). Malbim, an ardent defender of the faith against both the early reform movement and Higher Criticism, bolstered much of his innovative commentary on Rabbinic exegesis, along with his own philology.
    - Commentary on Pentateuch – *haTorah vehaMitzvah* (Warsaw 1874–80)

- Twentieth century
    - **Cassuto, Umberto** (Moses David; 1883–1951), Italian historian and biblical and Semitic scholar.
        - Commentary on Genesis (2 vol.)
    - **Elitzur**, Yehuda (1911–1997). Professor Elitzur, head of the Bible Department at Bar-Ilan University, contributed greatly to the "modernization" of *Parshanut**, introducing the finds of archives and near eastern documents as aids in interpreting and understanding Biblical text. He helped launch the Da'at Mikra series, published by Mosad Harav Kook (Jerusalem, 1976–2003), which integrates traditional commentary with contributions from a vast array of fields, including archaeology, numismatics, cartography, etc.
        - Da'at Mikra (see above).

- **Nechama Leibowitz** (1905– 2001). Leibowitz was a renowned Bible teacher in Jerusalem, where she lived from 1930 until the end of her life. She contributed weekly study sheets that were eventually disseminated internationally, that teach the reader to address the text through the eyes of the great commentators.
  - Studies in the Book of Genesis (English translation): Studies in Bereshit (Genesis) in the context of ancient and modern Jewish Bible commentary / by Nehama Leibowitz; translated and adapted from the Hebrew by Aryeh Newman. Jerusalem: World Zionist Organization, Department for Torah Education and Culture, 1981.
- **Breuer**, Mordechai (1918–2007) Professor Breuer has contributed greatly to the dissemination of modern methodologies in the teaching of Bible in Israel through his essays and the many students who continue and expand his methodological tools.
  - Essays on Genesis (Hebrew *Pirqei Bresheet*) Alon Shevut 2000.

GLOSSARY

- **Ashkenaz(ic)** relating to the Jewish communities in Northern and, later, Eastern Europe
- **Book of the Covenant** the first legal text committed to writing according to Exodus 24:7
- **Cantillation Marks** special markings designed by the Masoretes in the 6-9th centuries, indicated in codices of the Bible, used for punctuation, stress and cantillation in the synagogue
- **Chiasmus** a literary structure of A-B-B-A or A-B-C-B-A, using related ideas or common words to associate symmetrically.
- **Contemplative School** the school of medieval and modern Bible commentators who utilize the text as a springboard for observations about interpersonal and human-Divine interaction
- **Contextual School** the school of medieval and modern Bible commentators who focus their interpretative orientation on gaining a greater sense of the context of the narrative in order to solve its thorniest problems
- **Documentary Hypothesis** the approach, developed in the late 18th and 19th centuries among European Bible scholars, that the Pentateuch is a combination of several documents, originating in the 10–6th centuries BCE and edited together in the 5th century BCE
- **dualistic perspectivism** an explanation of apparently conflicting stories in the text which holds that each story is presenting one of several simultaneously accurate perspectives
- **Eisegesis** literally "reading into"; the practice among some commentators and students to read their own "agenda" into the text of the Bible
- **Exegesis** literally "reading out"; extracting meaning from the text
- *hapax legomenon* a singular and unmatched occurrence of a word or phrase in the canon
- **hermeneutics** the devices of interpretation
- **Hexateuch** the "six books" i.e., Pentateuch and Joshua

- **Historiosophy** recitation of historic narrative as an argument
- **Karaites/Karaism** the movement of "fundamentalist Judaism," popular in the 9–11th centuries throughout the Near East, that espoused complete allegiance to the Written Law but rejected much of the methodology and rulings of Rabbinic Judaism
- **Leitwort** key word (Heb. *Milah manhah*), a word which appears an inordinately high number of times in a given passage
- **Libation/Meal Offering** the ritual pouring of wine and grain offering that is brought with most animal offerings on the Altar in the Tabernacle or in the Temple
- **Ontological Truth** a statement whose truth value can only be ascertained against the full reality of the being of whom it is being stated
- **Masoretic Text** the canonized version of the Bible, known as *textus receptus*
- **Pascal's Wager** argument suggested by the mathematician Blaise Pascal wherein belief in God is the recommended path of action
- **Postdiluvian/Antediluvian** after/before the Great Flood
- **Qumran/DSS** the series of caves above the Dead Sea at *Khirbet Qumran* where the Dead Sea Scrolls were discovered in 1947
- **Rejectionists/Integrationists/Teleologists** schools advancing three different responses to the apparent contradiction between the knowledge imparted by the Bible and that which is discovered through the scientific method. Rejectionists typically dismiss either the Bible or the scientific method; integrationists attempt to harmonize the latest scientific claims with the text, and teleologists reject the question, assigning each discipline to a separate realm
- **Tetragrammaton** the four letter ineffable name for God, consisting of a *Yod*, a *Heh*, a *Vav*, and *Heh*

HEBREW TERMS

- *Aggadah(ot)* legend(s)
- *Akedah* binding (of Isaac – Genesis 22:1–19)
- *Aliyah(ot)* lit. "ascent"
  - Occasion(s) of being called to publicly read from the Torah
  - Moving to the Land of Israel or ascending to Jerusalem
- *b'khorah* birthright
- *B'rit* (**pl.** *B'ritot*) covenant(s)
- *D'rash* homily

- **Darshanim** preachers, using homiletics which relate to the Biblical text
- **Eretz Yisrael** the Land of Israel
- **Ger** stranger (Biblical Hebrew) convert (Rabbinic Hebrew)
- **Halakhah** "the way" – Jewish Law which guides all facets of life
- **Halakhah l'Moshe miSinai** a tradition that dates back to Moses at Sinai
- **Hashem** lit. "The Name" – i.e., God
- **Hazal** acronym for "Hakhamim zikhram liVrakhaha" – the sages, may their memories be a blessing. Generally refers to the Talmudic and Midrashic authors of the first 700 years of the common era
- **Kehunah** priesthood
- **Mefarshim** commentators
- **Mesorah** tradition
- **Mitzvah** commandment
- **Mophet('tim)** wonder(s)
- **Ot(ot)** sign(s)
- **Parasha(ot)** lit. "paragraph(s)" –
- **Parshanut** hermeneutics
- **Pashtanim** commentators who focus on *P'shat
- **P'shat** straightforward meaning of the text
- **Rishonim** "early ones"; rabbinic sages and commentators operating from the 11–15th centuries
- **s'mikhah** "laying of the hands", either as a preparatory act of an offering or a transferring of blessing/authority
- **Teshuva** "return" (akin to repentance)
- **Tol'dot** – generations
- **Tzaddik(im)** righteous or innocent person(s)
- **Yesh Muq'dam uM'uhar baTorah** – chronological sequencing; the position that the text has chronological fidelity
- **Yeshiva(ot)** House(s) of Torah Study

GENRES OF POST-BIBLICAL
LITERATURE AND RESEARCH

NOTE OF EXPLANATION OF RABBINIC SOURCES

Premedieval Rabbinic literature consists mainly of compilations of statements and analyses from an assortment of rabbis. The primary sources of early rabbinic literature are the Mishnah and Tosefta, both composed in the third century CE and consisting mainly of legal material. These were later expanded by the Palestinian (or Jerusalem) Talmud in the fourth century CE and the Babylonian Talmud in the sixth century CE. The Babylonian Talmud is often referred to as "Gemara," lit. "learning."

A passage from the Mishnah will be abbreviated M. followed by the name of the tractate, and the chapter and paragraph (e.g. M. Bikkurim 3:1). The Tosefta is cited in the same fashion (e.g. T. Bikkurim 3:4). Passages from the Babylonian Talmud are abbreviated BT, followed by the name of the tractate and the folio and side (e.g. BT Pesahim 94a).

Additionally, much exegetical and homiletical material was compiled in a vast literature called the Midrash (see Chapter 9 on the methodology of Midrash). There are many different compilations of Midrash (plural: Midrashim) and below are listed the books used in this study:

Midrash Aggadah (non-legal exegetical literature):
Midrash Rabbah, Midrash Rabbati, Midrash Hagadol, Aggadat B'resheet, Tanhuma, Midrash haHefetz

Midrash Halakhah (legal exegetical literature):
Mekhilta, Sifra (Torat Kohanim), Sifri